Robert,

Endless gratitude and appreciation for your enormous contribution to this book.

Fondly,
Brenda Cavanaugh

Mr. MacNeil,

This book could have NEVER happened without your help. Thank you for your incredible generousity

Yours,
Jymi Jynes

ALMOST BACK

ALMOST BACK

The Brenda Cavanaugh Story

By Jami Janes

Introduction by Robert MacNeil

NEW CENTURY BOOKS

Copyright © 2002 Jami Janes

All rights reserved. No part of this book may be reproduced or transmitted in any form or by any means, electronic or mechanical, including photocopying, recoding or by any information storage and retrieval system, without permission in writing from:

New Century Books
P.O. Box 7113
The Woodlands, Tx., 77387-7113

Library of Congress Number:
2001098787

ISBN: Hardcover
   0-930751-33-7
ISBN: Paperback
   0-930751-34-5

This book was printed in the United States of America.

For more information on this book
and author go to JamiJanes.com

Material from THE PROPHET by Kahlil Gibran, copyright 1923 by Kahlil Gibran and renewed 1951 by Administrators C.T.A. of Kahlil Gibran and Mary G. Gibran. Used by permisison of Alfred A. Knopf, a division of Random House Inc.

For Dick

Table of Contents

Acknowledgments		ix
Introduction by Robert MacNeil		xi
1)	Devotion . . . Duration . . . Desperation	1
2)	Windows of the Soul	3
3)	Magic Enchantment	8
4)	The Sweetest Summer	27
5)	Once Removed . . .	33
6)	Compulsory Crossroad	54
7)	Budding Bliss	74
8)	Dreams Demolished	80
9)	Twice Removed . . .	86
10)	Wasted	101
11)	Hopeful Holidays	134
12)	Ripped Apart	151
13)	Corrupt Confusion	158
14)	Almost There	171
15)	Kindred Summer	206
16)	Coming Up for Air	218
17)	Last Out	222
18)	Shattered	225
19)	Fall Out	226
20)	All Over Town	235
21)	Disillusioned	239
22)	Five Flags	242
23)	Conviction	248
24)	Never Okay	255
25)	Affirmation of Life	259
26)	Forever Removed	263
27)	A Call to Peace	267
28)	Eternal Love	274
29)	The Bond of Father and Son	295
	Epilogue	298

Acknowledgments

I don't know how I could adequately thank all who made the telling of this remarkable story possible. How can one properly show gratitude to people like Brenda and Dickie and the Genests and the Cavanaughs and George Pavlidis and Roland Provencher, who courageously and unselfishly tore open the deeply-scarred-and-scarcely healed wounds of their hearts, minds and spirits?

It seems impossible to express the absolute awe I feel when I think about how Brenda, day after day, month after month made herself available to me. Knowing full well that each minute we spoke would spawn hours of tears and pain, not to mention the days of recovery from having her heart and soul ripped out over and over again.

There were so many times when I wanted to quit because I was so tired of making people cry. But there was something or someone pushing me to continue. I want to thank Edgar and Fleurette Genest, Charlotte and William Bowers, Nancy Lou Buciak, Bill Starr, Jill and David Knowles, Tom Cavanaugh Sr., Nancy Cavanaugh, Jim Cavanaugh, Tom Cavanaugh Jr., Richard Murphy, Roland Provencher and George Pavlidis for so bravely sharing their pain. As bad as I felt at times about prying into such a private and painful place, I am sure that I could never really feel or know how traumatic and exhaustive it must have been. For their courage and generosity I am forever grateful.

Of course there are those who did not have to dig as deep into their souls but without whom this book would have never happened. Jim Gilbert's constant willingness and availability to help sort out facts, people and places was invaluable. Robert MacNeil, who from the first contact, was the embodiment of grace. Jack Doherty who opened his home and heart. Sean and Chris Doherty who encouraged this journey and were so helpful in finding photos, letters and pictures. My mother — Donna Tiedemann de Bazan, Judy Taylor, Grant Brown, Sheree Smit, Marnie Hassler, and Liz Hanly, all who listened to me for hours and hours about how I was going to write this story and then spent hours and hours reading draft after draft. Karl Motsenbocker who not only encouraged me but also allowed me, to take the time to do it. To Jim Adams whose military knowledge was unparalleled and who spent so many hours assembling research and preserving photos. To Jeff Sherman who so eloquently and thoughtfully gave us the very appropriate title. To Thomas Fensch, the best ally I could ever have.

I owe special gratitude to Jason Janes who generously shared his incredible knowledge of grammar and language to copy edit.

And there is no way this book would have been completed without Kelly Norris and DJ Dart whose knowledge of writing is unparalleled.

Finally, I never could have done this without Dick. My love for him inspired and motivated me. However, it is because of his courage to face what he lost, that made this possible. I can say with absolute certainty that his father is indubitably proud of the man he has become and that I am so very blessed to have him in my life.

Introduction
by *Robert MacNeil*

The Vietnam Memorial in Washington is an inspired design because its symbolism is so rich and so fitting. It is a gash, a wound, a scar cut into the sacred turf between the Washington Monument and the Lincoln Memorial, as the war wounded the psyche of this nation and left permanent scars. When viewed from one side, the Memorial (as originally designed) was invisible, as the Vietnam War was for many Americans, virtually out of sight and out of mind. The Memorial's gradual, downward incline evokes the deepening, and increasingly hapless, engagement of the United States in Vietnam's civil war. Then the path rises to mark the gradual disengagement, an uphill struggle costing almost as many lives as the way in. Finally, in the heartbreaking wall of names lies the truth of the war, the irreparable loss of those lives. In confronting their engraved names, in the reflection from the polished stone, we confront ourselves and our responsibility as the citizens whose nation sent these men to fight.

Partly in reaction to the trauma Vietnam has left in the American psyche, we have recently been celebrating the men who fought in World War II. Now a memorial far more grandiose, even vainglorious, is to be built in the same area. In future generations Americans will pass from one memorial to another, one glorifying, the other starkly deglorifying war, and they may wonder how, within one generation, this country could experience both sentiments so strongly.

But if those future Americans bother to read what the men who actually went to war, whatever war, felt about it in their most intimate and honest moments, they will find little to glorify. Yes, they will find patriotism, courage, patience and loyalty to comrades — all beyond the call of duty. They will also find resentment, resignation, anger at their superiors and bitter humor. And they will find all of the above in this book about one man who lost his life in Vietnam, Richard Genest, and his widow, Brenda. Their story is remarkable. Richard, a National Guardsman from New Hampshire, serving a compulsory one year in Vietnam, "spoke" to his wife, that is, he tape-recorded a message to her, every day. Those messages are more intimate and more candid than most soldiers tend to be in their written letters. But Brenda herself behaved remarkably. Women down through the ages have mourned when their men were sacrificed on the battlefield but, unable to do anything more, accepted their loss. This young woman refused to accept it passively. She turned her personal tragedy into one of the most eloquent statements of protest Vietnam produced.

Finding their story was a notable moment in my journalism career and the details remain buried into my memory more than three decades later.

Anyone who wishes to know what those years were really like, cleansed of glorifying rhetoric or political cant, will find it, searingly, in these pages.

1) Devotion . . . Duration . . . Desperation

He wrote to her everyday. Like a composer, whose soul demands to be heard, like an artist, whose vision commands to be seen, like a genius, whose mind screams with logic that requires recognition, he wrote to her everyday. For his letters were the only protection he had against being sucked into the deepest, darkest, bleakest place he had ever known.

The torrential rain that soaked his bed, the debilitating heat that beat and sickened even the strongest among them, the deafening noise of the guns that shattered and then destroyed all that was near, the mosquitoes who took blood and gave disease all at once, the infestation of cat sized rats who conquered his bunker and delighted in ravaging everything in their path, the wind and sand that would pelt his body as his bunker crumbled around him, the despair, depression, desperation and all the doom and death that is vital to war, could not keep him from writing to her everyday.

It was through his letters to her, his parents and his sister that he lived. It was then and only then that he could bear the burden that he and so many other young men were forced, even commanded to embrace. He, like so many others there, reluctantly possessed the terms of the future and the fate of all those who loved them.

The happiness, hope, promise and expectation of an entire family and the generations of that family to come, hinged solely on his survival. As he battled through each oppressive day, his wife, his father, his mother, his sister and even his infant son delicately and desperately suspended their hopes and dreams upon the precarious promise of his return.

His father based all his decisions about family matters and the family business solely on the return of his son. His mother greeted every morning with thoughts of her son. She would bask in the image of her family united and she embraced every night as one less they would be without him. His sister counted the days until she could finally share all the growing up she had done during his absence. She anxiously awaited the day that she and her brother would be able to bring their families together and experience adulthood as they had experienced childhood — together.

And then there was her. She whose existence mandated his presence. His wife, whose life had been exiled, the moment he had had to leave. Every breath she took, every thought she thought, was in anticipation of the day he would finally be home and they could begin to live the life together for which they desperately longed. The life that was ripped out from underneath them just six months into their marriage. A life in which all they needed, desired or required was to be with each other. A life in which their son was fed the love of his mother AND his father. A life in which all that they had been told was supposed to be; was.

2) Windows of the Soul

As soon as the plane landed on St. Croix in the U.S. Virgin Islands, the excitement of two weeks in the Caribbean with my boyfriend was overshadowed by the uncomfortable reality that the main purpose of the trip was to meet his mother and grandparents.

While Dick watched the other 150 passengers anxiously exit the plane I tried to melt into the seat I had squirmed in and wrestled with the last twelve hours. Even as Dick gently prodded me with words of comfort, "You look great. She is going to be so happy we are here. You have nothing to worry about, she is going to love you," I could not force myself to leave my aisle seat.

My mind was flooded with doubts. What in the hell had I been thinking when I told Dick I would love to go with him to see his family? Never before had I been compelled to meet the family of any of the men I had been seeing. Never mind travel 5000 miles to meet Mom. What was I going to say to her? "Hi, nice to meet you, I know I have only known your son a few months, but I really am madly in love with him and instead of moving back to New Hampshire after the ski season where he has family and a career, he will be staying in with me in California. And by the way, we will be living together and oh yeah, did I mention I don't like to share him? So, I hope you did not plan on spending too much time with him while we are here."

The longer I sat, the more panic-stricken I became. Gripped

by fear, I wondered how the seemingly confident woman who boarded the plane in San Francisco had turned into an insecure, irrational girl somewhere around Puerto Rico.

Realizing we may never have gotten the plane, Dick gently pulled me out of my seat. Before I even knew what had happened, I was thanking the pilot for a smooth flight. As I stepped onto the jetway, the tropical heat washed over me. I took a deep breath and felt the thick humid air coat my lungs. The sun was so bright, my eyes actually ached. I clutched the steel handrail and cautiously stepped down. Dick was close behind. With each step I descended, I could feel the strong thump of his heart backing me up.

Once on the tarmac, I began to adjust to the heat and light. Dick briskly walked toward the entrance of the airport. He acknowledged me with a playful grin as he sped past me. As I cautiously waded through the sticky air I surveyed the airport. It was a small building, resembling a double wide tin shack that had been cut to be a parking garage. There were so few people in or outside the airport I wondered if we were the only plane to arrive that day.

I was grateful the airport was small and appeared easy to navigate. It would be relatively effortless for me to find the luggage carousel. While Dick and Brenda greeted each other, I could easily maneuver myself away from them without losing sight of Dick. Mother and son could reunite and I could safely stand back without appearing obviously rude or distant.

Feeling a bit brave, I marched through the garage-like door into the airport. I was blinded by the dramatic change in light. I closed my eyes while white flashes darted through my head.

Suddenly I felt someone's arms around me. Startled, I flung my eyes open and attempted to step back. As I began to adjust to the light I became confused. I was looking into Dick's eyes, but standing before me was a striking blonde woman. Her hair rested just above her golden shoulders. Her tan was just dark enough to be dramatic but not so dark that her flesh looked tired. Her face reminded me of a reflecting pond on a calm summer day. Her eyes brown, soft and inviting. I could feel the warmth that flowed from her slowly wrap around me.

"I am so glad to finally meet you," she said with genuine sincerity as she tenderly squeezed my shoulders. She kept her hands on my shoulders as she stepped slightly back. She looked at me as if she was taking in the last few moments of a sunset. Not quite the disapproving judgmental look I had been expecting. I gave her a nervous smile and wondered to where Dick had disappeared. Sensing my concern, Brenda grabbed my hand and led me to Dick, who had easily found his way to the rum punch hospitality booth. She greeted her son with a tender affectionate hug. He peered over his mother's shoulder and I shot him a nervous disapproving glare. He returned a mischievous smile and winked at me.

I made an attempt to slip out of Brenda's view and hide behind Dick, but she caught me. She put one arm around me and led me to the baggage carousel. Dick, never one to miss an opportunity to see me squirm, walked to the other side of the carousel.

Brenda stood by my side as she described the island. She told me we had picked a great time to come because the weather in April was perfect and most of the tourists were gone. She said that her parents Tom and Nancy were excited to meet me. She said she had heard many wonderful things about me and she was thrilled that Dick and I were there.

I could not help but feel a bit dumfounded as she spoke. Several times I had to remind myself that her warmth and openness had to be some sort of trick. I was very suspicious. Why in the world would this woman be so kind to me, so soon? I was sure, it would only be a matter of time before she would judge me unfit to be with her first born.

"Are you on the Pill?" The words slammed into the side of my head. Instinctively I tried to shield my ears. My elbows were resting on the bar and I quickly lowered my head into the safe haven of my hands. I rested my cheeks on my now sweaty palms and placed my index finger very close to the now numb opening of my ear. Shock rippled through my body, followed by a sharp whisper of pain that was eclipsed by loud and throbbing numbness. Damn, she tricked me. How could I have not seen it coming? As I sipped my little tropical drink I anxiously wondered why I had let my guard down.

We were sitting at a bar less than fifty feet from the water. Dick was at the other end of the bar talking and laughing with a native. The steady, smooth trade winds sailed in and out of the sea side bar with confident tranquility. The evening air was brimming with infectious calm and soothing contentment. After three days of basking in the sun on soft Caribbean beaches, snorkeling, sailing, laughing, and swaying to the ebullient beat of steel drums and cautiously analyzing almost every move, intention, inflection and question Brenda had sent my way, I finally had decided to relax and enjoy the company of such a warm, loving, interesting, strong, and giving woman. Well, that was a brilliant decision, I thought to myself as I felt Brenda's powerful gaze sear through my head.

"Jami, are you on the Pill?," she repeated slowly and distinctly. Her tone was strong and sharp. The words came out of her mouth like staccato notes. I had hoped by pretending not to hear her the first time, she would not have the impulse be to ask again.

I stared straight ahead and tried to let the sound and smell of the sea calm me. "Yes," I tentatively mumbled in a cracking, high-pitched voice. I sounded like a fourteen year old boy whose voice had changed while asking out the most popular girl in school. I shifted uncomfortably on my barstool, made an attempt to release the strain that was building in my neck, and hoped beyond all hope that another question would not follow.

"Do you want to know why I asked?" Out of the corner of my eye I could see Brenda leaning ever closer to me. Her face was intent. It felt as if her eyes were penetrating my soul. I was too much a coward to face her. I continued to stare at the electric sea as the waves and the beach shamelessly flirted. "No, I don't want to know why," I said hoping the steady beat of the steel drums would obscure her voice. But Brenda had no intention of letting me off the hook. With conviction and compassion she said, "The reason I asked is because Dickie's eyes are the shape of his father's and your eyes are the color."

Suddenly, and much to my surprise, I turned to face her. Tears began to well in her eyes. As the waves waltzed with the white, sandy shore before us, silent, raging tears crashed down her cheeks. With a slight but piercingly painful quiver in her voice, she continued, "And I was just wondering if," she looked away from me and cupped her hands as if she was cradling someone's face, "I was wondering if ever I will see those eyes on this earth again, because that is what I have been living for all these years."

Her hands were trembling as she released the face she had held in her hands. She looked at me and with a sentiment that soared from the core of her being she said, "Oh, what I would give to look into those eyes just one more time."

3) Magic Enchantment

"STOP! STOP! THAT'S DICK GENEST! STOP, STOP!" It was a dull gray, Saturday in February 1965. Brenda and three of her girlfriends were doing what most sixteen year-olds do when they receive their license and a car; drive anywhere and everywhere over and over again.

The girls had been cruising Union Street, the main thoroughfare in Manchester, New Hampshire, when they spied Dick hitchhiking. The three passengers again screeched at Brenda, "That's Dick Genest, that's Dick, STOP!"

The shrill of their voices caused Brenda to slam on the brakes of her yellow convertible. The street was neatly coated with a thick layer of New England ice and the car that Brenda had possessed a mere four months rambunctiously slid toward Dick. She squeezed the steering wheel with all her might, as the car careened toward the sidewalk. Her elbows were rigid, her knuckles were white and Brenda felt panic sweep over her. She could vaguely hear her friends shouting as she silently begged for mercy, "Please, let me stop. Please don't let anything happen. Come on, please STOP." Her car hit the curb, jerked toward the sidewalk and came to rest just a few inches from Dick.

Dick wore a cool and confident smile as he carefully opened the passenger door and climbed into the compact sports car. As Dick deftly maneuvered himself into the back, Brenda could not help but stare. Like most everyone else in town, Brenda knew who Dick was, but never before had she been this close to him.

He was very handsome. He had lustrous brown hair that could appear black at certain times and golden at others. His hair was just long enough to be dangerous in 1965, but not so long it would offend anyone. He parted it to the left, although it was hard to tell because of the big, soft curls that rested on his forehead. His presence was large — although he was not. He weighed no more than 130 pounds, he was just shy of five feet seven inches, but his slight body was replete with spirit and charisma. He walked with a casual and proud stride. His smile seemed to consume his whole face except, of course, for his eyes.

His eyes outshined everything. They sparkled with a deep, crisp blue that was so stunning, it was almost shocking. Kindness, humility, and compassion confidently and playfully danced with humor and mischief inside the sapphire pools that were the windows to his soul.

Brenda found herself taken aback as she let her shy glance become a strong gaze while Dick squeezed himself between the two girls in the back of her car. Once situated, Dick made sure to knowingly lock his eyes onto Brenda. She was instantly mortified. She could not believe she had let herself be caught. Quickly she cast her eyes away from him. She defiantly whipped her head around and thrust the car into gear.

Brenda had never experienced a more intense look. Its power and force was forever and saliently seared into her.

It was a hushed ride down Union Street. The girls suddenly found themselves speechless once they actually had Dick Genest in the car. The anticipation and the silly excitement that proceeded Dick was replaced by vulnerable discomfort. Dick, never one to make himself the center of attention — although he almost always was — sat quietly between the two girls in back. He spoke only to inform Brenda of his destination, which of course, was a moot point, since most everyone in Manchester knew Dick worked for his father at the family bakery, Genest Better Bread.

10 ALMOST BACK

The Genest Bakery was the largest bakery in Manchester. Edgar, Dick's father, took control of the bakery after his father, Albert, died in 1954. Edgar was barely thirty-two when he inherited the family business that had sixty employees and was losing money. By the time Edgar sold the bakery in 1977, he had 450 employees and gross yearly sales of twenty-five million. By 1965 Edgar had increased the business and profits many times over and was well on his way to owning and operating the largest independent bakery in New England. Naturally, he was very busy and worked long hours. Having Dick work at the bakery served two purposes: he was able to spend time with his only son, and he was able to teach his about the business that, of course, Dick would one day take over.

Richard Edgar Genest was born to Edgar and Fleurette Genest, August 7,1945. Many people had told Fleurette she would be unable to bear a child while others asked Edgar why he had married a woman who appeared much too small to have a child of his. Edgar was an average sized man who evenly wore 180 pounds. However he towered over his wife, who was a least a foot shorter and close to a hundred pounds lighter.

Fleurette had been stricken with polio at age seven. When Fleurette's father Oscar learned that the treatment for polio required he leave his daughter in Boston while she was kept in a body cast, he decided to take charge of her recovery. Oscar took the unorthodox approach of physical therapy. Every day after he closed his general store he hurried home and took Fleurette for a swim in the river. Oscar would row his canoe while Fleurette grasped the back and kicked. No matter how weary Fleurette would become, Oscar insisted Fleurette kick and exercise her legs for half an hour. Fleurette believes her father's commitment to her is the reason she can walk effortlessly today. However, despite her father's dedication to rid her completely of any remnant of polio, Fleurette's growth was surely inhibited by the disease.

The name Fleurette fit her well. She was petite, delicate and beautiful. Her personality was much like a budding blossom: full of promise and life. She wanted so much to bloom as a mother. Edgar was madly in love with Fleurette and had no doubt they would have a great life together. They were married on 12 September 1944 and they immediately made plans to start a family.

Fleurette became concerned three months into the marriage because she was not yet pregnant. She began to wonder if maybe all the talk about her size and bearing a child was true. She worried she would be unable to give Edgar the opportunity to be a father and that she would never experience the joy of motherhood. She was about to approach Edgar about adoption, when in December, she learned she was pregnant.

She was elated and relieved. She and Edgar were beside themselves with joy when she gave birth to a baby boy. How fortunate and blessed they felt to have a beautiful son. And they were doubly thrilled and felt infinitely blessed when, four years later, Fleurette gave birth to their daughter, Charlotte.

Edgar and Fleurette strived to make their children's life safe, fun and filled with love. Edgar worked diligently to build a business that would amply provide for his family and Fleurette devoted herself to Dick, Charlotte and to their comely home. Theirs was a life like so many others in the United States during the 1950's and the early 1960's; comfortable, prosperous, and filled with hope for the future.

There was never the slightest doubt that Dick would follow in his father's footsteps at the bakery. Dick began working at the bakery when he was sixteen. One of his first duties was as a relief driver. During his summer breaks from high school, he would take over routes for vacationing drivers. All the drivers loved him, not just because he enabled them to take their much needed vacations, but also because he was did such a good job covering their routes. They knew that Dick took his duty very seriously and when they returned they always found their routes at least as good as they had left them.

It always impressed everyone that Dick not only knew every route in the state, but even more so, that he knew exactly how each and every driver liked his route handled. Dick's attitude and efficiency were appreciated by even the most skeptical — who initially openly questioned the usefulness of the boss son. Dick's undeniable charm, coupled with his work ethic was an irresistible and powerful combination.

Although Manchester was the largest city in New Hampshire, it had a small town feel to it. Just like Genest Bakery, most of the businesses were family owned. (And had been for many generations.) Generation after generation patronized and supported the same businesses. It was a given that whomever your father did business with, you would, too. Insurance agents to car dealerships to general stores (and everything in between) were chosen not so much for what they provided, but for whom they had provided. This unspoken tradition had both grand and grave effects on Dick's generation.

Dick graduated from Manchester's Central High in 1963. That fall he began attending classes at Kansas State University, where not surprisingly they had an extensive and respected baking school. He would end up attending only two semesters there. No one remembers the exact details of his dismissal from the school, but everyone is certain that his involuntary exit stemmed from him being caught on or around campus with a case of beer in his possession.

Upon Dick's somewhat shameful return to Manchester his father punished him by giving him the most mundane job the bakery had to offer — packaging English muffins all day. Although Dick prided himself in not being above any job that needed to done, he did not want to spend the rest of his life putting muffins that all looked the same, into bags that all looked the same, all day long. Therefore, to show his father he was serious about taking over the business, he enrolled in classes at Saint Anselm's college in Manchester and constantly asked his father questions about every detail of operation of the bakery. Gradually Edgar began to teach Dick all the aspects of working in and running the bakery.

By 1965 Dick was an integral part of the bakery. On any given day he could be found washing delivery trucks, baking bread, delivering bread, making donuts, cleaning the conveyor belts and anything else that needed to be done. No one can be sure what tasks were on the agenda for Dick when Brenda deposited him at the entrance of the bakery. What is certain, is, above all else, from the moment Dick had entered Brenda's car, he vowed his first and foremost task of the day, was to find out who the breathtaking, blonde, driver was that had baited his eye and snared his heart.

When they arrived at the bakery Brenda could not help but notice the brick structure with cement trim consumed the most of the block. It was an imposing building that at first glance had the personality of an impenetrable fortress. Upon closer inspection though, the building tempted even the most timid with the sweet smell of baking bread that wrapped around the building and engulfed the street. Dick swiftly exited Brenda's sunflower yellow car. As he shut the passenger door, he surrendered to Brenda a smile that was sweetly confident but masked in sly shyness. Brenda pretended not to notice, for if she smiled back, she would be forced to look him in the eyes and if she were to look at him again there was no way she could hide her attraction to him. She dismissed his smile as mere politeness and turned her eyes intently to the car's shiny ebony dashboard. Once Dick's back was to the car she intently watched him push open the glass door to the bakery. She let her eyes pursue him as he crossed the threshold under the massive cement marquee that proclaimed in bold letters "Genest's Better Bread" and finally she let him escape her gaze when the glass door lightly rocked shut.

Brenda had barely put her car in gear before her friends regained their courage and voices. "He is so cute," squealed one. "Cute?!?!, he's gorgeous," shrieked another. "I would give ANYTHING to date him," cooed the third.

"He's too short for me," Brenda plainly stated, as if the subject matter bored her. Of course, it was amusing that as Brenda proclaimed he was too short, she could barely see over the steering wheel of her car. Her father often wondered how at just over five feet tall, she managed to see where she was going AND reach the gas pedal at the same time.

Fortunately for Brenda her friends did not comment on the absurdity of her statement. They just continued to proclaim the wonders of Dick Genest as they headed back toward Union Street. Brenda paid little attention to the squeaky chatter of her friends and tried to just concentrate on driving. However, the only thing she could think about was Dick.

She quickly and forcibly squelched the soft sentiment that was budding inside her and firmly planted unquestionable logic. She could not understand why her friends would even be talking about it. Why waste time thinking about something they could never have?

She knew there was no way Dick Genest would be chasing after high school girls. What in the world made them think that one of the most desired young men in Manchester would ever dump his girlfriend — a woman his own age who was pretty, popular, well-known, well-mannered and whom he had been happily dating for a year, to pursue some random sixteen year old girl from a working-class family?! Boy, that would be funny, if it was not so stupid, thought Brenda.

After two more hours of cruising the streets of Manchester, Brenda dropped off her girlfriends at their respective homes and returned to her home. By the time she walked into the busy kitchen of her house she had managed to rid herself of any fantasies about herself and Dick Genest. As she settled into

Saturday night with her family, Dick was busy asking everyone he knew, how he could find the petite blonde with enchanting brown eyes, who drove the yellow Rambler.

Although Brenda did not think this to be true, many people in Manchester knew of and admired her family. The Cavanaughs were not as wealthy as most of the families who lived on the North End of Manchester, but their name held prestige in the community. In 1876 Brenda's great-grandfather, James Cavanaugh, began selling horses in Manchester and it took little time before Cavanaugh Bros. became the largest horse dealer in New England. In 1916 Cavanaugh Bros. progressed to cars and became one the first Ford Dealers in New England. By 1965 Cavanaugh Bros. Motors was a well recognized and permanent fixture in the city selling American motors. Brenda's father, Tom, a tall, handsome, dark-haired Irishman was very proud of, and took very seriously, his job of running the dealership.

Besides the dealership, many people knew of Brenda's mother, Nancy. Nancy Cavanaugh was a striking woman. She had thick, smooth hair that sparkled like a polished ruby. No matter if she styled her hair in the look of the latest fashion or in a regal bun, when she passed by men and women were obliged to take notice. Nancy's hair, was only one of many distinguishing characteristics: she walked with proud elegance, she had an extraordinary figure — a shapely model's figure — and when she spoke it was obvious that her ancestry included Ralph Waldo Emerson. These traits were magnified by the fact she was the mother of six children ranging in age from two to sixteen.

Brenda was the oldest of the Cavanaugh children. In all there were three boys and three girls. The children came to Tom and Nancy in alternating order of gender. After Brenda came Tommy then Jill then Mike then Nancy Lou and finally Jimmy. With such a large and recognized family it took very little time for Dick to find someone whom he had in common with Brenda.

"Hi, Brenda it's Mike," Brenda was used to getting phone calls from boys but she was a little baffled why Mike Burns would be calling her. She had gone to grammar school with him and had been in the same class as his sister at Mt. St. Mary's (a small private Catholic school). That was all they really had in common. She wondered if Mike was about to play some prank on her. "Brenda I have somebody here who wants to talk to you." Great, Brenda thought, Mike has nothing better to do than bug me with prank phone calls.

"Hello," said a voice that Brenda could not place. "Hi," Brenda said wondering what Mike had up his sleeve. She was getting ready to hang up and then the voice said, "Hi, Brenda, it's Dick, Dick Genest, you gave me a ride a couple days ago." Brenda was silent, she felt her stomach creep into her throat she quietly gulped, held her breath and waited for Mike to start laughing. "Brenda, I was wondering if maybe sometime you might want to go out?" Brenda was scared to even blink. She held the phone tightly, her stomach retreated from her throat, but she felt as if she was at the top of a teetering roller coaster that was about to uncontrollably surge down.

Dick continued, "The Beach Boys are playing in a couple weeks at the Manchester Coliseum and I have tickets, I mean it's no big deal but I'm sure it will be fun." Brenda felt if she opened her mouth and moved her tongue there was no way any words would find their way out. Maybe some familiar sounds but definitely not anything comprehensible. Taking what felt like the biggest gamble of her life, Brenda coerced her lips to move and in one breath she said, "Um, yeah that's sounds like fun." Brenda took a quick breath and before Dick had a chance to respond she said, "I was going to go with some girlfriends anyway." Dick waited a moment and then said, "Good see you then."

Brenda hung up the phone with both relief and regret. She was relieved she had been able to speak without stumbling over her words or blatantly showing her delight, but she regretted not talking more with Dick. She was unsure if he had asked her on a true date. Had he invited her to the show or was he just telling her he was going to be there? Was he going to pick her up or was she going with her friends and take the chance of finding him there? And what about his girlfriend? Or for that matter what about her boyfriend. She knew she was much more interested in dating Dick than her present beau but what about Dick? Everyone knew he and his girlfriend were fairly serious. Brenda decided she would go with her original plan of attending the concert with her friends but she told her friends in no uncertain terms, "If he shows up I'm going with him."

No one really knows how Dick learned where Brenda lived but, just as Brenda had convinced herself he was not coming by to take her to the concert the door bell rang. Brenda jumped when she heard the bell. She pretended she could not feel her knees buckling as she walked to answer the door. She told herself that it could be anybody and Dick surely had to be on his way to the show with his friends or his girlfriend or both. She opened the door enough to see who was there but not enough to expose herself. If she had not been clutching the door knob so tight she probably would have stumbled or fallen backward when she saw Dick.

Oh, this is so unfair, she thought. Why does he have to be so good-looking? Dick was grinning, the promising and comfortable gleam in his sparkling blue eyes was almost more than Brenda could take. She widened her eyes, threw her shoulders back, swallowed the fear that had been choking her and opened door completely. Still smiling Dick cast his eyes to the ground and said, "Wow, you look great." Brenda was often told she was pretty but to hear Dick say it made her feel as if she was the most beautiful girl in the world.

Beautiful, Brenda certainly was. At five feet and maybe two inches, weighing one hundred two pounds she was thin but robust. Her oval-face and shapely figure kept her from appearing waif-like. She had her mother's posture, refined and proud but never vain or forced. Her voice was soft and thoughtful, her sun-brushed blonde hair made her satin brown eyes sparkle.

Brenda instinctively allowed Dick to guide her from the alcove down her drive way to his cobalt blue '65 Mustang. Dick opened the car door for Brenda, she slipped in and Dick confidently shut the door. As Dick turned and walked around the front of his car Brenda slumped into the seat, threw her head back, and wondered how she could make through the evening without melting into his arms. Just as Dick climbed into the car, she sat up straight, composed herself and vowed not to let him know that she was mad for him.

Brenda remembers little of the Beach Boys performing that night. What stands out in her mind about the night is the adoration for Dick that consumed her. It felt natural for her to not to pay attention to the concert because Dick made her feel as if they were the only two people that existed during the show. He was kind, funny, charismatic, personable and charming. For the first time in Brenda's life she truly understood what chemistry meant. A charged and excited energy constantly and effortlessly surged and flowed between them. She half expected to wake up any minute, because she felt, there was no way the euphoria she was feeling could exist anywhere but in her dreams.

By the time Dick took Brenda home she knew that she was in love with him. She did not feel giddy and silly, she felt remarkably calm and sure that this man was put on the earth solely for her. However, she was not about to let him or any one else know of her feelings. She did not want to appear as of she was chasing him, she definitely did not want to expose herself to rejection or pain so she decided to play it cool, very cool. Dick had pulled into her driveway and even though Brenda knew they could easily sit in the car and talk all night, she reluctantly turned her head toward her home and said, "I better go." She purposely kept her head slightly turned away from him. He leaned toward her, slid his arm behind the head rest on which Brenda's right cheek was slightly resting and tenderly kissed her left cheek. Brenda called upon every ounce of will power reserved in her diminutive body and answered his kiss with a smile. She bolted from the car, ran to her house, and quickly closed the door. She slumped with her back against the door and took her first real breath since arriving home.

Brenda and Dick went on a two more dates with the same result each time. Brenda remembers having more fun with Dick than she had ever had with anyone. It made no difference if they walked alone on the beach for hours in the rain or if they were surrounded by other people, whatever they did seemed like the best and most exciting time of her life. Their connection to one another became stronger and more undeniable with every encounter.

Dick, though, still had a girlfriend and Brenda recalls asking him what he intended to do. Dick plainly told Brenda that he had been trying, rather unsuccessfully, to break off his relationship with her. He told Brenda that she was a good friend of his sister and that his parents liked her immensely. He also told Brenda he was very fond of her, but he could never imagine being with her now that he had met Brenda.

Less than a week later, Brenda spied Dick pulling out from the street where his girlfriend lived. Brenda was not normally allowed out on school nights, but on this particular week night she had been allowed to go to her friend's (Sue-Ellen) to work on a project for their French class. As Brenda was leaving Sue-Ellen's house she thought about going by Dick's house since he lived just a block away. Quickly, she thought better, because she did not want to betray her parents' trust or give Dick the wrong impression. She decided to go straight home. As she was exiting the street where Sue-Ellen lived, she saw Dick. There, right in front of her, was his blue Mustang and he was not alone. She could easily tell his alleged ex- girlfriend was in the car with him.

Brenda was livid. She began to follow him. When she caught up with him she was really going to let him have it. With each passing moment of the pursuit, she became more hurt and more angry. She stayed on his tail until she realized that, if she was actually to confront him, she probably would not be able to recite all the names and nasty phrases that were ricocheting in her head, instead she knew she most likely would break down and sob. She was not about to give him that satisfaction. So, she drove her parents' station wagon home, limped to her room and after berating herself for being so stupid and naive as to think that Dick Genest actually cared for her, she began thinking of all the nasty things she would say the next time she saw him.

Dick made a point to track Brenda down the next day. He found her at the soda fountain where many of the teenagers in Manchester hung out after school. Brenda's heart leaped into her throat when Dick walked in. She had spent most of her day at school plotting and rehearsing exactly what she was going to say to him.

She was going to give him a piece of her mind. How dare he think he could play her! Just because she was still in high school and she could not go out on school nights, did NOT mean he could lie to her and then see her on weekends. Who did he think he was? He had pursued her! Oh, she could hardly wait to tell him what she really thought. (Of course if she told him what she truly thought and felt she would tell him she loved him and they belonged together.)

She pretended not to see him as he walked toward her.

"Hi," Dick said as he leaned even closer to her. He twisted his head down and around trying to catch a glimpse of her eyes that were sternly cast down.

"Oh, hi." Brenda said as if she were talking to no one in particular, keeping her eyes glued to the magazine she had been flipping through. She closed the magazine and made a half-hearted attempt to escape. Dick stepped in front of her and locked her in place with a concerned but firm stare, "Brenda, I know you were chasing me last night."

"WHAT??? I don't know what you are talking about. And why in the world would I chase YOU?" Brenda said with as indignantly as she muster.

"Look, I know it was you because the ski rack on your parents station wagon is always open on that one side and as soon as I looked in my rear-view to see who was riding my tail, I could see the top of the rack bouncing up and down as you chased me."

"Well I can't help that you pulled out in front of me while I was on my way home, after doing homework at Sue-Ellen's. What exactly were you doing and why didn't you stop if you knew I was behind you? Were you hiding something?" Brenda was grasping for the anger and hurt that had flowed so effortlessly inside before he had been looking at her and talking to her.

"No, Brenda I have nothing to hide from you. I did not pull over because Pam was with me. I was in the process of telling her that I did not want to see her anymore and she was not taking it very well. So, I was trying to explain to her that she was a great girl but she is just not the girl for me, that I just did not feel any spark or chemistry. And then there you were, right on my butt, with your high beams all but blinding me. I was having a hard enough time concentrating before you came along."

Dick wanted to tell Brenda he could barely concentrate because as he was talking to Pam, all he could think about was her. He wanted to tell Brenda that she was the greatest person he had ever known, that she sparked a fire in his soul, that she had made his black and white world fill with vivid, vibrant, and living color, but he was afraid she would think he had lost his mind.

"Anyway Pam and I will NOT be seeing each other again."

Brenda lifted her head and allowed herself to look in to Dick's eyes. She knew from the tenderness of his voice and the earnest look that leapt from his face that he was telling the truth. She felt herself trembling and prayed he could sense her excitement. "Well, call me when you can." She stepped around him, all but skipped down the aisle, exited the building and jumped into her sports car leaving Dick slightly confused but mostly exhilarated and proud, watching his girl, his beautiful girl, drive away.

By April of 1965 Brenda and Dick were inseparable. Dick adored Brenda's family and the feeling was mutual. When Dick and Brenda were not at his house, they could be found playing with Brenda's brother and sisters or skiing with the whole family or at the Cavanaugh family beach house in York Beach, Maine. Dick loved spending time with Brenda's family and although he came from a loving and secure home he truly enjoyed being with and thrived while with the Cavanaugh family. He loved the atmosphere of their family. The Cavanaughs were always doing something and Dick reveled being in the thick of the family activities. Brenda loved being with her family as well, but growing up in such an active and busy house she was always grateful for the calm time she and Dick were able to spend at his house.

The Genest home was a large and stylish residence that was perched upon a slight slope on Union Street. It had a sizable, manicured front yard and a luxurious swimming pool in the back yard. The home had three levels. On the top floor were four bedrooms, one of which was turned into a den. The second level had a massive kitchen, a marble tiled dining room and a living room that also had the tan marble tile. The first floor consisted of a large family room that contained couches, a player piano, a television as well as many other pieces of furniture. It was enclosed with large picture windows, which enhanced the view into the back yard and made the room elegant. It was in this room that Dick and Brenda spent most of their time when at his house.

They had been dating two months when while watching television in the family room and eating Pepperidge Farm Goldfish Brenda found the nerve to ask Dick a question that had been eating away at her for some time.

She was gripped with fear as the words started to stumble off her tongue, but she knew if she did not ask at that very moment she may never have the nerve again. In a soft, bashful ,almost trembling voice Brenda looked away from Dick and said, "I need to ask you something and please don't get mad at me." She ducked as if she were about to be hit in the head and said, "Will you go to my junior prom with me?"

"Sure, yeah of course." Dick said with relief and slight puzzlement. Brenda tried not to choke or spit out the goldfish she had crammed into her mouth after asking him the question.

She managed to swallow most of the orange crackers. "WHAT did you say?" She felt as if she was choking and absolutely no oxygen was finding its way to her head, but she continued in an unfamiliar, high-pitched voice, "I mean my friends told me there was no way you would go with me especially since you did not even go to your own prom. Everybody said I was totally crazy to think that a nineteen year old guy would go to a high school junior prom."

She now was speaking so forcefully it was as if the safety had been released from her tongue and the words were shooting out of her mouth automatically. Dick was not intimidated. Actually he was slightly amused. Before she had a chance to fire the next round next he interjected, "Well, Brenda I WANT to go with you."

As with every date Brenda and Dick had a great time. They double dated with Brenda's dear friend, Sue-Ellen and her date,

Arthur. Brenda wore a beautiful white cotton and lace sleeveless dress with a satin pink ribbon that hugged her waist. Dick dressed well for the occasion in perfectly pressed tuxedo pants and shirt, a bow tie and a very hip, subtly plaid dinner jacket. They were the best dressed and most admired couple at the dance. After the prom Dick, Brenda, Sue-Elien and Arthur drove to Rye Beach together.

On the thirty minute drive to the beach from Manchester they stopped to buy a bottle of champagne. They all sat together on the beach, sipped champagne and marveled at the beauty of the star filled sky. Brenda and Dick gazed at the sky and each other. They let the salt air and the sounds of the Atlantic wrap around them. They stayed out on the beach talking and laughing, not tiring for even a moment until sunrise. It was a time that they would never forget. Neither had known such wonderful feelings and sense of belonging existed until they were together. The prom was in May and when the summer of 1965 began they wondered how they had ever survived without one another.

Brenda spent the summer working as a nurse's aide and Dick worked at the bakery. Brenda's shift at Elliot Hospital started at three in the afternoon and ended at eleven at night. Dick's shift at the bakery began at three in the morning. Even though their schedules appeared to leave little time for one another, they always found ways to see each one another everyday.

In August it seemed they were going to have a chance to be together more often because Brenda's parents, brothers and sisters were going to spend the entire month at the Cavanaugh family beach house in Maine. However, working forty hours a week in the hospital, going out late at night with Dick and friends and getting little sleep took a toll on Brenda. During the last two weeks of July she contracted mononucleosis. Brenda did not want her parents to know she was sick for fear they would make her go to Maine and she would miss an entire month alone with Dick. She pretended she felt good and continued to work full time.

When the first week of August rolled around Brenda was so ill her throat had just about swollen shut. She could not eat anything and was barely able to drink water. Her mother demanded she go to the doctor. The doctor said she had gotten there just in time — her spleen was about to burst — and he ordered her to total bed rest. Much to her disappointment, her mother insisted she go to Maine with the family.

She spent most of August resting and recovering in bed. Fortunately for Brenda her room not only faced the ocean, but also it was less than a hundred yards from the beach. Dick would drive to Maine whenever he was not working to see her. They would sit in her room talking, laughing and listening to all the sounds the Atlantic Ocean had to offer.

Brenda had mostly recovered when her family left Maine toward the end of August. She was able to convince her parents to let her stay at the beach house until school started. Naturally, Dick joined Brenda there. They spent countless hours in the beginning of September walking along the beach, eating lobster and steamed clams, gazing at stars and talking to the moon. They spent night after night perched upon boulders talking and laughing while the mist from the sea drifted over them.

During the winter of 1965-1966 they went on ski trips together, played in the snow in Manchester, hung around Dick's house, entertained and supervised Brenda's siblings, went out with friends, really it was of little significance what they did as long as they were together.

By spring of 1966 Brenda and Dick were seriously discussing their future. Brenda would be graduating from high school in June and Dick wanted to continue his education not only because it was the best way to avoid being drafted and going to Vietnam, but also because he would be taking over the bakery one day and he wanted an education as well as experience to run the business. Because they knew they were going to marry they agreed their first priority for their future was to secure educations. Brenda applied and was accepted to the University of New Hampshire. Dick agreed to go to the baking and business school at Oklahoma State University. The summer of 1966 was to be last care free time of their lives.

4) The Sweetest Summer

The summer of 1966 began with Brenda's high school graduation on 17 June. Dick purchased a gold charm bracelet as a graduation gift. Included with the bracelet was the first of many charms Dick would give Brenda. It was a stunning gold oval charm with her birthstone — an opal — and of course a gold diploma and cap resided within the charm. On the other side 6-17-66 had carefully been engraved. Dick was proud of Brenda. She was going to pursue her dream of being a teacher and he chose a gift that not only showed his love but also his pride in her accomplishments. More than anything else though, he was thrilled to have purchased something that he could add to and enhance as they celebrated all the triumphant and significant moments that were bound to bless their life together. Brenda had never received such a gift and she was overwhelmed by its beauty and Dick's thoughtfulness. Whenever she wore it she felt as if an armor of affection enshrouded her.

After graduation Brenda was again a nurses' aide at Elliot hospital. Her shift was the same as the summer before, three p.m. to eleven p.m. Dick was again working the early shift at the bakery which began at three in the morning. Their time together may have seemed limited but they made the most of every moment.

Almost every night in August when Brenda's family was in Maine, Dick would sneak into Brenda's house and have lobster and steamed clams waiting for her when she got home from work. He could not bear the thought of his girl coming home to an empty house, hungry and tired. He would park on the street behind Brenda's parents home walk across a small field, climb over the hill that led to the Cavanaugh's back yard and discreetly climb in the kitchen window, all while carrying a bag of clams and two live lobsters. He slyly slipped into Brenda's house because in the curious and talkative community of the North End it would have been big news to see a young man entering a home of a young lady late at night and then exiting in the wee hours of the morning. Mostly though, he loved to surprise Brenda. She would come home and find the table set, candles lit and a feast of seafood awaiting her. They would talk in hushed voices, dip the lobster in butter, eat clam after clam, laugh with and at each other, savor the food and even more so, each other.

There are many nights during that summer that Brenda vividly remembers. The taste, smell, temperature — everything seemed to permanently saturate every pore of her body. But there is one night in particular that really stands out in her memory.

Brenda had just finished her shift at the hospital and Dick was waiting for her at her father's car dealership. He was going to help her in the exchange of her sport car that had not been running so well for another car her father had for her to use. Ironically Dick's uncle, Roland Genest, owned Genest Ford, next door to Cavanaugh Bros. Motors. As Dick and Brenda were making the exchange, the Manchester Police arrived. Naturally the police wanted to know what they were doing out at eleven at night getting in and out of cars at a car dealership with no one else around. Brenda began to explain that this was her father's dealership and she was just picking up a car her father had left for her. The police asked both Dick and Brenda to produce some identification. Nervously they handed the police their driver's licenses and after one policeman carefully examined both of their licenses he said, "Well, I never thought I would see the day that a Cavanaugh and a Genest were together."

Whenever Dick and Brenda could during the summer they would take trips all over New Hampshire and the coast of Maine. Brenda describes Dick and his zest for life, "Dick loved life, he loved to do things, he loved to be outside and active. We always were doing something adventurous or fun."

Sometimes they would drive west and hike Mt. Sunapee. Other times they would get a bottle of champagne and a bushel of steamed clams drive east to the coast sit on the dock sipping champagne and eating clams. At the top of Mt. Sunapee there was a wooden ski lift shack that provided a brilliant, panoramic view of Sunapee Lake, the crests and ebbs of the surrounding mountains and the small New England ski village below. Brenda and Dick would settle into the shack for hours pretending they were married, talking about all the things they were going to do, taking in the view and cherishing each other's company.

Most of their dates were centered around the beach and ocean. The sounds, smell and power of the sea gave them great pleasure. They felt as if the ocean and beach spoke specifically to them. They would sit on the dock and admire the boats in the harbor. They would slowly drink champagne and eat clams as they watched the Atlantic Ocean command its domain. They would explore the seemingly endless miles of underground bunkers from World War II that extended from the harbor in Portsmouth, New Hampshire to the harbor in Kittery, Maine. They climbed the steep concrete steps into Fort McClary, an abandoned lookout post from World War II, and embrace the vista of varied life and landscape that generously shared the coastline. Brenda had spent much of her life on the coast of Maine, she had always appreciated its beauty and wonder but when she was with Dick it became glorious and magical.

Dick loved being with Brenda's family. He spent much of his time with Brenda surrounded by her family. When they went to the Cavanaugh home in York Beach, Dick would spend hours on Long Sands Beach playing with Nancy Lou, seven years old, Mike nine years old and Jimmy four years old. He did everything with the kids. He would wrestle with the boys, chase Nancy Lou, let Nancy Lou chase him, build sand castles just about anything that the kids wanted to do, he was game. The older Cavanaugh siblings would marvel at Dick's energy and kindness to the pesky little ones. Jill who was fourteen and Brenda at seventeen wanted nothing to do with the little monsters. The beach was for perfecting tans, not running around like lunatics. Dick enjoyed resting and relaxing on the beach as well but some think he got more pleasure running around the beach chasing the kids. No matter if it was a cloudy weekday with a few locals on the beach or a sunny weekend with hundreds of tourists Dick's antics with the children managed to amuse all. Tom and Nancy were not only grateful for a break and a chance to relax, but also they were thrilled to see the newest member of their family bring joy to everyone.

Whenever Dick had the chance he would pack up the three youngest kids and without Brenda or any other adults he would cart them down to the bakery. He would take them on grand tours. He would allow them (actually he would insist), to help themselves to anything they wanted. He would lead them directly to one of the many conveyer belts and tell them to grab what they wanted. Sometimes it was a Whoppie Pie other times it was donuts. After the kids got a treat, Dick would take them outside to the back of the bakery and let them play in one of the many tractor-trailer trucks that were used to deliver Genest products all over New England. He would encourage them to pretend they were driving the trucks, or he would open the back and they would run around in the bed.

Jimmy, Nancy-Lou and Mike felt privileged and special while with Dick. Jimmy remembers, "It was like we owned the place. He just let us do pretty much whatever we wanted."

Before he took them home, he would fill their arms with all sorts of pastries and day-old goodies. In a house with six children it was impossible to always have treats on hand for everyone, but Dick made a valiant effort to keep the Cavanaugh household supplied.

During that summer whenever Dick had the delivery route in Maine he would stop by the old but grand, brown-shingled Cavanaugh home. Everyone in town would take notice as he parked a Genest Bakery truck squarely in front of the beach house. He would quickly exit the siren-red GMC cab, open the side door of the trailer, grab an arm load of various fresh baked items, sprint up the stairs, take several giant steps around the porch, gingerly open the side door that always greeted him with a muffled groan, proceed to the kitchen and discreetly unloaded the bounty of Genest products. On his way out, he would take a moment to join whoever might be sitting on the oversized porch. Words were seldom exchanged as Dick and one of the Cavanaughs let the vista of the ocean wash over them.

Then just as quickly as he arrived Dick would bounce from his seat, leap down the ten stairs and be off to make his deliveries. If for some reason they did not notice him coming into the quiet coast town, they surely must have noticed the large vehicle as it chugged along Ocean Avenue. Even though Genest trucks were a common and familiar site in most of northeastern United States, it was virtually impossible not to take notice every time one left town. Like a large banner behind a small plane, the trailer, in blood red and white, caught your attention with its message; CALL FOR **GENEST'S** BAKERY PRODUCTS **NEW ENGLAND'S FINEST.**

Several times Dick brought Brenda's brother Tommy along on his delivery routes. Dick was five years older than Tommy and at sixteen, Tommy did not consider Dick part of his "group." But as was Dick's nature he never considered that their ages would or should matter. Dick made sure Tommy was paid in cash when he worked. Tommy remembers how great it was to receive money for something that was a fun adventure.

Tommy valued his friendship with Dick and Dick was genuinely fond of Tommy.

There was one event that probably brought them to be closer than anything else. Tommy had been arrested with some of his friends for drinking beer. Tom went to pick up Tommy at jail and father and son got into a minor fisticuff once home. Tommy left the house in a huff saying he would never return. Dick went out, found Tommy, gave him some money and eventually convinced him to go home. All the members of the Cavanaugh family held a special place for Dick in their hearts and lives. He made everyone of them feel special and in turn they cherished their time with him.

But it was Jimmy with whom he had a special bond. Jimmy being the youngest of six many times "got lost in the shuffle." He was too young to play with his brothers; Brenda and Jill had had enough of playing with kids, and even though Nancy Lou and Jimmy were close in age they shared little interest in the same things.

Tom, Brenda's father, remembers, "He loved Jimmy and he was awfully good to Jimmy."

When no else had much time for Jimmy, Dick made him the center of his attention. Nancy recalls, "He taught Jimmy how to ride his bike without training wheels. I remember it so well. It made Jimmy so happy and we were so proud. I mean I'm sorry, but by the sixth kid you don't care if they still have training wheels on at twenty. You are just so busy trying to take care of them; their true needs, as well as maintain your home and a small piece of your sanity. He really meant a lot to us and of course to Jimmy."

By 1966 Dick had become a permanent fixture in the Cavanaugh household. Nancy Lou recalls, "I remember him being there. I don't remember him first coming or being introduced to the family, it was just like he was always there. Like a brother. We loved him."

5) Once Removed

It probably took Dick about fifteen minutes to realize he had made a mistake.

He was nervous and hesitant to go when he kissed Brenda good-bye at Logan airport in Boston. Some how after leaving Manchester, they got lost in Boston and had arrived at the airport with little time for anything other than getting Dick to his flight. It was Sunday, October 2, 1966, four days before Brenda's eighteenth birthday when Dick stepped on the flight from Boston to Tulsa, Oklahoma.

Throughout the flight he kept telling himself that they were doing the right thing and it would be the best for their future. However, once he actually arrived on the campus of Oklahoma State University School of Technical Training in Okulgee, Oklahoma, he began to doubt the value of being separated from the girl he called his "Sunshine."

He had never seen such a wide-open space. He had not known what to expect when his father had told him it was time he went to a baking and business school, but he did not expect to be as surprised as he was at the open terrain.

Monday, October 3, 1966

Hello Sunshine,

Speaking of sunshine you have the type I really enjoy, not the type over here. It is so hot I think I am going to die. It was only 94 today. The only consolation for the heat that I can think of is, I was lucky enough to be put in the new dorm which is air-conditioned.

My room is really very nice and quite large. In fact the bed is larger than the one I have at home. But the one thing that really brightens up the place are the pictures I have of YOU. My roommate is really a pretty good guy.

Brenda, I can not count the times I have asked myself what am I doing out here?! But it is only for one year and it will pay off later on. So, I guess I will stay confined to my room and maybe even study.

I have not gone to class yet. I start at 7:30 to 11:30 then 1:30 to 4:30 five days a week. I doubled up on just about everything. I figure I may as well get everything out of this place as I possibly can while I am here.

I now know what you mean when you say starvation. I have had one meal here and it took me about three minutes to finish off and it was a poor meal.

The area they call a campus around here is really large. I get just as confused walking around here, as I did going to the airport Sunday — if that is possible. I certainly hope you did not have any trouble leaving the airport. If you did only have half as much trouble as I did getting there, I would have to say you did a mighty fine job, as you always do.

Love and Miss You Very Much Love, Dick.*

Brenda sat on the foot of her bed in her dorm room on the second floor of Scott Hall on the University of New Hampshire campus in Durham, reading Dick's first letter to her. She envied only the large dorm room he described in his letter, as the single room she shared with an acquaintance from high school was painfully small. It was obvious the college expected a large number of first year dropouts judging from the amount of freshmen they had doubled up in single rooms. Brenda decided that the

---

*Author's note: Here and throughout the book Dick Genest's letters have been edited — usually for brevity — without, the author hopes, diminishing their sentiments.

lack of space was a minor issue after reading Dick's letter. She was grateful to be within a twenty minute drive of York Beach and was pleased it would take only forty-five minutes to be back in Manchester if she so desired. She wondered how it must be for him to not know anyone. Although she had not been friends with her dorm roommate Barbara in high school they knew many of the same people and it took little time before the two became great friends.

Brenda had applied to two colleges: Wheelock in Boston and U.N.H. Even though Wheelock had been her first choice, she was quite content to major in early childhood studies on the beautiful and somewhat familiar campus of U.N.H.

Brenda loved the campus at U.N.H. for several reasons: the large brick ivy colored buildings, its provincial setting; green fields with cows and horses close to the campus, its close proximity to York Beach, and most of all its size. She was thrilled that she was attending a large college. "I liked the fact it was large because I don't like to stand out. I like to be anonymous and the campus and classes were large enough there that it was really easy to blend in. I don't like to draw attention to myself, so I just loved it there."

As she sat on her bed reading Dick's letter she realized that for the first time in over a year she would not be spending at least the weekend with Dick. She felt herself slipping into a quagmire of depression, doubt, and loneliness. Quickly, she shook her head and thought of all the possibilities she had for the weekend. She could go to the beach, she could go to the mountains, she could visit her friends in the city, she could stay on campus, the possibilities for her were endless and yet empty. She could not imagine any of those activities being remotely fun without Dick.

At least I have options, she thought to herself. No matter how down she felt she knew she was in a much better place than Dick. She knew that instead of feeling sorry for herself she should be grateful. Should, should, should, she thought. She wanted to look on the bright side of things, but nothing seemed that bright without Dick at her side.

At that moment she decided, whenever she read Dick's letters she would imagine he was sitting right there by her. Just the thought of Dick put a large smile on her face.

Thursday, October 6, 1966

Dearest Sunshine,

I imagine by now you are probably recovering from homecoming. I certainly hope your float came out okay and you had a wonderful time. Things have been really exciting around here — LIKE HELL!! There really is nothing to do here except drink and that is quite a problem since none of the kids from Boston own a car and we have to walk about a mile to a bar, unless we drink in our rooms. But I suppose it is to our advantage because among other things, drunken driving in this state can get you up to a year in jail. I have heard the town up to par in the area is Tulsa. It is about forty miles from here and Tulsa University is located there. It is a fairly large school, about twice the size of U.N.H and very modern. Have I told you the school I am presently attending, is located on an Indian reservation?

I just read this letter and there is no doubt it is one of the worst letters ever written. If you speak to or see your parents say hello for me. Brenda darling I love and miss you so very much and hope to see you soon.

Love Dick.

Tuesday, October 11, 1966

Dearest Sunshine,

Believe it or not I just received your two letters TODAY! They probably have been here since Saturday. The fools over here thought my name was spelled with a J instead of a G. Today I slowly spelled it out for them so I guess I won't have that problem any more.

I think I was food poisoned today. I'm just getting over it but I may have a relapse at any time. This afternoon I was in class and an attack came on. I had to leave and go to my room. I just laid on the bed and for awhile I was sure I was headed for the great big pasture in the sky.

I finally wrote a letter to my parents and speaking of parents please make sure to tell your parents hello. You asked in your letter about my roommate, well he is really from California and then lived in New York.

Just to give you an example of a typical nut around here, I was with the boys from Boston and we saw this kid walking up and down the hall clapping his hands in all directions. We watched him do this for awhile and finally asked him what in the heck he was doing. He replied, "I'm killing flies," and then he proceeded to tell to us of his unique fly-killing system. He told me he had different methods of killing them. And then he told me "off the record" he kept track of how many he killed daily, weekly, monthly, etc.

I don't want to give you the wrong impression of this hole . . . the department I am in is actually quite good. We have a lot of math formulas we must work out and they are quite hard. It is great they only keep us here one year.

The three pictures I have of us are really the only bright spot around here. I throw a kiss to the one of us standing by the dock in the morning; a kiss to the one of us in the snow around lunch time and a kiss to the best one, the prom picture — I see your cute beautiful face and your beautiful body, your lovely gown, OH just your entire self which I love and miss so very much — during the evening. Of course the best part of all comes before I go to bed when I throw one big kiss to all three. If my kisses could only travel as fast as air mail you probably would have received one by now. And I am sure they are strong enough to fight all the storms they encounter in flight. They will get there soon, providing you do not have a snow storm in Durham, but I am sure they are warm enough to melt snow right out of their path. By now you probably think I have gone crazy or am right on the verge, but I'm still sane, I think. It is going to be quite a battle not to lose my mind here. Miss you so very much and love you more than anything, Dick.

Sunday, October 16, 1966

Dearest Sunshine,

I am at the moment stranded in Tulsa. I have been in Tulsa since I about seven last evening. Please forgive the paper as I am now at the bus station and it was the only thing I could get my hands on. I borrowed it and I probably should ask the lady who gave me the paper for an envelope before she leaves. I now have the envelope and another piece of paper. Concerning my roommate I have no idea where he is. The last time I saw him was last night around midnight. I just miss you so much Brenda it is unreal. I know if you were here we could have a good time. I just go crazy thinking about you!!! Last night I managed to sleep in some apartment. It was a nice apartment.

I have not eaten a good since I have been here. I am so depressed. It is awful not knowing where I am, not knowing anyone, just sitting here in this bus station like a real bum. I have been here since one o'clock and now it is quarter of six and the bus comes at quarter past nine. Please excuse my writing I am so tired and shaky. Would you believe I have been writing this letter two and a half hours now? You should just see some of the people in this bus station, some with real class and some real bums. There are two sections one for colored people and one for whites. It's crazy.

More than anything I wish I was with you, sitting by the ocean eating clams. Brenda love and miss you more than anything.

Dick.

Tuesday, October 18, 1966

Dearest Sunshine,

Just want you to know that I now have a pillow to sleep on and I only wish you were by my side. It has been quite an exciting day — my trunk finally arrived! Just think, tonight I have a pillow a blanket AND clean sheets! My wardrobe has been expanded to now include four pairs of pants, five shirts, two sweaters and one winter coat. I mean how plush can things get? Actually I would not have the nerve to wear anything decent around here because of the environment and for fear that I could give up lunch anytime. One other important thing: my clock radio was in the trunk, so we have a little sound in the room. I don't mean to knock the room because as I have said it is fairly nice.

Well get ready for a shock, I had my first exam mid-semester (the semester ends in mid December here) and I received a B+. The exam was quite difficult with formulas and the like but between you and I really just lucked out. I did not know what I was doing, I do now, but I did not understand what I was doing then. I just looked above my desk and the picture of us skiing is really starting to curl up. Tomorrow I will have to get a pin or some tape to straighten all the pictures out because they are my only source of energy or life around here. The food around here just tears me down by the day. My greatest challenge of the day is not knowing whether or not I am going to survive the meal or have another attack. By the way, I had my 225th cheeseburger today. Well lover you know I miss, love and think about you, so I will say good night. Study hard and be good. Love you so much, Dick.

Saturday, October 23, 1966

Last night was really quite a time. I came back from class around quarter past four, had two beers in the room with Paul. Then some girl Paul had not seen in a few years called and he left with her. So I just sat around here for awhile, had many thoughts of you, asking myself what I was doing here. Knowing I could not take it much longer I went over to the kid's room from Boston and watched television until three a.m. Then I started to walk back to the dorm and got stopped by the campus police for no reason at all. I had to stay with them for about fifteen minutes giving them all kinds of identification, etc. It was really quite an experience. Be good, love and miss you, Dick.

Sunday, October 24, 1966

Dearest Sunshine,

Just a short note to inform you that we did go to Tulsa last night. I'm really getting bored with the place it is always the same old thing. We arrive about ten thirty p.m. and leave at four a.m. and then I go to bed completely exhausted from doing nothing. I don't know what I am doing next weekend for we have Friday off but, I know that I can't stay here because I really go crazy, haunted by thoughts of you. I knew things would be bad here without you but I could never have possibly imagined that it would be like this missing and loving you so much. I just keep telling myself that it will someday pay off. I suppose the old saying that if you do want a little out of life you so have to suffer a little, does hold true.

Even if I had to make the decision to come here again, knowing how awful it is, I'd do it again. I know if things come true for us, which as I have said before, I pray to God everyday they will, I will be able to give you and a family just a little bit more. For the first time in my life, I really feel that I am learning something. Seriously, I am working quite hard, even though there isn't that much that I do. I can't wait to get into business law school and leave this place. I am sure I won't have to come to Oklahoma, providing I can get into school in Chicago or the one in Hartford, Connecticut. The one in Hartford is not Yale.

It all depends on my marks. Well love I guess I will take a shower before the savages start to file in after being gone for the weekend. Be good and study hard. I do love and miss you so much, Dick.

Wednesday, October 26, 1966

Dearest Sunshine,

What a day! You would not believe it. Just call me accident-prone. I am lucky to have lived through the day. I woke up with a wicked backache and got dressed. (I am surprised my pants are not walking around the room by themselves that is how dirty they are.) Anyway I got to the stairs, (I live on the third floor) and yes, you guessed it, I fell down the stairs. Thank God there are only eight stairs at a stretch.

The rest of the morning was okay except for a few things like having a pen I borrowed spring a leak and having ink all over my hands and all over the formula sheet I was working on, and of course by the end of the morning the ink was all over my face.

Everything went rather smooth during the afternoon except, I was listening to some professor giving a lecture and I don't know if I fell asleep or what, but I was sitting in this chair, sort of leaning against the wall and BANG! it slipped and there I went crashing to the ground. I must have turned about ten shades of purple.

Besides all that, it is warmer here today than any other day since I have been here and it's really taking it out of me.

Well Hon it is almost five and I have got to go wait for my ride to the Tulsa airport so I can pick up my tickets for Thanksgiving. I just hope I don't get a depressing attack while I am there and fly home. I do love you so much, Dick.

Wednesday, November 2, 1966

I've decided that this letter is not going to be depressing. I mean how could things be depressing in this room when in my closet there is so much life and happiness? Yes, in my closet. You see I have quite a community of pet ants. I put a half can of beer in my dark romantic closet for my little friends. Boy are they having a blast. They never sleep, they are constantly intoxicated and they pass out once and awhile. There is a real orgy going on as far as I can tell. Every once and awhile I open the door and when the light hits them, if they are too bombed to notice the light, hey turn sort of purple I guess maybe they are blushing. I only have one problem hon, I cannot tell the males and the females. Well anyway the ants do add a little life to this place.

To the science lab for I cannot stand the library. You should see the library, I bet if you asked for a Donald Duck comic book they would have it, but if you asked for a certain encyclopedia they would not have it.

The ants are still having a wild time. Tomorrow is the day I just have to find out my marks. I am completely starving, I'll just have to drink water to take care of the pains. Wish so very much I could be with you for I do love and miss you so miss. Love You, Dick.

Thursday, November 10, 1966

The weather has taken another drastic change, the temperature is in the low forties compared to eighty-seven the other day. Well I am quite sure that the new generation of ants are coming to life for I have seen a few marching across the room. I must say they do look exactly like their parents. I have not put anymore beer in the closet because they are still a little too young to drink, even with my liberal age limit. Besides I don't want a bunch of lushes on my hands. Well Brenda it is time for me to take a shower, then read a little and go to sleep. And if I am really fortunate I'll have a neat dream in which we are together. Do love and miss you truly, Dick.

Friday, November 11, 1966

I forgot to tell you that the night I got really bombed this week, me and this kid from Boston chased this horse around a cow pasture. Thank God we were not able to catch him because our plan was to ride him bareback. If we had caught him I would most likely be in the hospital with broken arms, legs, etc.

Saturday, November 12, 1966

Hello Sunshine,

Well guess what hon I finally spent the entire weekend here and it was not that bad. Today did start with good laugh. Paul (by the way he did not go home for the weekend) had three warm beers and he decided to cool them by hanging them out the window by way of a small rope and tiny foam cooler. Of course it was sixty degrees outside and I could not convince him that the beer would never get cold.

Well anyway after about an hour he decided they were cold enough and he started to pull them up and yes, the handle on the cooler did break and it smashed into many pieces on the ledge which is below the window about four and a half feet. But luck was with us and the beer did not fall off the ledge.

Our main concern was getting the beer off the ledge before it was seen. So, I sort of held his legs while he was hanging out the window trying to reach the ledge. I was laughing so hard I almost dropped him a few times. Well, anyway there we were, Paul hanging out the window, me just about pulled out the window by his weight and here come the campus police followed by one of the dorm supervisors. Talk about being trapped in a crazy position. I was laughing so hard I could not answer their questions. Somehow before they got upstairs we did get the beer in the room. When they got to our room and saw the beer (we did not try and hide it) I just looked at them, biting my lip to prevent myself from laughing, but I could not help it, I started laughing so much it was ridiculous. The really funny thing was they laughed too. They did not even take the beer. Probably because it is a weekend and there are not many people around.

Miss you so very much, love more than anything in the world. Do love you, Dick.

Sunday, November 13, 1966

Dearest Sunshine,

You would not believe this day. It was so perfect. It was a beautiful beach day, the only problem being there is no beach in this desolate place. I took another hike today in order to get some decent food. I have never walked as much as I have since being here. The big moment came, I finally did wash and it was worse than last time. I just hate it so much. Of course I only did half of it because the rest can be done when I get home.

On the way back from doing my wash I ran into the kid's from Boston and they talked me into going to the movies with them. So, off I was again on another hike. My feet are really in pain.

Just think Love, you have a complete biography of my life over here and maybe some day it will be worth millions. Like Hell! What an existence. I do love you so much and miss you and cannot wait until I'm with you. Do love you so very much, Dick.

Monday, November 14, 1966

Hello Sunshine,

Well love it has been another beach day. I finally caught up with the head man around here in my department and now prepare yourself for a real shock, I have a 3.4 overall. I still do not believe it myself. All in all though I have worked for it. I have studied here more than anywhere else.

It has finally happened, I have gone a little soft or crazy. I knew that the environment would at one time another catch up with me. This afternoon after I took my little nap I caught myself saying, " Hello light. Hello wall." Yes, I was actually speaking to a light and a wall and I was too tired to pay much attention to it so I let it pass. But this evening it happened again, "Hello wall. Hello light." etc., so as fast as I could, I left the dorm and walked over to the kid's from Boston's room and listened to the Casious [sic] Clay fight on the radio.

Love, when we get married just forget about my working or anything all we are going to do is get a great house on some beach and write about some, rather all of my experiences over here, and for contrast maybe put in a few of yours. I guarantee you hon, we would have a best seller. It will be so great. Kids running around everywhere, it will be so great.

I bought a bag of peanuts tonight but I have to hang them from the ceiling or the ants will get at them. The new generation is really full of life. I will give them a beer in a few days. I cannot wait to get out of this place and be with you Love and miss you truly, Dick

Wednesday, November 16, 1966

Hi Sunshine,

What a day this has been, talk about being tired. Speaking to you last night was great the call really helps me along. Last night I got on this whiskey and sour kick. I had never had one before and they tasted great. A friend of mine was the bartender at the Driftwood last night. For awhile he had so many beers on the bar for us that there was no room for our hands or even an ashtray. We had a great time but what topped off the evening was when we got back on campus we were picked up by the campus police. Love, I SWEAR we did not do a thing.

We just got picked up for walking around on campus after midnight. They took us to the office and took our names. I was so disgusted by the whole thing, I just looked at one of the cops and said, "I hope you like your job because in the morning you will not have it!" and I went on saying things like that. Drunk I was to say things like that. But, I was so disgusted for we really had not done a thing. Nothing happened today concerning the whole ordeal and I doubt anything will. I think probation in this place would be a joke unless my parents found out about it. Well hon another so called letter, another twenty-four hours closer to the time I will be with you. Do love you very, very much, Dick.

Dick departed for New Hampshire on Saturday 19 November. It seemed like an eternity before the plane that he boarded in Tulsa, Oklahoma landed in Boston. He was excited and nervous to see Brenda. He was eager to spend every minute of his Thanksgiving break with Brenda, but he knew a week with her, would only magnify his desire and longing for her. He wondered if maybe their time apart had the opposite effect on her. He worried maybe her time at college had made her realize that there was more to the world than him and their relationship.

Of course deep inside Dick knew nothing could ever come between them. They had written each other every day. Brenda had with great amusement told Dick of all the boys pursuing her. She told him how none of them interested her in the slightest and how silly she found their pathetic attempts to get her attention. She too had been counting the days.

When Dick saw Brenda standing next to the terminal door on her toes looking as intently for him as he was for her he knew he had been foolish to think for some reason they would experience anything other than bliss together.

The week passed quickly. They wondered how the time they spent apart seemed to move in thick and slow motion while the time they spent together seemed to race past them.

Sunday, November 27, 1966

Hi Love,

Well I am back on the reservation. I walked in the door about two minutes ago and once here I just had to write to you. It seems as though I was just beginning to relax and be comfortable and I had to leave you. I imagine it will not be as bad at Christmas since it is not that far away. I know the time is just going to drag. I mean I just look around this place and get so depressed.

Friday, December 2, 1966

Hi Sunshine,

Believe me when I say this has been one of those days that you wish never had come along. The only good part of the day was receiving three letters from you. The day started out with me completely freezing to death this morning while I was walking, no running to breakfast. Class was the same dull thing. During lunch I decided to get a haircut in a barbershop. Well that is last time in my life that I ever go to a barbershop. I could have killed the barber. If I could only have seen a mirror I think I would have stopped him. But no, like a fool, I just let him clip away.

Well anyway I got back to the room and read my mail and I had a letter from my mother and I was classified 1A. That made me feel real great. Like Hell! But, I am not worried too much because I have been classified 1A [high priority draft ranking]. Anyway my mother called this friend of hers on the draft board and they said all I had to do was write a letter saying I was in school and I would be all set for another year anyway. Love and miss you more than anything, Dick.

Saturday, December 3, 1966

You would not believe what just went crawling by, a little ant! It is the first one I have seen since I have been back. Like a fool I caught it and I have it wrapped in cellophane. I am thinking of sending my new friend to you. Please just tell me I am not going crazy. I think I will wait and see if he lives through the night. If he does, tomorrow I will buy him a little food and send him on his long journey by way of the mail. I hope he doesn't get crushed on the way. Please tell the people who handle your mail to be careful with your letters. Oh, just tell me I am not cracking up. Love and miss you more than anything in the world, Dick.

Thursday, December 8, 1966

It is now six and I just got back to my messy disgusting room that I have not yet cleaned. I left here at three in the morning and stayed in class and science lab until five thirty. I did take a half hour break for lunch. I did not go to bed until midnight last night and I am so tired. Tomorrow I am going to get up early again but Monday, Tuesday, Wednesday I plan to rest. One good thing about being so tired is, I will be able to sleep a lot this weekend. But at this stage I don't even think of weekends as anything to look forward to; they are just a time of existence for me.

With my luck next Thursday it will probably be snowing or foggy and my flight will be delayed or canceled. if anything like this should happen I will call you no matter where I am and I will call.

Friday, December 9, 1966

Well it has been another swell night. I sang a few Christmas carols to a bush with a few lights on it and watched a little television. I hope my father sends money for the plane ticket. It should arrive Tuesday or Wednesday. It's a good thing the money is not going to arrive until next week because I believe I would spend half the money since half of the money is supposed to pay for the flight back here. And I am very serious when I say there are many doubts in my mind as to whether I will return.

Dick's flight arrived in Boston on time and in tact. He was exhausted, but once out of airport, the familiar coastal air revitalized him. The weak and dragging feeling that had plagued him the past month became a vague distant memory as he walked through downtown Boston at two in the morning. At one point he even considered walking the sixty miles to Manchester. However, before he left Oklahoma he had called his long time friend, Mike Burns and had asked Mike to pick him up in Boston. Dick decided he might as well stick to his original plan and he soon found a hotel room in the heart of the city.

Dick awoke up early Thursday morning. He marveled about how rested he felt in spite of just four hours sleep. He called Mike and told him where to meet him. Mike and Dick had known each other since grade school. They were part of a group of neighborhood boys from the North End which included Richard Murphy, John Howe, and Dick's closet friend Bill Starr.

They all had been friends as boys and now each one was creating his own path into manhood. Of course each of their paths in life went in different directions but they all seemed to be headed toward the same location. Dick often told Richard Murphy one day Richard would be the vice president of the bakery and Bill Starr would be the lawyer for the bakery. The camaraderie between boys that began with playing Little League, swimming in the Starr's pool, terrorizing the neighborhood on bikes, chasing each other through every backyard and field around, had become a strong friendship and bond that each one valued and appreciated in a way that none could really express but each knew absolutely existed.

But as with most friendships, the only real way to weaken the chain of shared experiences that brought the friends together would be the introduction of a serious girlfriend or boyfriend. Richard Murphy put it this way, "I did not like Brenda and she did not like me. I mean I never gave her a chance. There had been other girls but she was different and I did not realize until years later that I was just jealous of her. I was mad at her because she was taking Dick away from us."

Dick was happy to spend some time with Mike as they drove from Boston to Manchester. An hour with Mike seemed just right.

Before Dick was ready it was time for him to return to Oklahoma. He was convinced in all the hustle and bustle of the holidays coupled with his family and friends as well as Brenda's family and friends that somehow time had fast forwarded and robbed him and Brenda of their rightful time together.

Friday, January 13, 1967

Hi Sunshine,

Things have not changed at all since I left this desolate place, in fact they maybe a little worse. Once I got on the plane in Boston I knew I had made a mistake. So, I stayed in New York Wednesday night and decided I was not going to come back here. But, I was on a plane Thursday morning and arrived here in the afternoon. I called my parents Thursday night and my father told me I had given him a real snow job by not coming back here on the fourth but I really did not. I don't know whether or not he believes me. When I walked into class this morning I was kind of scared to meet this one professor because I know him so well. He was really surprised to see me. He did not expect to see me until next week. If my parents would have only been away I don't think I would have come back for another ten days. Particularly after finding out he did not expect me for awhile.

It was sixty-eight here yesterday — cold winter isn't it? I can't stand it being so warm. Tomorrow it will probably be about thirty below. I just hate this place so much. I guess one of the reasons for this hate is because I miss you so much.

Sunday, January 15, 1967

Hi Sunshine,

Well it's been another swell day in the prison without walls. I did manage to make it to mass this morning. The Mass lasted over an hour, but the most important thing is, I am really happy I went. I plan to go every Sunday while I am over here. I am going to pray everything goes okay between us and life is good to us while we are separated and that things are the same when we are together.

Monday, January 16, 1967

You Cute Hunk of Sunshine,

You are definitely driving me out of my mind. I cannot take it much longer. Concerning the picture, I love it! It is really great. I added to my collection. Between the high school picture and the one you just sent me I have your beautiful face constantly starring at me whenever I am in this hole of a room. I am going to go crazy, I just miss you so much.

I am going to get my semester marks in about twenty minutes and I am a little scared. Sometimes I feel that I really don't care anymore, but that is a foolish statement to make, especially since I am back in this place.

You would never guess what I forgot at home, yes, my toothbrush. I did buy a new toothbrush, a Dr. West Special, and I thought I was getting a great deal at thirty-nine cents but it turned out to be a child's toothbrush. It's a real joke brushing my teeth at present.

I just got back from class. It is two which is a lot better than four last semester. I got a 3.0 overall for the semester. I missed the hot shit list by one point. I am really broken up — like hell.

I've decided I am going to grow a mustache. It will take some time but it will probably keep my mind away from how desolate this place is. I have not tried to find a job yet, but I am going to go and look tomorrow afternoon. I am going to save all the money I make for our trip to Florida or for when we get married. How could you ever think that I could forget that we are going to be engaged next Christmas? Many many thanks again for the wonderful snapshot. I just hope I don't crack up when I look at it, but you know I see more in you than your beautiful physical features. Miss You and Love you so much, Dick.

Thursday, January 19, 1967

Hi Sunshine,

    A little incident happened in the prison today, I was called into the Deans office. The reason being is that I had a beer can in my closet. It was the beer can from months ago when I put it in there to feed the ants. I had completely forgotten about it. We must of had a room inspection sometime this week and the fools must have found it. Anyway when I got into the office, the idiot brought up the time I got stopped by the campus police last semester (when I was really found innocent), and he said the beer can made it my second offense. He put me on disciplinary probation for the semester and told me one more offense or school rule broken and I would be thrown out.

    You cannot imagine how mad I am. All this trouble over a beer can that I did not even remember I had! They are such idiots around here. Maybe I wish they would throw me out. No, my parents would go crazy. I would not give them (the school) the satisfaction. I would leave on my own before I would let that happen. I will never bring a beer back to my room because I know they will be checking it frequently. Isn't it a bastard the fools go right to my closet? For all I know they probably check the pocket of my clothes and go through my drawers.

    I just wish I could be with you and live with you and have fun times and do as we wanted, have a family and just live a good wholesome life together. It will be so great when the time does come.

I have a lab report due next Wednesday and I have done all the experiments but I really do not know what I did, so have to do them all over. I could borrow someone else's but I don't trust them plus and since I have to suffer in this prison I may as well learn something. Love you always, Dick.

Saturday, January 21, 1967

Dearest Sunshine,

At this moment I am just so mixed up, if you only know this day which you will. Today I got up at ten-thirty, took the two mile hike downtown and did nothing. I got back here and watched television. Okay get ready for a jolt — I got kicked out of school. In simple words I did! I tried to call you and when I tried to charge the call to my home phone the operator said my mother wanted to speak to me. So I spoke to my mother for awhile (did not tell her about school) and then my mother said okay go ahead and call Brenda. So I started to call you again but when the operator checked with my house, my father answered and said he would not accept the call. So I bought a six pack and now I am writing to you. I now realize that even if I got through to your dorm you would not have been there. I cannot write anymore for I am going to be sick. I am a bum and I am disgusted with myself and life. Please still love me for you are all I have. Do love you, Dick.

P.S. Please not a word about me getting kicked out of school for no one knows.

6) Compulsory Crossroads

National Archives and Records Administration

                                        8601 Adelphi Road
                        College Park, Maryland 20740-6001

Unfortunately, we do not have any records of the 3rd Battalion, 197th Artillery, for their tour in Vietnam. When we began processing the records in 1988 it soon became clear that there were no records for National Guard units called up in 1968. The army denied all knowledge of the existence of these records as did the various State Adjutants General.

We cannot help you locate any records of the 3rd Battalion, 197th Artillery, for the simple reason that records do not seem to exist for this unit.

We regret that we cannot be of more assistance in this matter.

Sincerely,

Charles Shaughnessy
Modern Military Records (NWCTM)
Textual Archives Services Division

NWCTM 2001465

Dick was devastated by his expulsion. In reality he had very few options as what he could do. That truth however, could not keep his head from feeling like it was going to explode. Countless thoughts of what he should do pounded on his skull. He considered going to Colorado. He was not sure why he thought of Colorado. Maybe just because it was not Oklahoma, or maybe because he really wanted to learn to ski well, or maybe because Coors beer was made there and as long as he had been thrown out of school for having a beer can in his closet, he may as well go somewhere were beer was somewhat vital to the economy. His head really began to throb as he tried to figure out how he was going to explain this to his father. After all the complaining he had done about school, he doubted that anyone was going to believe he was truly upset about being expelled.

How and why Dick's expulsion transpired is not entirely clear. Oklahoma State University enrollment record for Dick indicate only that he, "Entered October 3, 1966 (Baking) — Withdrew January 23, 1967." Clearly from Dick's letters he was did not withdraw voluntarily. As best as anyone who was familiar with the situation can recall, soon after Dick was summoned to the Dean's office on 20 January 1967, it was decided that disciplinary probation was not sufficient punishment for someone who had two prior offenses.

As was Dick's luck, it appears that he was chosen to be the example what would happen if a student was caught with, or suspected of, using and/or possessing alcohol on campus. It is believed that the humorous incident Dick describes in his letter dated 12 November regarding holding his roommates legs while his roommate attempted to retrieve the beer that had fallen onto the ledge below their window, being stopped by the campus police 15 November (even though Dick was with at least four other inebriated dorm mates, only he and one other were forced to go to the office and produce identification that night) and finally the beer can he put in the closet to feed the ants he did not have the heart to kill, apparently were all taken as flagrant violations of the rules by Dick.

By Sunday, two days after Dick learned of his fate, the shock and disappointment had turned to anger and disgust. He was angry for allowing himself to be put into a situation where he had such little control over his future and he was disgusted that his school career had ended in such a ridiculous fashion. He called Brenda, told her he would be home in a few days and made her promise not to tell anyone of his circumstance.

Dick probably left Oklahoma Wednesday or Thursday. Brenda remembers she was able to meet him at the Holiday Inn in Manchester as soon as he arrived in town. Since Brenda frequently left U.N.H. on Fridays and went to her parents' house in Manchester, she figures Dick must have arrived on Friday. She remembers they spent most of the night discussing how Dick was going to tell his parents. It is worth noting that Dick and Brenda were not sexually active at this time.

After talking through the night with his dearest and most trusted friend, Dick felt he had the courage to face his parents with the news he knew would anger, upset and disappoint them. Dick had waited until he was sure his father would be at the bakery before he and Brenda left the Holiday Inn Saturday morning. Dick dropped Brenda off at her house, told her he would call her in awhile and with great trepidation he proceeded to his home. His sister Charlotte remembers him slowly shuffling up the walkway to the house. Oh boy, she thought, why is he here?

Dick went into the house, gave his mother a kiss, threw his sister a hopeful smile and proceeded to tell his mother what happened emphasizing that he was home for good this time. Once the shock of having Dick standing before her wore off, Fleurette found herself mostly concerned for him. She found herself really only worried about Dick having to tell Edgar what had happened.

Dick knew he had to tell his father immediately. But the thought of going into his father's office and not only having to face his father but also to have to look into the eyes of his grandfather who watched over the bakery from his portrait that was prominently hung on the wall behind Edgar's desk, made Dick's stomach twist and turn so tight he almost doubled over.

Fleurette parked her olive green Thunderbird convertible in front of the bakery. She turned off the car and she and Dick sat in silence. After a few moments Dick turned to his mother, bowed his head and in a way that only a vulnerable, scared, son who was in need of their mother could, he asked her to please go in and tell his father.

Fleurette said nothing to Dick as she left the car. She went in and told Edgar Dickie was home from school and he was not going back. She remembers that even she was nervous talking to Edgar. Although Edgar was very upset, he had little to say. He seemed to know that he could not make his son feel any worse than he already did and to fight this battle would be futile.

When Edgar came home that night he and his family sat down to dinner. During the quiet and reserved meal he told Dick to be at the bakery at four a.m. Monday. Edgar had decided that since Dick was no longer in school, that he would now completely take charge of Dick's education. He was going to show Dick every thing about the bakery and he had decided that he would be the one to teach his son how to run a successful business. However, first he wanted Dick to suffer a little.

When Dick got to the bakery on Monday morning he found the first lesson his father had planned for him could have been titled, "How to start at the bottom and work your way up," because he had been assigned to the lowly task of packaging English muffins (a job he was not above doing but had always disliked). It did not take long for Dick to convince his father he had learned his lesson and was once again a vital part of daily operations.

ALMOST BACK

It is evident from the following letter that Dick was the happiest he had been in months. He may have failed to complete his academic education but he really felt like his future was promising as he got back into the swing of the bakery.

Monday, February 27, 1967

Hi Brenda,

The events of the day have beer so exciting I simply do not know where to start, but, I will try. I started work today by first going to the post office to get the mail. When I got to work they gave me a whole mess of spreadsheets to add up on the electric adding machine. Well after about six hours I finally finished what should have taken about an hour to do. You would not believe how much I hate adding machines that is the electric ones — if I kept my finger on one key just a split second too long, the damn thing just kept on adding. For a period of time I was ready to completely smash every one of the adding machines we have. The rest of the day I spent on the phone, taking orders and calling different places, which was actually kind of fun.

As was their ritual and necessity Dick and Brenda wrote to one another everyday. It did not matter that they were less than a 45 minute drive from one another, they had to be in daily contact with each other. For them, the letters were as important to their days as eating or sleeping.

Brenda continued her studies at the University of New Hampshire while Dick worked for his father. She stayed in Durham at U.N.H. during the week and came home on weekends. She had been delighted at the end of the first semester when she and her roommate were able to move from their single room on the first floor of Scott Hall to a larger room on the third floor. However now that Dick was home she had little interest in her new spacious room and she was always excited to leave so their weekends together would begin.

Their weekends almost always ended with a Sunday dinner or cookout at the Cavanaughs. It was during the family dinners and the afternoons that preceded them that Dick's place in the Cavanaugh family became a permanent position. He often took the kids to the pool at his house. Jimmy remembers, "It was really neat, he would take us swimming or to play in their playroom. It was a great house and he always let us have so much fun. I mean imagine this guy, here he was dating our sister but he always took time to play with us. He was just really something else."

Dick worked hard with his father during the rest of the winter and the spring of 1967. He was so busy with work and Brenda he had little time to be concerned with anything else. However, like most every man during the 60's and early 70's, the threat of being drafted hung over his head, like the ruthless blade of a guillotine that was tethered by a tired and frayed rope. Having been expelled from three colleges (it seems that he was caught with a beer in hand one night on the campus of St. Anselm) because of beer, his options of avoiding the draft were limited.

Dick and Brenda decided to go to York Beach to their favorite boulders to discuss what Dick could do to avoid being drafted and ending up in Vietnam. By the beginning of 1967 the "conflict" in Vietnam had become a zone of death and destruction that most of the country watched with horror and disgust every night on television. Brenda recalls, "It was not like these boys were going off to fight for some noble cause — I mean our government would not even declare war — it was like they were being asked to die for a cause that not even our government would outwardly support. It was just crazy. And on top of that every night on t.v. they would show all the guys that were dead or dying every day over there. It was like if you went to Vietnam — you were going to die — and for what no one could really say."

It was an unusually warm day in February when Dick and Brenda walked to the Nubble Lighthouse in York Beach. The Nubble majestically and proudly marked the dramatic and beautiful Maine coast line. The Nubble both invited and warned visitors to the sea. Dick and Brenda walked to the rocks that lined the shore. They climbed down to a large rock with a smooth, square flat top. They sat down, dangled their legs over the edge, watched the waves clash with and then retreat from the rock. They savored the air as the ocean mist draped over them. It was awhile before they spoke and then they both began at the same time. They laughed and smiled at one another. Brenda leaned next to Dick and he put his arm around her. They molded into each other, and searched the sea and the sky hoping maybe the stars or the water held the answer. Dick began to tell Brenda he had been talking to Mike Burns and Mike had said he could get Dick into the National Guard because his uncle was a general.

Although Brenda did not like the idea of Dick joining, she knew it was about the only way to keep him out of Vietnam at this point. Brenda, as well as just about everybody else in 1967 knew, that if you were not in college and you did not want to go to Vietnam, if you joined the National Guard you would be safe from the draft, jail and Vietnam. Thousands of men from every imaginable background and belief had already joined and were falsely secure in knowing that they were safe from being activated. It was a common misconception that was perpetuated and continued in part by the army. (It becomes easily understood why everyone — except those who actually went from the National Guard — still, even today, believe that the National Guard was not called and never did go anywhere near Vietnam when one reads a letter Brenda received from the National Archives and Records Administration in December of 1999, that states, "When we began processing the records in 1988 it soon became clear that there were no records for National

Guard units called up in 1968. The army denied any knowledge of these records as did various State Adjutants General.")

A six-year commitment that consisted of six months of training, followed by two hours a month along with one weekend every three months seemed a small sacrifice to keep Dick alive. When Dick and Brenda returned from the beach Dick called Mike and set up a time to go to the armory.

The National Guard Armory in Manchester, was an imposing brick building that sat a few hundred yards from the Merrimack River. The 197th Field Artillery's revered and honored history in Manchester imbued the entire building and grounds, where the tools of the war trade impatiently rested. Dozens of olive green trucks in every shape and size surrounded the compound — a fence around the trucks served a warning that only the approved were permitted access.

The 197th evolved from the New Hampshire Militia which was organized in March of 1680 and served in all of the Colonial Wars as well as the Revolution and Civil War. The 197th was a field artillery with large mobile guns. The guns could shoot 98 pounds of artillery at an effective range of eight miles.

As early as 1966 the 197th was classified as a Select Reserve Force meaning, they were to be 100% ready to be activated. It is very likely that Mike's uncle, General Burns was well aware this when Dick went with Mike to join and it is highly unlikely that Dick was informed of the imminent probability of activation, before he made the commitment.

After joining the National Guard, Dick continued to work at the bakery and spend most every night and weekends with Brenda until May of 196, when he had to begin to fulfill his obligation to the National Guard. On Thursday, May 4, 1967, he arrived at Fort Campbell in Kentucky to begin boot camp and basic training.

Friday, May 5, 1967

Hi Sunshine,

I suppose I could give you a rough idea of what this place is like, but you would never believe me. We arrived here Thursday about one in the morning. They had us fill out paper work until quarter past four in the morning and then they said we could go to bed; until four-thirty. Yes, they did give us a fifteen minute sleep period in two days. Tonight they really did give us a break, guess what we can go outside in front of the barracks until quarter past eight!! Isn't that great!

Oh yes today I received my new army haircut. A lot of time went into it, I'd say maybe, ten seconds. Brenda, they cut so close to your head that they actually cut you. I really saw quite a few kids bleeding quite a bit. I was fortunate and only got a small nick. I don't think you would recognize me if I was walking down the street. I look kind of like Mr. Clean. It is really gross, I can't stand the way it feels more than the way it looks. The way I see it, even if I do not get another haircut until September, it still would not be close to what it was.

Dear Love, I cannot see any possible way that I will be able to make it without you until September. I am just going to crack up. I do love you so very much and cannot wait until we are married and together forever and ever.

They gave us four minutes to eat tonight. Pretty good huh? When the time is up whether you are done or not they make you throw any food left away.

I plan on calling you sometime. I will let you know in advance so we can make arrangements. At present we are restricted from the phones. Love tomorrow I plan on writing a more detailed letter. I am running out of time at present. I have to make mail before a certain time or it's curtains, so they say. Do love you very much, Dick.

Sunday, May 7, 1967

Hi Brenda,
    I feel like a cow with all the different things that are hang-

ing around my neck, two keys two foolish metal tags and another medal thing. Saturday we had to cut the lawn with our hands. They really are a bunch of nuts around here. Friday after I wrote I went to bed at nine and at nine-thirty some guy came in and woke five of us up to go clean the officers club. I could have killed him, I was so tired. You just would not believe how warm it is here but, in the morning it is so cold that my head feels like it is frozen. The fools over here will not let you close the window. The food is bad — not as bad as Oklahoma — but it's bad. They give you enough but they do not give time to eat it. You have to eat like a pig in order to eat half of it. I met a pretty neat kid from Illinois that is a nervous wreck. I thought I was bad but he is just unreal. Boy, I think I have it bad now, but I have not even started basic.

Tonight I have fire watch, that is I have to walk around the barracks and outside and look for fires. Now, tell me that is not stupid. Oh Bren, I just love you so much and want to be with you. But I know it will be a good thing when all of this is over and out of the way. It sure is a bastard now though.

Some of these guys here really scare me. You would not believe all the swearing people do. We are sworn out for doing nothing at all. It is really disgusting. We have to get up at four-thirty every morning and wait around until six before we can eat. This morning they let us sleep. But about nine someone come over to me and said, "Okay get up." I thought it was some kid and almost said, "Fuck you." Well good thing I did not because it was a sergeant asking only it I wanted to go church. Well Brenda I will try and write tomorrow. Do love you so much, Dick.

Tuesday, May 9, 1967

Hi Bren,

Well to tell you the truth, I really do not like this army stuff at all. All this walking and being pushed around is really getting to me. All you do is get pushed around, I just thank God I am not here for two or three years. I do not think I will mind the weekend meetings anymore after this.

I am really missing you very much, thinking of you often, wishing so much I could be with you.

Tomorrow we have to get six shots, in the arm I hope. Tomorrow we might get shipped out to basic training and receive permanent barracks. I hear it is a real bitch when you get off the bus at Basic. They make you run about thirty minutes with the heavy duffel bag we have. I don't mind saying that I am a little scared.

You should see the Basic Training sergeants. They wear these Smoky the Bear looking hats and definitely don't look at all like the Good Humor Man. God, they look mean.

They are also a bunch of neatness fanatics around here. We have to sweep, wash and scrub the same floors everyday. It does not matter if we have walked on them or not. You can not even go to the bathroom during certain hours of the day and you cannot go until the bathroom has been inspected, which could be any time during the day. After you finish smoking a cigarette, you have to tear the paper let the tobacco fly away and then put the filter in your pocket. When I get out of here I am going to be a real slob in retaliation for all the crap I have taken. They are a bunch of nuts about making beds here. It only takes me about twenty minutes to get the blankets and sheets the right way. I am telling you, they are REALLY crazy.

Well Love, l will write as soon as possible, but when I get to basic tomorrow night I am pretty sure they will keep us going for a couple days around the clock. Love you so very much and miss you very much and cannot wait until we are together permanently. All my love Bren, Dick.

Tuesday, May 16, 1967

Hi Bren,

Well I guess I lucked out a little today, I had to stay in the barracks all day, cleaning and guarding them while the boys were out marching and playing games. I am now guarding, so to speak, because really there is nothing to guard. Truthfully, I was more of a janitor than a guard today. Tomorrow back to the same old crap.

I forgot to tell you, I cannot make a bed properly. Every morning I make it and then sometime during the morning, some sergeant tears it up. So, I have to make it twice, which really gets me mad. No matter how hard you try, you are always wrong and someone is always screaming at you. I feel more like a caged animal everyday. I don't know if I told you but the bed's mattress are about one inch and a half in thickness, but you are so tired at night, it doesn't really matter.

I just love you so much and like being with you, it is just so great. I just wish I could at least speak to you. I think the boys are on their way back, I hear, "Left, left left." Love and miss you more than anything in the world, Dick.

Sunday, May 21, 1967

Hi Bren,

I have a little time before we go and crawl in mud holes, swing on bars and run around like fools. Today has been a swell day around here. One kid had some kind of attack and was giving up blood by way of his mouth. I could not even look, just hearing about it gave me the shakes. Another kid had an attack of appendicitis. It's a real healthy place around here wouldn't you say?

Oh Lover, just thinking about you, I go crazy. We had so many good times and I want so many more. I am already missing the beach with your company. I just looked down toward my feet, what a joke these boots are. I feel like such a clod with them on. I really have to laugh, it is so ridiculous here. Everyone is walking around in green baggy pants. Really it is not funny but I just have to laugh. I am really surprised I have not been called to go run and swing like a monkey on the bars.

Monday, May 22, 1967

Well here I sit on the floor in the bathroom writing you a letter at three in the morning. I am so tired I can hardly keep my eyes open. Man, am I sick of this army stuff. I am on fire watch, looking for fire in a barrack no one smokes in. Be back in a minute I have to do my rounds. I just walked around upstairs and man some people are really restless. Oh Baby, I just want to get out of this place and be with you. I need you Bren, I honestly and truly do. I need you and your company throughout life.

I just had to wake up the K.P.'s (it's three-thirty) and I have never heard so much swearing in my life. I cannot say I blame them though.

Tuesday, May 23, 1967

Hi Love,

You would not believe how tired I am. I did okay firing the rifle today. Or maybe I should say I am not scared of it as I was before, but, I still do not care for guns. I do not think we should have any in our future home. Unless, you really want one but I do not believe you like them anymore than I do. Today when I was standing in formation, I coughed and out of habit, I put my hand over my mouth. Well I had to do push-ups with the rifle in my hand and I could not let the dumb thing touch the ground. These Smoky the Bear hat wearing sergeants really tend to piss me off.

I had a really neat dream last night (during my twenty minutes of sleep) and you, my love, were the main character. I don't remember what it was about but, I remember it was great.

Tuesday, May 30, 1967

Hi Love,

It has been another great day. I washed plates, pots and pans all day and got back to the barracks at 7:00 p.m., just in time for the run. I'm not too mad about the whole day! Of course it was the first day we could do anything and I had to wash dishes for twelve hours. Some of my friends went bowling here on post and drank 3.2 beer. The fools snuck a beer into the barracks for me. I refuse to even look at it or know where it is. They are kind of upset with me, but I have just gotten into too much trouble in my life because of beer. I promised myself it would not happen again, nothing is going to interfere with me getting out of here and being with you. After this I am not going to leave you again, there is just NO WAY.

Thursday, June 1, 1967

Not much has happened since I last wrote to you. We did get paid, I received $39.00 for a months work plus $25.00 for a grand total of eleven to twelve cents per hour! Pretty good would you not say? We have been going to the rifle range the past two days. What a walk, I heard it is eighteen miles one way, but I am not sure. I have improved a little bit with the rifle, but you have to shoot in a crouched down position and it feels like your are off balance. Anyway several times after firing, I have been knocked down on my ass.

Sunday, June 4, 1967

Went to mass today and followed in my little book. It was really great. The army turns some people into swearers and drinkers, but it is having the opposite effect on me. It is making me a nicer guy. I don't want to sound conceited, but once out of here I am going to be or try to be the most pleasant person around. I have just had all I can take of yelling, screaming and being called dumb, stupid and idiot.

ALMOST BACK

Brenda completed her freshman year of college the second week of June 1967. After working four summers as a candy striper and nurse's aide she decided she wanted to spend the summer in York Beach. She applied for and got the coveted job of candy sales girl at The Goldenrod, a candy shop that was (and is) renowned for its salt water taffy throughout New England. It was the perfect job as far as she was concerned. The Goldenrod was just a block from the beach house and the beach. Most satisfying though, she was able to spend the summer on the coast.

Except for Jill, Brenda's family went up to the beach most weekends. Her sister, Jill, had convinced her parents to let her spend most of the summer with Brenda at the beach house. During the week Brenda and Jill had the grand beach house to themselves and just when the house seemed a bit lonely, their family would converge upon the house.

Brenda's was constantly reminded her of how lucky she was to be spending her summer in such an ideal fashion, but her heart would not let her, even for a minute, forget how much better things would be if Dick was with her. She almost found herself angry that things like walking on the beach, swimming in the ocean, sitting on the porch with her family and even her all time favorite, eating freshly caught lobsters and clams seemed almost meaningless and certainly boring without Dick. She was amazed how the year she had spent with him had changed her life. Everything she had once held dear paled in comparison to Dick. For the first time in her life she could hardly wait for the summer to be over, because come the end of August, Dick would be done with his training for the National Guard and they would be able to be together again.

Wednesday, June 14, 1967

Hi Bren,

I just got off guard duty. I did not have K.P. yesterday, but I did have it today. We got a ten minute break plus eating time in fourteen hours of work. Last night we had night fire until twelve, you could not even see the targets. I got to throw a hand grenade on Tuesday and you would not believe the noise they make. After hearing them, I would never want to be around when a bomb goes off.

Thursday, June 22, 1967

Hi Bren,

Well I am back from life in the woods. It was really different. The march out there was something else. We carried all different kinds of equipment, sleeping bag, first aide kit, ammo, rifle, canteen, plus countless other things. At one point if it were not for you, I was hoping to die. What a gross thing to say, especially considering I love life so much.

We hardly got any sleep at all. The whole experience was based on a visit to Vietnam. It was really bad. What an experience being attacked at night. They use machine guns, flares and tiny bombs. Of course none of the things could really hurt you. It was really gross. I hope your able to read this because I am writing dark and I am not supposed to be writing now. Bren. I just want to marry you and have little children that look like you.

Friday, June 23, 1967

Only one person got bit by a snake while we were out in the woods. He is still in the hospital. I was fortunate and did not even see one. Just about everyone has broken out in a rash of some kind, but I have not, yet. The person I shared the tent with is completely ruined. He has these little chiggers embedded all over his leg, it is really gross.

Wednesday, June 28, 1967

Hi Bren,

Well I got caught writing you last night. I was sealing the envelope when the lieutenant happen to walk in about five after nine. There were three of us in the bathroom at the time. He did not say anything except to get to bed.

Yesterday I lost my temper for the first time in a long time. I almost hit this person who is one of my best friends over here. I don't know what happened. I was just constantly being teased all day and all these aggravating things were being done to me, nothing bad, just annoying things. Anyway, I was so tired and sick from the shots the previous day, I retaliated. Any one who witnessed the whole thing would say it was nothing, and really it wasn't anything. It was just strange to me because I never lose my temper and rarely get real mad. I just was so tired and the bastard really got on my nerves.

I hope you are not finding work to hard or tiring. I just cannot wait until we are married. Life will be so great for us and don't you worry I am going to make you such a happy married person.

Thursday, June 29, 1967

I am going to tell you about the gas chamber we had to go through today. Well it was pretty bad once inside. The sergeants made you take off your gas mask and say your name, serial number and date of birth. If you could do that you were doing pretty good because the gas really burned your eyes and skin. They made myself and this other kid sing "Happy Birthday," because it did not look like we were in enough pain.

Sunday, July 2, 1967

Hi Bren,

Well it is fourth of July weekend and sure does not feel like it here. I imagine you probably have been working like a slave. In my life I have never been as scared and nervous as I am right now about the test we have to take tomorrow. If I flunk it, it is all over, eight more weeks of this crap. I hope I do okay. If I pass, I most likely, will leave here on Friday after graduation for Oklahoma (to finish training). I just hope the time in

Oklahoma goes by fast, because I cannot take being away from you much longer.

I wish I could use the phone today. I need to talk to you and I would like to call my mother too. I have spoken to my mother once since I have been here, but she has written me a lot of letters.

Yesterday I did my good deed and gave a pint of blood. I really think they took more than a pint. They said the blood would be in Vietnam in three days, so I really did not mind how much they took.

Tuesday, July 4, 1967

I did do well on the test yesterday. I guess I got all nervous and everything for no reason at all. Only three more days here and basic is over.

Dick was transferred to Fort Sill in Oklahoma the weekend of July 8–9. At Fort Sill he would fulfill his training obligation to the National Guard. The purpose of this phase of the training was to have National Guardsmen pick or be assigned their "job" in the service. Dick was assigned to be a driver, which was one of the better jobs to have. The irony of Dick ending up back in Oklahoma for advanced training, less than a year from when he was thrown out of school in the same state was not lost on no one.

Monday, July 10, 1967

It was really warm over here today. I had it pretty easy today and I will have it fairly easy Tuesday, Thursday, Friday and next Monday because I am taking driver education. I was selected to be a driver, which is quite fortunate. I never will be able to figure out why I was selected, if they only know how I really drive.

I just found out it's 105 degrees right now. Man, is it ever crowded here. In Kentucky there were six-teen people per floor, here there are thirty-six. Brenda I am really missing you. The more I think about it, the more I realize you are the greatest person I have ever known. We just have so many things we have to do together.

Monday, July 17, 1967

I passed my drivers test and received my license to drive heavy trucks. The type of trucks that pull cannons, ammunition, etc. As crowded as it is in here, they just moved six more kids in here. Please do not take all my complaints seriously. I mean what I say is the truth even if I exaggerate a bit.

Sunday, July 23, 1967

Hi Bren,

Well here I sit in my truck on guard duty. I am thankful I don't have to walk, I simply drive the boys to the various posts. I don't even have to get out of the truck to let the tailgate down because I have an assistant for that. When I was on guard duty on Thursday all I did was drive some lieutenant around. It was really a snap. I was kind of nervous at first, but once I got to know him it was really easy. Again I must say it is really hot in the land of nothingness. I am watching the sweat roll off my head and hands. Of course the uniform does not help. I think when they manufactured the uniforms they had the North Pole in mind.

Brenda, just looking around this place, really kills me. Every building is painted the exact same color. I found out the place I live in was built in 1941. It was built to last just six years so you can imagine the condition they are in. There are some nice places here, but it just so happens I live in the slums. I could not go to Mass because I had to be on guard duty. That really upset me. You will have to pray extra for me. Love and miss you so very, very much, Dick.

Dick celebrated his twenty-second birthday on August 7, quietly by himself in the Enlisted Man's Club.

> Tuesday, August 22, 1967
> Another day just about over and they still have not told us when we will be able to leave. I will be the first to know because I am very well known driving for headquarters and the orders will go to headquarters first. I have all the messenger boys on alert and asked them to tell me when they come in. It will be so good to leave this place. The best part will, of course be, that I will be with you, my best friend. I am looking so forward to being with you.

Dick was released from training in Oklahoma on August 30, 1967. Brenda picked him up at Logan Airport in Boston and after a quick stop in Manchester to see his parents, they went to York Beach. The two weeks they spent in York Beach together were as glorious and delightful as they both had fantasized. They sat on the pier and ate clams and lobster, they walked for miles hand in hand on the beach, they spent hours soaking in the sun and basking in each other. They spent every evening sitting on their favorite rock with the Nubble Lighthouse watching over them, talking into the wee hours of the morning.

Although they savored every moment the time flew by. They reluctantly returned to their respective responsibilities — Dick to the bakery and Brenda to U.N.H. for her sophomore year. Even though they had dreaded the end of their beach vacation it did not take them long to became content with their fall schedules. They talked every night, wrote one another every day and spent every weekend together. It was plainly obvious to them that it made no difference what they were doing as long as they were together, nothing else really mattered.

7) Budding Bliss

Surprisingly, as much as they were in love and as sure as they were of their future together, Dick and Brenda were not sexually active. In the two years and six months they had been together, only once had they "let things go too far." That one time had spawned so much guilt and shame for the two young Catholics that they decided it was not worth it. They believed they should, and could, wait until they were married. However, they were not immune to the radical changes that were creeping across the country.

As Dick and Brenda struggled to maintain some of the values they had been taught to hold sacred, "The Summer of Love," was expanding and accelerating from West to East. As many drastic changes in society were weaving their way through America, Dick and Brenda found themselves questioning much of what they had been taught to believe. They could not help but notice that the world in which they now lived had become dramatically different from the world in which they had grown up. Their generation was becoming increasing distant and independent from past generations. They began to wonder if the beliefs they had been raised to revere still held the same significance as they did when they were children.

Toward the end of September there was a large bakery convention in New Castle, New Hampshire. Edgar, Fleurette, Dick and Brenda all went to the convention that was held at a resort know as The Wentworth-by-the-Sea, a grand old hotel that majestically watched over the Atlantic Ocean. After a full day of presentations and a formal dinner at the historical hotel, Dick and Brenda wanted to get away from the appearance and ego motivated socializing and so they went for a long, lazy walk along the beach below the hotel.

As the full moon slowly blanketed the horizon, the ocean quietly spoke of flirtation and romance. Soon Dick and Brenda became seduced by temptation and anticipation. They decided to go back to Dick's house. Fleurette and Edgar had made plans to spend the night at the hotel and Dick and Brenda longed to be unaccompanied by anyone but each other.

Brenda and Dick were overwhelming distracted with love and desire by the time they completed the sixty-mile drive. Being separated for the entire summer, having the house to themselves and having had the beach seductively taunt them, proved to be too much for their will. Brenda remembers the only apprehension they felt was a fleeting and momentary doubt when she said, "I know if we do this tonight, I will get pregnant."

To the shock of both of them Brenda's matter of fact statement neither struck fear in them nor seemed to be a strong enough reason for them not to express their deep love for one another. Perhaps because they knew that they were always going to be together, that they were going to have many children and because they felt more committed and connected than any married couple they knew, they did not hesitate to express the love that overflowed the brim of their being that night.

Not surprisingly, two weeks later Brenda was two days late for her period and there was no doubt in her mind that she was pregnant. She told Dick and though he may have been slightly taken aback, he was not shocked or upset by the news. However both Dick and Brenda wanted a doctor's confirmation. Brenda felt that going to a doctor in Manchester would be equivalent to placing an advertisement in the local newspaper announcing her pregnancy. Fortunately, Dick had a friend who was a doctor in

Nashua, New Hampshire. Both he and Brenda felt the inconvenience of traveling to Nashua was outweighed by the benefit of retaining their privacy.

Brenda did not even have to get out of the car. Dick brought her urine sample into his friend's office. When Dick came back to his Mustang half an hour later, and simply said, "Yes," Brenda just nodded her head and said "I know."

On the hour drive home they discussed the options. Of course their conversation was just a token discussion because they both knew and agreed not only should they get married but really they truly wanted to be married.

The next day Dick told his father he was going to marry Brenda. Edgar was not overly happy nor he was he surprised. Edgar was a smart man who had hoped this day would come later, but knew the day had been inevitable from the moment he first heard Dick talk about Brenda.

That same evening Dick went over to Brenda's house to tell Tom and Nancy with Brenda. Tom remembers it vividly, "I had no idea he was going to marry Brenda. I mean she was my first child and with all the other children were still at home and the LAST thing on my mind was one of them would be getting married.

"Anyway, they came into the living room and said they wanted to talk to me. I could not imagine what the two of them needed to talk to me about. Marriage was the last thing on my mind. When they told me I almost fell off the couch! It was a shock to me. It took a little thought on my part, but it did not take long for me to recover and I thought if she going to get married she could not ask for a nicer guy."

Dick had told his father that Brenda was pregnant but Brenda could not bring herself to tell her parents until after she was married. Tom and Nancy most likely figured it out long before Brenda told them. After all, Brenda had quit school soon after starting her second year and had married just a month after the announced engagement. Tom and Nancy saw no reason to state the obvious. They had faith in Brenda and her choices. And they too, knew that Dick and Brenda were destined to be together.

Brenda A. Cavanaugh and Richard E. Genest were married on Saturday, November 2, 1967 at St. Catherine Church in Manchester. Monsignor Philip Kenney presided over the simple ceremony.

Brenda's beauty that day was radiant. Her face was reminiscent of a perfect porcelain doll. Her veil lightly covered her face, cascaded over her shoulders and came to a rest high on her waist. Her blonde hair was tastefully pulled away from her cherub-like face and crowned with a large soft white silk bow that perfectly matched her full length A-Line dress that was discreetly jeweled at the neck line and wrists. She was a picture of elegance and happiness as Tom walked her down the aisle. Dick stood at the alter waiting for his bride and although he felt like he could not wait one more minute to be married to his love, he also felt like he wanted to freeze this moment forever. He could not imagine there was a better feeling than the one that he was experiencing as he watched his angel glide toward him.

The dinner and reception at the Manchester Country Club following the service was a fun and loving merger of two families and their friends. After many speeches and toasts, tears of laughter and tears of joy, slow and tender dancing as well as impulsive and joyful dancing, Dick and Brenda said good-bye to their parents in many ways and set out for a two week honeymoon in Acapulco, Mexico.

Brenda and Dick's shared zest and passion for the ocean and the beach was one of the strongest links in the bond that pulled them so close together. Immediately after checking into the Acapulco Hilton they took the one-minute walk from their room to the beach. They soon discovered that the turquoise water and the chestnut beach considerably upped the ante of their love for the sea. They quickly realized that sometime in their future they would live somewhere where the water and land were welcoming and warm.

Brenda and Dick relished each moment they experienced in Mexico. Their exuberant happiness was noticed by everyone they came in contact with. They were the picture perfect model of two young people in love, relishing in and marveling at each other and the life they were about to begin. So much so they were asked to pose for pictures to be used in a travel brochure promoting one of the major hotels. The photographer for the brochure had approached them an the beach and said, "I have never seen two people look more happy or having more fun than the two of you." Of course Brenda and Dick found the experience entertaining. They howled with laughter and giggled through the entire photo session.

Not even Brenda contracting the legendary Montezuma's revenge would dampen their spirits. While she was ill they spent the day in bed, laughing and talking. Dick left her alone just once. While Brenda was napping Dick went out and purchased a gold charm for her cherished charm bracelet. He chose a gold Aztec calender so that she would always be reminded of the incredible time they had together that November of 1967.

At the end of the two weeks, they decided it was just too soon for this once in a lifetime vacation to end, so they extended it by three days. Neither was ready to surrender the one time in their life that they were both without outside commitments and they were able to completely devote every moment to one another. Brenda remembers, "If there was a way to freeze time we would have done it. It was just the most beautiful, carefree time of our lives. It was a time that we had to totally invest it in each other." Brenda and Dick half seriously discussed staying there permanently. Dick told Brenda they he could not think of one good reason why they could not stay and sell beads on the beach like the other locals.

It was bittersweet when their three "bonus" days expired and they boarded the plane that was to take them back to New England. As much as they wanted to stay they were genuinely excited to get back to Manchester and begin their married life.

The woe of leaving Mexico was quickly overshadowed by the pure excitement they felt as they moved into the second story apartment they had rented before leaving for their honeymoon. It was neither a small nor large apartment. The front door of the apartment opened to the living room. A modern kitchen, with a dishwasher and ample cabinet and counter space, served as their dining room. Their bedroom and bathroom were comfortable and clean. They were instantly comfortable as most of their furniture came from various rooms in their parents homes. They had everything a young couple should: a simple but absolutely adequate home, a baby on the way, and true love. Any one who entered their world left feeling like they had been given a potent shot of optimism that had a mandatory booster of joyful anticipation.

Dick spent his days at the bakery working and learning with more ambition an commitment than ever before. Brenda spent her days carefully constructing the nest for her new family. By Christmas of 1967 they effortlessly settled into a gratifying routine that they planned to continue for years: Dick worked during the week, Brenda took care of the house and often went to her mother's to help with the kids, they spent every evening together discussing their respective days, laughing and loving, and usually found themselves at the beach or in the mountains on weekends. They felt incredible fortunate for the life they had been blessed with and they greeted 1968 with sanguinity.

8) Dreams Demolished

"I'm fed up with old men dreaming up wars for young men to die in."
—George McGovern,
1972 Democratic Presidential Candidate

As the winter of 1968 acquiesced to spring, Brenda and Dick believed that their life was evenly in step with the world around them. Each spring day that delivered a blossoming bud, or a young blade of grass, or the fresh song of a recently arrived bird also brought a slew of new experiences for Dick and Brenda. There was the child that was growing inside Brenda. There was the increasing thrill they felt each day as they awoke side by side. There was the smile that inevitably crept up whenever they said, "My husband this . . . " or "My wife that . . ." Oh, there were so many things that fostered their optimism and joy. But it took just one thing to knock the wind out of them so hard they feared they would never catch their breath.

It was a sleepy afternoon early in April when Brenda felt the first pieces of her world beginning to crumble. As usual, she was listening to the radio as she cleaned the apartment. She had been singing to her unborn child before the top of the hour news rudely interrupted. She felt her knees buckle as the lead story marched out of the radio speaker. She reached for the kitchen counter as her stomach violently twisted and turned. She felt as if she had just been kicked in the stomach.

Instinctively she let go of the counter and cradled her unborn child. She tried to make herself breathe as she reached for the phone. She could not keep her hands from trembling as she dialed. With each ring she became more despondent. By the time Dick answered she was crying, "Dick, is your unit the 197th Artillery? Is that you? Is that you?"

"Yeah, Bren, are you okay? What's the matter?"

"What's the matter?!? What's the matter!!! You just got called up. Your unit just got activated to go to Vietnam!" By now the floodgate of terror had opened and consumed her. She became hysterical as she heard herself say the words.

"Bren, Hon, calm down. Just calm down and tell me what happened."

"I told you what happened!!! Your unit was just called up. They just announced it on the radio."

"Bren, it's okay it's no big deal. Please calm down. I am worried about you. I don't want you to be upset, it might hurt the baby."

Feeling like she had just been slapped in the face, Brenda had stopped crying and screamed, "Dick, what's the matter with you?!? How could know about this and not tell me?"

"Bren, this is the first I have heard, please, please calm down baby. I am coming home right now and we can talk. Please don't worry. I'll be right home."

Brenda was shaking uncontrollably as she hung up the phone. She weakly walked over to the couch and slumped into it. She began to weep. How could this be happening? She felt like a bomb had just detonated in her heart. She found herself wishing that she had an atomic bomb that she could drop on the rest of the world so they would know what she felt like. So they would know what it felt like to have their world disintegrate in seconds.

Dick rushed to his car. While he drove home he found his mind flooded with thoughts: How could the National Guard use the radio as a form of notification? What if it was true? What if they actually planned on sending the National Guard to Vietnam? No, no, that can't be right. The National Guard does not get sent to wars — particularly not undeclared wars being fought on foreign soil. For crying out loud, he and about every man he knew had joined because it was the only sure to stay out of Vietnam. Dick pounded the steering wheel of his Mustang as he tried to convince himself that there was nothing to be worried about because he knew he HAD to believe it for himself otherwise Brenda would see right through him. He took a long deep breath and before he exhaled he forcefully swallowed any doubts that plagued him as he pulled into the parking lot of his apartment building.

Dick certainly was not alone in his alarm and uncertainty. Roland Provencher, who became one of Dick's closet friends in the National Guard remembers, "I was driving home when the news came on the radio and said we had been activated. I was on the turnpike and almost drove right off the road when they said the 197th had been activated. . . . I never thought we would go."

George Pavlidis who was not only a close friend of Dick's in the National Guard but also had been a friend of Brenda's since grammar school remembers the day he found out vividly, "I was traveling for work one day and on the radio I hear 25,000 National Guardsmen have been activated and I thought 'Oh my God.' They did not give any more details so I headed home. I was living at my mothers at the time and by then, the local news had picked up on it, and they had distinguished the units. They confirmed that in fact the 197th 3rd Battalion had been activated.

"Anyway, I got to the door and my heart was in my throat. I walk in the door and my mother is crying and she says, 'Haven't you heard?' She was cooking and she had an apron on and a towel in her hand. She sat down on a stool, put the towel on her lap and said, 'You have been activated.' I just said, 'Oh is that what it was. Oh that 's nothing, don't worry about it.' Meanwhile, I was dying inside."

Dick ran up the stairs to their apartment, and when he opened the front door Brenda leapt from the couch into his arms. He rubbed her back and softly spoke to her, "Bren, we will only be support in North Carolina or something like that. We won't have to go to Vietnam. There is no way they are going to send the National Guard to Vietnam." Brenda looked at him with hopeful disbelief.

"We'll just have to provide stateside support. Please stop it. PLEEEAASE don't worry, Hon."

Brenda was temporarily soothed by Dick's words and touch, but something deep inside her would not allow the sickening, hollow pit in her stomach to be subdued. Dick wiped the tears from Brenda's face and asked what smelled so good because he sure was hungry. In his own delicate and unpretentious way, he signaled to Brenda he did not want to discuss anymore, period.

That night Brenda decided the only way she could live with the impending doom was to take the matter into her own hands .While General McSwiney was telling the citizens of New Hampshire that the only way they were going to take the National Guard from New Hampshire was if the Vietnamese sailed up the Merrimack River into Manchester, Brenda was doing everything and anything to find out if the 197th was going to go to Vietnam. Virtually everyday she pursued every avenue she thought might lead her to a definite answer as to her husbands fate.

She went to the Armory and talked to generals, she called state representatives, she talked to anyone in the community who she thought might have some information. Finally on June 20th, one month after Dick had been sent to Fort Bragg in North Carolina for field training, Brenda went to New Hampshire's U.S. Senator Thomas McIntyre's office in

Manchester. She was nineteen, five days overdue in her pregnancy and her husband was hundreds of miles away.

Brenda had tried to make an appointment but was told it would be months before the Senator would be available to see her. Fearing that Dick and the others could be sent to Vietnam at any moment, she decided to just go and wait in the Senator's office lobby until the he agreed to see her. She defiantly and diligently waited four hours before she was ushered into Senator McIntyre's office. Once inside Brenda discovered Senator McIntyre to be everything she expected: uptight, pale, old, aloof, distracted, and obviously uninterested with whatever this pregnant teenager in his office had to say.

Brenda spread her arms as she placed her hands on his massive desk. Carefully she cast her soft brown eyes dead on him. He could feel her gaze searing through him. "Senator, I just want to know one thing: Is the National Guard of this state going to Vietnam."

The Senator lamely cleared his throat, squirmed in his chair like a rat caught by its tail and then in a pitiful attempt to shake this girl from his system, he rolled his head around like he had an annoying kink. Brenda was unwavering in her resolve to get an answer. She stared at him with dubious hope.

He looked down at the papers that were neatly bundled on his desk, unwilling to make eye contact with her and said, "Honestly, Honey, I do not know."

Brenda could hold on no longer. The dignity and spirit that had thus far propelled her suddenly shattered into millions of shards inside her. She began to weep uncontrollably. The bitter taste of anger and sorrow coated her lips, as tears pelted her cheeks and marched down her face, "Yes, you do know! And you won't tell me! Why won't you tell me?"

"I don't know. I really don't know." His meek voice and demeanor sickened Brenda. His paltry dismissal and denial of broke her. The weight and burden of the past months began to collapse on her.

"I am nineteen years old, this is not the way things are supposed to happen. I need some help. Why won't anybody help me? Why won't they help me? Why won't anybody tell me? Why will no one help me? My father, Dick's father, everyone says he has to go. That it's the right thing to do. How can sending my husband to die be the right thing to do? Do they want him to die? Am I the only one who understands what is happening? What is the matter with these people??"

Brenda staggered out of McIntyre's office, hugging and rocking her unborn child. Everyone in the lobby watched with detached fascination as she left alone and hysterical.

9) Twice Removed

"The military don't start wars. Politicians do."
—General W.C. Westmoreland, United States Army

Dick and most of other men of the 197th reported for active duty 13 May 1968 (each unit reporting to its own armory). After months of speculation and rumors that were peppered sporadically with fact, the members of 3rd Howitzer Battalion, 197th Artillery reported to Fort Bragg in North Carolina on 20 May 1968, to prepare for and receive advanced training for war.

One of the many ironies of the mobilization is that, "President Johnson refused to declare a national emergency, to seek congressional legislation for a mobilization or to seek a declaration of war.[1]" The men were acutely aware that they were training to go to a war that the President, their Commander-in-Chief, refused to officially acknowledge as a war. To some this meant they were being sent to die not for freedom and liberty, but as a final desperate attempt to salvage the reputation of one man who had already sacrificed many in his quest for prosperity.

It is nothing short of appalling to consider that on 31 March 1968, when President Johnson addressed the American people on television, within minutes of stating he had authorized the call up the Reserves, he announced, "I shall not seek and I will not accept, the nomination of my party for another term as your

[1] Taken from Mobilization of the Army National Guard and Army Reserve: Historical Perspective and the Vietnam War. 15 November 1984

president." George Pavlidis said, "I thought to myself, what kind of activation and commitment is this?"

It is amazing to think that of 680,000 combined members of the Army National Guard and the Army Reserve just 24,500 were activated. Of the 24,500 only 10,000 would be scheduled for deployment to South Vietnam. Therefore if you were in the National Guard or the Army Reserve in 1968 you had less than 1.5% chance of ending up in Vietnam.

At first, statistics like this one helped quell the fear and anxiety the men in the 197th were surely feeling from the moment they found out about their activation. However, it became obvious, even to the most oblivious, that with each day that passed day at Fort Bragg, the odds of them having to go increased. Beside the conspicuous reasons (like having been actually activated), members of the 197th had numerous reasons to suspect that they might end up in Vietnam: the 197th was a mobile artillery unit (a unit possessing cannons and guns that were designed to be mobile would surely be useful in Vietnam), members of the 197th were citizens of a notoriously conservative state that overwhelming supported the war, (despite the fact that, at the time, New Hampshire had the highest per capita death rate in Vietnam), there was little, if any concern, that any significant protests in the state would occur if the state militia was sent to foreign soil, and with weekly regularity the men were being issued some sort of new jungle and/or war paraphernalia.

George Pavlidis remembers the time like this, "I'll tell you the truth, right up until we were at Fort Bragg, in the unbelievable heat of that summer, even in the middle of training, we were in denial. We thought and said things like, 'They won't take us. We are too special. We are too this, too that. They don't want to take civilians. We are not combatants.' We would look at the Green Berets who were training every single day across the way from us and say, 'Those are the guys they want. Those guys are applying for tour after tour. They don't want us.'

"But then every week something would come down to us. First it was like camouflage poncho liners, then jungle fatigues, then one thing or another that we would need in a jungle. But the denial would continue. We would say, 'Oh that stuff is just in case.' And then one day they opened up these crates and unpacked the M-16 rifles. We all looked at each other and went, 'Well guys there is no denying it now.'"

Denial was the only emotion Dick allowed Brenda to see from him. He was fraught with concern for his wife's and baby's well-being. Not for one minute did he want her to think about anything other than their baby and the great future they had in store. At Brenda's prodding, they discussed him refusing to go. Brenda implored him to consider jail instead of death. Dick told Brenda he would contemplate jail if were not for their child. He did not want anything to haunt or harm his child's life in the future. Dick made every effort to convince Brenda that everything would soon be okay. Brenda though, could not shake the doom and dread that loomed over her head like a black cloud.

In one of many efforts to comfort Brenda, Dick along with some of fellow guardsmen, chartered a plane whenever they could so that they could come home and be with their families on weekends. Every minute that he was home Dick assured Brenda there was nothing to worry about. He told her the government was just using the National Guard to make a point. He tried to convince her that there was no way the government would deploy the National Guard to anywhere other than American soil. They would never use a force, whose purpose was to give Congress the power to, if necessary, "to execute the laws of the union, to suppress insurrection, and repel invasions."*

Brenda wanted to believe Dick and she even let herself believe him sometimes. But, most of the time she knew danger for her husband and the others was painfully clear and present.

*U.S. Constitution, Article 1, Section 8

Once Dick was activated he and Brenda reluctantly decided that she needed to move in with her parents. Just six months after creating a home, they were forced to give it up because they realized they could not afford the apartment on Dick's minimal army wages. While Dick was being acclimatized to the conditions and elements of Vietnam in North Carolina, Brenda was packing up their home and preparing to move back into a tiny bedroom at her parents' house. During this time about the only thing that kept Brenda from having a nervous breakdown as she saw her world collapsing around her was her mother, Nancy.

Nancy stood by and with her daughter, facing every challenge that presented itself to her first born, with dignity, dexterity and strength. When it was time to move from the apartment, of course Nancy was there. Mother and daughter carried box after box down the stairs and transported them to the Cavanaugh house.

When Brenda was asked how she was able to hold up as she moved from her home — how she was able to cope with the first of many losses to come she chuckled as she recounted moving, "Here I was nine months pregnant, moving these heavy boxes and my mother is helping me. My mother and I are moving everything and I will never forget, I get hysterical laughing and my mother is hysterical laughing. I'm so pregnant and I can't stop laughing but somehow I say 'Mum wait a minute, I have to stand in the garden,' because I was laughing so hard I was about to wet my pants, I mean I just could not move. So I had to stand in the little garden outside the apartment and well, let's just say I watered the plants. Which of course made us laugh even harder.

So, there were some comical moments. Fortunately, I had my parents. I moved in with them and they did not charge me rent or food money. They did that for me so we — Dick and I — could save money. Because I lived there and my parents were so loving and open, Dickie (Dick Jr.) is really close to my family, my mother calls him their fourth son. He was born when I lived in their house and both he and I were nurtured there while Dick was gone."

Brenda was not the only one who feared for Dick's well being. His father, Edgar tried as best he knew how to keep his son out of harm's way. It was excruciating for Edgar to think that his only son could end up thousands of miles away as a target for death, but Edgar had come of age during World War II and just as Brenda's father had, Edgar had come of age at a time when the most noble, honorable thing that any man could do was serve their country during war time. He did not want his son to suffer or die; conversely he wanted his son to do the right thing. He did not want his son to disgrace himself or his family by going to jail or fleeing to Canada. It was a struggle that in 1968 had an unflinching stranglehold on this country. Jill Cavanaugh's husband, David Knowles, commented, "The generation gap in America has never been as wide as it was during that time."

Edgar did what he thought he could to protect his son. He went to see Congressman Louis Wyman and General Burns to plead for his son's safety. He expressed to them that Dick was both a husband and a father. He made sure they knew that Dick was his only son. He clearly stated that he wanted his son to do his part, but he thought it was unnerving and unfair that an only son, a husband and soon-to-be father, was being shipped to what seemed to be certain death. Edgar's plea fell on deaf ears. He was told it did not matter that Dick was his sole son. He was told if Dick had one brother or more who had died in battle then and only then would it matter that Dick was the lone son. He was informed that although it was unfortunate that Dick would have to leave his wife and child, there were countless men with families serving in Vietnam. Edgar let it be known that, although he did not want his son to go, he understood why his son had to go and he did not think it was asking too much for his son to be at least given the chance to serve where his talents would be used to their fullest — in the kitchen. It seemed very logical to Edgar — Dick was a baker and as a cook he would most likely be safer than if he was driving ammunition trucks — the job for which he had trained when he first joined the National Guard.

Dick began his career as an army cook while at Fort Bragg. It was during this time that so many men in the 197th came to know and love Dick. It was not unusual for a cook to be a popular person among the men, but the fondness for Dick was exceptional. Just as in his civilian life, his presence and charisma won over even the most skeptical and hardest of men. Roland "Rocky" Provencher said, "It's important he (Dick Jr.) knows his dad was the most loved guy in the company . . . Everybody loved Dickie. Dickie was the most loved guy I have ever seen in my life and I am not just saying that, I have never seen a person loved that much, by so many people . . . everybody loved him. Everybody just wanted to take care of him."

Rocky, who was a gunner, came to know Dick very well at Fort Bragg when he suffered an injury in the field and while recuperating he spent time with Dick in the kitchen. He tells of how Dick was able to go home almost every weekend. "One of the guys who was in charge of the kitchen loved Dick like a son, everybody loved Dick like a son. Anyway the cooks did not have to make formation on weekends so this guy would cover for Dick all weekend. All Dick had to do was make sure he was there for formation Monday morning." To understand the significance of Dick's trips home to Manchester, it is worth noting, that Rocky who also had a wife and a baby, was able to go home just twice during the four months at Fort Bragg.

One of the hardest parts of training for Dick was being away from Brenda the last month of her pregnancy. From the moment he had learned of Brenda's pregnancy Dick had become jubilant about the prospect of being a father.

Everything about having a child excited him. He marveled at the beautiful changes he saw in Brenda's body. He was amazed that he and his love could create something so glorious. He could not wait to hold their baby, play with their baby, provide for their baby and live in peace with his family.

He had been forced to leave Manchester one month before Brenda was due. It had upset him to know that he would not be the one to bring his wife to the hospital when the time came. It sickened him to know that after Brenda he would not be the first one to hold their newborn. It angered him that he was not there to support his wife. However, he vowed not to let Brenda know how much being away from her upset him. Moreover, in spite of all the negative feelings that had invaded his body, he could not squelch the excitement and anticipation he felt about being a father.

Rocky describes Dick during this time, "Everyday I am with Dickie, and we go from the kitchen, walk about half a mile to the Cannoneers' Club and have a drink. Cook, drink, cook, drink, that is what we would do. All we would talk about is the war and the war and how Brenda is due, and how much he wanted to be home. Then Brenda became overdue and he'd be calling Brenda all the time. He was driving her crazy calling. So one night I got him real drunk. So drunk he could not call her and the next thing you know, she has the baby that night."

Dick was probably sleeping soundly (thanks to Rocky) for the first time since he had been activated when Brenda awoke to her first contraction at 4:30 a.m. on June 24, 1968. Her first reaction was to jump out of bed and call for her mother, but she thought better and stayed in bed. Carefully she watched the clock to see if another contraction came. At 4:45, 5:00 and again at 5:15 she felt contractions — each one stronger than the last. She went down the hall and woke her mother. By 5:30 they were en route to the hospital and as far as Brenda was concerned, they had left not a moment too soon because the contractions were coming faster and harder with each minute that passed. Nancy soothed Brenda on the ride, telling her not to worry, that she would have plenty of time to get settled and see the doctor. Nancy took Brenda to the maternity ward, checked her in and left her daughter alone. Naturally, Nancy had wanted to stay, but she had five children at home that she needed to tend to and she figured she would have plenty of time to come back and be with Brenda before the baby was born.

Richard Edgar Genest, Junior had taken his time deciding what day he was going to enter the world but once he decided it was time he wasted nary an instant in making his grand entrance. At exactly 8:30 a.m. — less than three hours from when Brenda had arrived at the hospital — he took his first breath of life.

Brenda was thrilled, relieved and maudlin all at once. As she held her son and gently stroked his beautiful, perfect head, she longed for Dick. She wanted him to see and hold this incredible, amazing and glorious being their love had created. Because there were no commercial flights from North Carolina to Manchester, no one remembers exactly how Dick got to Manchester but he managed to arrive at the hospital at 1:00 a.m. on the 26th of June. Without doubt Dick was overwhelmed and consumed by his son. He spent countless hours holding and cradling his namesake. He could not keep his eyes off Dickie — he could hardly believe that he had part in making such a beautiful baby. He found himself continually thanking Brenda. He had been excited to be a father, but he was surprised that this perfect, little seven pound creature provided him more joy, pride and fulfillment than he ever imagined existed. Before anyone was ready Dick had to go back to Fort Bragg.

When Dick returned to Fort Bragg, he and Rocky continued to spend much time together. Rocky recalls how haunted and obsessed Dick was by the war. "Everyday, the first thing he would do is show me the newspaper. He would show me how many people had been killed over there. He would figure out and tell me the ratio. He would tell me the odds. **Everyday!** He would say, 'My father is in business. I went to school for business and I know business. This "business" is just a numbers game. Rocky, we are just a fucking number. That's all we are, just a fucking number.'

"When we went over (to Vietnam) there were 500 being killed a week and there were 500,000 troops there. He would figure out the percentage and chances of dying."

In July of 1968, Dick began his journey to becoming one of the statistics he had been studying and analyzing, because the 197th received their orders to go to Vietnam.

Brenda remembers the summer of 1968 with her husband like this: "He got to spend a week with Dickie when he was born. Then he got two weeks in August and then he was gone . . . He did not think he was going. I mean the whole time he was at Fort Bragg anyone of the times he came home we could have had him in Canada — it was only hundred and some odd miles away. We could have been there so fast, but he was so torn about it and he really did not think they were going. Once that they got their orders, it was too late, there was no way he could leave. I mean they would have found him before he even got back to New Hampshire. He just called me one day and said, 'We got our orders. We are going.'"

According to several men in the battalion, they received their orders to go to Vietnam during the last week July of 1968 and that half of the men were allowed to go home (New Hampshire), get their affairs in order the first two weeks in August, while the other half was allowed to go the last two weeks in August. Brenda does not clearly remember what part of August Dick was able to come home, although she seems to recall it being later in the month. Although she can not remember exactly what part of August Dick was able to come home, she cannot forget the paralyzing fear and overwhelming sadness that toppled the joy of having Dick home.

She recalls, "There are many things that I just do not remember but then again I have these pictures in my mind that are so vivid. They are like snapshots that are just permanently seared into my memory.

"They are just so clear. I remember sitting down with Dick and going over our bills and our money and how much we would try and save while he was gone. Since Dickie and I were living with my parents we only had one bill that needed to be paid monthly — his life insurance. So anyway, Dick told me I did not need to pay because he had signed a paper that said he did not have to pay the life insurance while he was away at war. I told him we could afford to keep paying, I mean it was less than $10.00 a month, and since I was living with my parents, I knew we could come up with ten bucks, but he told me it was not necessary since the government guaranteed payment of certain things, like house mortgages and insurance, when a man is called to fight for his country. I did not know until years later that it was part of the Soldier and Sailor Relief Act of 1940. It's funny I remember that so clearly.

"As I think about it now, I clearly remember two other things. But, again they are so clear — like a movie playing in my head — I remember the way he spent every night just holding Dickie until it was time for Dickie to go to bed and even then he did not want to let go of him. He would jump out of bed when Dickie would wake up during the night and then he would just hold and walk up and down the hall, rocking him until he went back to sleep. He just wanted to hold him all the time. Then I could never forget the day he had to leave. I remember him and I and Dickie just hugging each other on the porch at my parents' house. I remember just standing there not believing it was happening. It was just awful."

The day Dick had to leave his family was the most heart-wrenching day of his life. Fear, grief, anger, depression and hopelessness invaded and began to aggressively consume his entire being. He felt as if he had been kicked in the stomach, stabbed in the back, and slammed in the head with a baseball bat, all at once, over and over again. Although he dared not say it — he truly felt this was the last time he would see his family.

Dick did everything he could to hide his anguish and terror from Brenda. As much as he feared and despised the reality that was before him, nothing hurt or caused him as much pain as knowing that his love, his wife, his meaning of life, was suffering. He was tortured not by images of the war he was about to enter, but by the image of Brenda holding their son, tears flooding from her eyes as he tried to comfort her, as he told her not to worry and as he tried to convince her everything would be okay.

It made no matter how much Brenda wanted to believe Dick. There was no solace in his words. It made no difference whether she tried to be strong. She just felt, that if he left, he was going to die. She recounts her thoughts at the time with what seems to be a straightforward statement of the obvious: "I just thought there was no way he could survive. I mean anybody who keeps ants as pets, because they don't have the heart to kill them, is going to get killed if they go to a war. He was just way too gentle of a human being to go to a war."

Brenda could not let go of Dick as they said good-bye. She felt she was about to allow her husband to make a mistake that would mean the end of his life. With every moment that passed, she became more and more convinced that she and Dickie were the only barrier between Dick and death. Brenda literally held onto Dick for dear life as they clutched each other and enshrouded their child.

Ultimately, their time as a family expired. Dick reluctantly stepped back from Brenda, looked intently into her tear filled eyes until he felt his heart shatter into millions of pain filled pieces, agonizingly forced himself to turn away, bowed his head and defeatedly walked to the car that was to take him to the Armory.

Whereas Dick held back his dread and apprehension to Brenda, he did not bridle his feeling with his friends and fellow soldiers. While many of the men had denied any possibility of actually going to Vietnam, while they were stationed at Fort Bragg, once the undeniable confirmation of their worst fear became reality, they boldly recognized and acknowledged the realities of their future head-on.

Rocky Provencher recalls a conversation with Dick. "We were leaving the Armory in Manchester to go to Portsmouth, New Hampshire to Pease Air Force Base. I'm sitting with Dickie at the back of the bus and they are getting ready to take down [rebuild] the bridge next to the Armory, and I said, "Dick, some of us aren't gonna make it back and they are going to dedicate this bridge to us."

No one could have known how prescient Rocky's statement would be. The Amoskeag Memorial Bridge would eventually be, "dedicated to the memory of Manchester's Vietnam War dead." It is worth noting that on the granite and copper memorial next to the bridge, not one name of the thirty-five Manchester sons who were killed in Vietnam appear. Instead, the name of the mayor, the city councilmen (aldermen), the city clerk, the Department of Highways commissioners, the surveyor, the engineers and the contractors of the structure, appear on the memorial. (Almost as appalling — is another memorial that lists the 35 names of "All of Manchester's Vietnam Dead," — that for close to thirty years sat on an area of diseased-looking grass, across from the bridge in the middle of a junction and intersection for three highway on-ramps, as well as, three city streets. Because of the danger and extreme difficulty involved to view or visit it, the memorial was recently moved to the Armory.

However, it is disgusting to know that it took 30 years and many complaints to move it to a more visible and less dangerous venue.)

Although it is likely that most of the men of the 197th felt as scared, sad and dejected as Dick, few, if any, had the fortitude to show the sorrow and pain they were feeling.

George Pavlidis recalls, "The worst day was when we left for Vietnam. All the good-byes were tearful. I remember I patted my mother on the back and you feel this sort of invincibility. Like, I am so invincible, I am so well trained. I was holding my father's bronze star from the 30th division in World War II and I thought I am doing this for my country. I am doing this because I am carrying on a tradition of what is to be an American. I mean there were a lot of good guys there, a lot of brave honorable men . . . but there also was this false bravado that Dick never pretended to have. Anyway I patted my mother on the back and said, 'I'll be back.'

"Then Dick and I get on the plane and Dick starts crying and he just did not stop. I tried to find the courage to say, 'Hey, look, we are going to be okay.' As we took off, I reassured him that we were going to look after each other, that there was no way anything was going to happen. He just put his head down and sobbed most of the way. I thought, 'My God, George,' you are not sharing what he just walked away from. He has a wife and a family. Those guys, all those guys who left children and wives, who had to leave that behind, what a big sacrifice they made.

"It [being with Dick when the plane took off] was one of the worst moments of my life, because it was like, you don't know. There was no guarantee of anything. We did not know where we were going to end up or what we were going to do."

It would not have mattered if any one of the men had wanted to talk as the Star Lifter C-141 strained to get off the ground; it was so loud they could barely hear themselves think.

The men sat on the rigid wood benches facing the rear of the plane, staring into the void of the cold gray fuselage. To keep the men company for the thirty hour flight that lay ahead, they shared their grim accommodations with Jeeps, army trucks and other tools of the war trade.

The violent noise that roared from the plane, the resistance of the atmosphere and the turbulence that bent the wings — all seemed to be obvious precursors. It was as if the plane's only purpose was to jolt the men into the truth of their situation.

Dick wept. He wept not for his fate, but for the pain he had caused his wife. He sobbed, for he, too, was convinced he was going to die, but his tears grew from the burden that he had not been honest with Brenda. As much as he needed to confide in his dearest and closest friend, he could not bring himself to tell Brenda of his grave truism. He sat crippled by sorrow. When the plane landed to refuel in Alaska and then again in Japan, Dick got off with the others to stretch his legs. Really, it was as if he were sleepwalking each time he exited the plane. He felt as if his feet were lead balloons and he was laboriously wading through a thick and ever-darkening black nightmare.

The men arrived in Bien Hoah, Vietnam, thirty hours after leaving the United States. As the plane taxied, Dick sat still and silent, hoping that any moment he would be awakened from this sickening dream. The plane jerked to a stop and the deafening noise that had escorted the men the entire trip died with a dull thud. No one moved. All the men sat apprehensively in the dungeon of the plane; every one of them wondering what was going to happen next. They carefully and cautiously searched one another's faces — trying to find someone/anyone who knew what they were supposed to do now.

Finally the eerie and nervous stillness became more than anyone could take, and the men conspired to find out what awaited them outside. George Pavlidis recalls, "There were only two small windows on the plane and both were about twelve feet above us. Anyway when we landed we HAD to see, we had to know what was about to happen to us. We almost expected to see fighting going on right outside because this was Vietnam, it is a bad place and we were there. So one guy hoisted another guy on his shoulders so he could see and I remember one of them saying, 'What do you see?' and he shot back, 'It's raining.'"

It was a hot sticky tropical rain that was more sobering than refreshing. The men were finally let off the plane and they began their journey to war.

10) Wasted

"God, I've been pounding on this damn door
until my fists are bloody
and my crimsoned fingers feel no longer.
What I want to know is:
WHERE ARE YOU?
And have you stopped listening to the music?
Are you deaf? Or are you just pretending?

Or did you die in Vietnam?"

Epilogue to "After-thought" by Amichaud — 1969

Thursday, September 19, 1968

Hi Hon,

Well I never really thought I'd ever see this place, but I am here now. The trip over here was really terrible. It took over thirty hours in an Air Force jet that had only two windows and the seats faced backward. We landed at Bien Hoa and they brought us up to this place called Phu Loi. It is a pretty safe place, inside the camp, but we live in a swamp. All there is, is mud and water. I could try and tell you how bad the living conditions are, but I could never really express myself correctly. Just imagine living right in the middle of a swamp, it is really gross, it is something no one could ever forget.

Although I am pretty safe over here, you definitely know

you are in a war zone. At night all you see in the distance are flares and flashes in the sky from cannons and big guns. Of course you also hear the noise that goes along with all of this. The food is all in cans and dehydrated, except for the meat and a few vegetables. The time is twelve hours ahead of you. At twelve noon it is twelve midnight at home.

The weather is extremely hot, in fact it is almost winter over here and the temperature is in the nineties and the humidity is so great, no one could understand unless they actually lived in it. It gets dark over here about seven and boy does it ever get dark, the darkest I have ever seen in my life. When it gets dark is when they start fighting. During the day there is very little action. (This place is about twenty-five miles north of Saigon.)

Needless to say, this is a very crazy war. The people during the day are normal and then at night they just stab you in the back. It does not seem as though you could ever get anywhere. I am no authority on these things, but from what I have seen it makes no sense at all.

The water tastes like it is from a cesspool and that is putting it mildly. I am talking about the water you can drink because actually you cannot drink most of the water here. You cannot find a Coke or soft drink of any kind anywhere. They have beer, but believe me it is just too hot to drink beer. Honestly, you just do not want to drink beer.

I will write tomorrow and everyday that I can. Give all my love to our son. You know I love you so much. Love you, Dick.

Brenda could not stop the tears that plunged down her cheek as she read the first letter from Dick. She peered at their son, who like most babies at three months, was starting to turn into a reflection of his parents. He had her smile. His eyes were the shape of his father's. She looked at his tiny peach fuzz head with wonderment. Would his hair be blonde like hers? Would it be satiny brown and curly like Dick's? Brenda put her hand in the crib and her son grasped her index finger with his tiny hand. She felt her soul let out a painful wail and her heart began to ache. How was it possible that the father of this beautiful child was not allowed to experience his son? How could it be that this newly formed family had been so cavalierly torn apart? Why was this baby robbed of his father?

Brenda was ambushed by feelings of disdain, anger and sadness. She tired very hard to have a loving, positive attitude, to be not consumed by so many destructive emotions, but they always seemed to creep up on her and slither into her thoughts no matter how hard she tried to suppress them.

The many things that supported and aided Brenda while Dick was in Vietnam also served as brazen reminders of their situation. Living with her parents was a great help emotionally and financially. However, Brenda could not help but feel confined. How could she forget that just a few months earlier she had lived in a 1200 square foot apartment when now she was confined to a 10-by-12-foot room with her son?

Brenda had been grateful that her brothers had agreed to move down to the basement so that she and Dickie could have their own room, but she could not help but feel a little bitter as the single room came to be her home. Brenda did her best to turn her brothers' bedroom into a nursery, a playroom, a bedroom for her and a haven for the baby. And she was able to find some solace in creating a loving place for her child.

Fortunately, through the entire transition, Brenda's siblings tried to be a tremendous help with Dickie. However, they all needed and loved Brenda in their own way and so they were demanding of Brenda's attention and time. Instead of being able to choose when her brothers and sisters could interact with their nephew as Brenda and Dick had imagined, Brenda was at the mercy of her siblings whims in their home. She was well aware that when she moved back home she would lose some privacy and freedom; what she did not expect was the resentment she felt at times toward her brothers and sisters. Brenda's friends sympathized with and tried to understand but their lives revolved around college, weekend partying, grades and dating; not diapers, budgets, doctor appointments and war.

Brenda had all the responsibilities that went with being a wife and a mother, but few of the benefits. She was a wife with a husband fighting for his life thousands of miles away. She was a lone parent of a child who had been brought into the world by two people whose only intention was to raise this child together. She was nineteen and her husband was at a war, that this country so far had done its best to ignore and despise.

Brenda has said, "After Dick went to Vietnam I would go to the grocery store or to the park or wherever and everybody was just going on with their lives as if everything was normal. I just wanted to scream at them, 'Don't you know what is happening? Don't you know how many of our husbands, sons and fathers are suffering over there? Don't you care that 500 of our husbands, sons and fathers are being killed a week?' I felt so alone. It was like no one cared what was happening.

"At least during World War II the whole country was at war. There were rations, women building ships and planes for their men, if you lived on the coast you had to be able to black out your windows at night. Everybody was involved in America winning the war. But nobody wanted to participate or talk about Vietnam except those of us who had to live with it and most of us were not even able to vote. I mean so many of those guys over there were 18 or 19 or 20 and in those days the voting age was 21. I was just nineteen and Dick had only been of voting age for two years. I was just so frustrated and angry that I had no say in something that was solely responsible for slowly destroying my life."

Brenda's sister, Jill, remembers the frustration and helplessness she felt herself and for Brenda during this time. "I remember I was a junior in high school and I remember when they came home and told us they were getting married and Brenda telling us we were going to be in the wedding and going to pick out the dresses for their wedding, and then I remember the wedding and reception, it was really nice, but then it seemed right after that he was gone. He was gone, he just got pulled into Vietnam.

"I used to think, 'I wish I had the courage,' because I knew, I just had this really bad feeling, 'I just wish I had the courage,' because I did not think it was right that he should be pulled away from his baby. I would think, 'I wish I had the courage to shoot him in the leg, or something, so he would not have to go. But then I thought that everyone would hate me. I mean I never got a gun or anything but I would just lay in bed thinking if I just shoot him in the leg then he wouldn't have to go.

"It wasn't even that I was afraid he was going to be killed. I mean of course I was really worried he was going to die, but it was more like, I did not think he should be taken away from his baby. How could they take a father away from his baby . . .

"It was a really hard time because Brenda had to give up her apartment. She moved in with us and that was really hard because of all the kids and she had to be in that little room. Dickie was more like our brother than our nephew because we were not that far apart in age, any of us.

"There wasn't anything right about it at all. It was just a total injustice. It just changed the whole world as far as I was concerned, because we went from this kind of 'Leave It To Beaver,' existence to a global existence, where they are plucking these kids out of a perfectly safe environment and putting them into this jungle where they got shot at. It just did not make sense.

"In my opinion that is when the world changed, because up until that point you always obeyed authority and you did not go against the government. I mean the government was the YOUR government and you had to go with them.

"Then we started thinking, this is wrong! Brenda I started going to meetings in downtown Manchester against the war. The meetings were in this dumpy little back room somewhere and there was no more than a handful of people there. I remember one of the organizers was my old girl scout leader. It was just really something to see this woman who we viewed as being so straight and conservative, the symbol of authority, leading these meetings against the war.

"We used to go to these meetings and to try and DO SOMETHING, anything. We had these chains and buttons that said 'Another Mother for Peace' and 'War is not healthy for children and other living things,' and we try would pass them out to people in Manchester. We just tired to do anything we thought could or would help to stop the war."

Brenda and Dick vowed to write everyday. It was through their letters that they were able to continue their married life in a small but exceedingly important way. It was through their letters that Dick got to see his son grow, participate in his wife's daily activities, and it was through their letters that Brenda became painfully aware of the horror her country was knowingly sanctioning.

Sunday, September 22, 1968

Hi Love,

Well another day has just about gone by and I honestly cannot see how I will be able to take this uncivilized life much longer. I just cannot take this going to the bathroom outside in a field, into a smelly old hole or this shaving with the use of a helmet to hold water.

Your beautiful and really necessary mail is getting to me really fast. Today is Sunday and I received the pictures of the baby. He really is a beautiful child but, of course, how could he miss when he has such a beautiful and wonderful mother as you are. I do not think Dickie boy will be crawling the length of his new bed very often at the present time. He really looks so neat and small in his bed.

Not this month but next month you should receive about $250.00 from the government. Presently I will keep $50.00 for myself and I told them to send the rest to you. If the $50.00 is too much, I will have them send more to you, but I just want to see how laundry, haircuts, etc. cost. You should see the funny kind of money we use over here. It is not Vietnamese but some kind of military exchange. I guess whenever the U. S. government has troops in a foreign country they make up some of this weird money and it is only good in that particular country.

Hon, you would believe how much I miss you. I just want to squeeze you so tight in my arms. I love you so very, very much and you are everything in the world to me. I just want to be with you and our son and to live together. Well my love, good night even if it is good morning for you, you know you are in my thoughts, a big kiss to you and our son, Dick.

Monday, September 23, 1968

Hi Hon,

Do you know that I miss you so much my love, I think I just might crack up. I've decided this base camp we are in at Phu Loi is really pretty safe. We are located on the perimeter of the camp and beyond us there is about 200 hundred yards of barbed wire, then there are the infantry troops and then after them, are the minefields. Really the only thing the Vietcong do, is send fire mortars in the air at us. When that happens all you do is jump in the bunkers. Also this place has not been mortared in four months. But, believe me, at night you can actually feel the ground shake from the big guns firing. The sky is constantly being illuminated by flares.

How is our little son? He must be getting quite big. I really miss him a lot. He was just so happy and smiling all the time when I saw him and that made me feel so happy. Hon, I just love you so very much and cannot stand being without you. When I get back nothing will ever separate us again. I promise we will live together again in our own little house, with our child and maybe we can even make another little baby.

Give my son a big hug and a kiss on his little nose for me and a big kiss to you my love, Dick.

Tuesday, September 24, 1968

Today we got a new mess sergeant and he seems to be a pretty good guy. At least I have something in common with him, we both hate this place to no end.

Do you know what? We have to burn all the mail we receive over here because if it were to get into the wrong hands, they would have our home address. Then they could send a letter to our families saying we have been captured or something to that effect and then they might demand thousands of dollars for our release.

Today they hired some Vietnamese women to do our laundry, wash our boots and clean around the area. It is going to cost each man eight dollars a month. Anyone caught messing around with any of these cleaning ladies will get sent to jail for one year and then will have to spend another year in this hell hole. Myself, I do not like to come within forty feet of them because I would not be surprised if at night they were out killing Americans. Who knows they are probably the ones that would find the letters and send false letters to your home; I just do not trust them.

The women are let through the gates at 8:00 a.m. and they have to be out by 5:00 p.m., because the road to the village is closed by 6:00 or 7:00 p.m. They say the road belongs to the Vietcong. That the U.S. owns the road during the day and the V.C. at night.

Okay Bren, figure this one out; these cleaning woman take

care of the equipment of eleven men and each man pays them eight dollars. So, that is eighty-eight dollars a month. In this country, that makes you wealthy. Anyway, if you take what the K.P.'s (who are also Vietnamese women) get paid by the government, which must be about a hundred dollars a month, and you figure these cleaning ladies get at least eighty-eight it just does not make sense. I mean look at the allotment you get of $100 a month or $105 with one child. So really these women are almost getting just as much, if not more, than you, when you consider the cost of living here. This is a very corrupt war and I just get disgusted thinking about it.

Wednesday, September 25, 1968

Hi Hon,

Again another day gone by, which means one less to put in at this place. I finally figured out how to give you an accurate description of this place. Imagine a World War II concentration camp, like the ones you see in movies. Well it is like that with wooden shacks, bunkers, etc., but imagine they are in a lot of mud and water, like a swamp. That is what this place is like.

I just wish you could see all the money being wasted over here. It is just unbelievable. Food is exposed to the rain, it's just left to sink into the mud. All kinds of waste. It is tax dollars that people in America are paying for nothing but waste. I just wish they could see how their money is being spent over here. It is a disgrace!

I get so disgusted at times I could just breakdown. I just sort of try and go on day by day. You never hear any news in the U.S. concerning this war and what the politicians are doing about it.

Saturday, September 28, 1968

I think of you every night when I lie in bed about 9:30 and I think it is 9:30 in the morning back home. I think you are probably giving the baby his bath and I imagine you are talking to him and he is laughing and smiling at you. Tomorrow, if I can, I am going to buy some kind of plastic envelopes or something to put the pictures of the baby in so that they do not turn moldy. The weather here will make them mold if I do not get something to protect them. The next time you send pictures of the baby, would you take some pictures with you and Dickie? I would really like that.

It is raining now. They say this is the end of the rainy season. I cannot imagine what it is like during the wet season, if this is what they call the end. I just hope I don't have to stay here a year. I hope and pray every day that I will not be here that long. I know I could not take it. I am just not cut out for this sort of thing. I just miss you so much sometimes I could cry. No, I have not forgotten about our wonderful son. I love him as much as I love you. I cannot wait to be with him again, to live with him and have him start to know me.

It is raining so hard I cannot even hear myself think. I have never seen anything like it before. I wish I were not here to see it.

Sunday, September 29, 1968

I went to get the food for dinner tonight and you should see the waste, it is just terrible. There are so many people making so much money because of this war.

Brenda celebrated her twentieth birthday on 6 October 1968. She tried her best to enjoy the party and presents from her family, but nothing could fill the void left by Dick's absence. The only present she wanted was thousands of miles away from her reach. Although she longed for her husband, she was grateful to spend her birthday with their son and she knew that Dick was experiencing more anguish than she could ever imagine.

Sunday, October 6, 1968

I just feel so disgusted when I look around where I am living. The best thing to do here, is not to think, otherwise you go crazy. The only thing is that you cannot help but think. I just wish that I could wake up one morning and this would have been a bad dream. Some day when I get out of this place I will be able to get up and just forget about this entire mess. I will just put everything here out of my mind forever.

Well I just sang Happy Birthday to you. I only wish I was with you to celebrate. I want to be with you so badly, no one could understand. I love you Darling.

Monday, October 7, 1968

I guess we will be moving to Thunder II. The day we are supposed to move has changed three times. I imagine the regular army, who has direct control over us, is kind of scared about the National Guard supporting the infantry. The infantry will be in front of us out in the field and all it would take is one mistake and we could drop a bomb on our own men instead of the enemy.

Tuesday, October 8, 1968

I found out today that I will not have to be the driver who drives from Thunder II to Laikee to get food. Laikee is about eight miles from Thunder II and I did not fancy the idea of being on the road every day for that much distance. What they are going to do is have one person stay at Laikee and all he will have to do is pick up rations and bring them to Thunder II daily. It is actually a very easy job and the living conditions the driver will have are much better than we have. They did ask me if I wanted the job but because of the fact you have to be on the road so much, the road is not to be trusted, I declined.

It appears from Dick's letters that on or around October 11 Dick's unit, 'A' Battery was moved into the field where they would be backing up the infantry and firing their guns every night. A Battery was one of the three firing units of the 197th, which included B Battery and C Battery. A Battery was the first of the three artillery units to be assigned to a field camp. Rocky Provencher remembers the ride to and arrival to the camp called Thunder II like this: "People were flipping us off as we drove by their hooches [Vietnamese huts or houses] and they would be taking a crap in front of their hooch and they would be flipping us off. I turned to Dick and said, 'I have to die for this country? I don't want to die for this country. I don't want to die here.' . . . Three weeks after arriving in country they put us out there and we never left. We were supposed to be out there three months then rotate with 'B' and 'C'.

" So we went out there to Thunder II. We never should have been out there. First of all we had the worst battery going over (to Vietnam) because we had not done good at Fort Bragg and we had the lowest shooting scores. Second, it was a place for self- propelled guns, like big tanks, not the guns we had. Third, there were no bunkers, we had to build this place while we were there. We slept like animals. It was a shit hole."

George Pavlidis recalls Thunder II like this: "We were put in a place that was completely different from anything we had anticipated as far as sacrifice goes. There was a hole there that had been previously occupied by other guys.

"Anyway, you were required to put in a twelve hour day of doing your job and chores, then and only then, if you could find the time to make your 'accommodations' more comfortable, fine. Otherwise, 'Put up and shut up.'

"We lived in a hole. Rodents crawled all over us. There were two kinds, big ones and the really big ones. When it was dark you would feel one jump and bump into or crawl over you. We [Dick and George built and shared a bunker at Thunder II] set up a trap and when the trap would go off I would have to go outside to kill the rat because no matter how much Dick hated living with them, he could not kill them."

Saturday, October 12, 1968

Well I am in the new area called Thunder II. It is getting dark and we have no lights so I do not know how long I will be able to write this letter. The trip over here was unbelievable. The roads and villages that we went through were just unreal. Everyday I just ask myself more and more what am I doing here.

This place is just unbelievable. I could not describe it accurately if I wanted to. When we pulled in I actually thought it was a dump. One thing that did happen when we pulled in that I thought was pretty funny was, that I almost flipped the kitchen truck over. Now, don't misunderstand, I know I told you I would not drive over here, I only drove to this place because I figured it was better than being a passenger while someone else drove. Anyway, to get the truck out, they had to get a wrecker to hold it on one side so it would not flip over while another truck pulled it out of the mud. After that stunt, I do not think they will want me to drive anywhere anymore.

It was so hot when we got here I honestly thought I was going to drop from heat exhaustion.

So you will not miss a letter, I did not write yesterday. It was impossible for me to write, but I will try and write everyday from now on.

One thing they do here at Thunder II is fire all night, so it is pretty hard to sleep because the ground is always shaking and the noise is unbearable. But, I am thankful that I am cook and not on the guns all night.

I just miss you so much my darling. I just cannot take being away from you. You are just the greatest person in the entire world as far as I am concerned. Any moment now I may have to stop writing because they are commencing to fire and not even a candle can be lit when they do start. Tomorrow I am going to make a point to write in the afternoon so I will be a little more at ease.

I took a shower tonight and I cannot believe it. I thought

the barrel over our head was bad. Nothing compares to the showers we take now where someone stands on a truck and holds a five gallon water can and pours water all over you.

Give our son a kiss for me and many to you my love, your loving husband, Dick.

Sunday, October 13, 1968

Hi Hon,

Well here I sit in my little bunker writing by candle light which can be difficult because the flame jumps around whenever they fire the cannons which is all the time. If you saw the place I sleep in, you would simply not believe it. I do sleep on a cot and I share the bunker with my mess sergeant. In this bunker you can fit two cots and nothing else. Of course you share the bunker with all kinds of bugs and rats. Life over here is uncivilized. We actually live like animals. You get so dirty and filthy, it is a real shame. Between the dust, mud and heat there is nothing you can do to avoid it.

I would like to see a few politicians come to this place; here, not Saigon. I would like to see them live like this for a few days. I bet if they did, there would be some real action concerning ending this war. My mess sergeant was in Korea and he says that the whole time he spent in Korea, was nothing like this hole. I have gotten so that I can sleep pretty well even with the guns firing all night. If I am awake though I still jump every time they go off.

There is an infantry battery over here with us and they drive in and out with tanks all the time. I guess, we primarily support the infantry, which is right in front of us. I think the way it goes is Thunder I-VI then another place then Danang and then the border. The reason they call the road Thunder, is because there is so much artillery and noise. I do not know why they call it a road because all it is, is a dirt pathway. It is really called Highway 13 and it goes all the way to North Vietnam.

I miss you and our child so much, my love. I think so often of the time we will be united again. How is my little son doing today? Is he crawling around yet? How old does he have to be before he starts crawling? Well Bren you know how much I love and miss you. No one in this world could ever take your place for me, you are just the greatest. I know these are only words, but I honestly feel them in my heart. Give our son a big kiss for me. Your loving husband, Dick.

Tuesday, October 15, 1968

Oh, this is just such a gross place and I just cannot see what the U.S. is doing here. The French could not do anything here for twenty years and so they left. I don't know why the U.S. came here. I cannot really see any accomplishment at all. Maybe I am wrong, but I cannot see any sense to this place at all. I will just be so happy to get out of this place and forget it ALL.

I don't know if you realize this but, in the 197th Artillery, there is A Battery, which I am in, and B, C Battery and Headquarters Battery. Anyway, A Battery is at Thunder II. B is at Phu Loi (where we were previously) and they get to do their firing from there, those lucky bastards. Headquarters are at Phu Loi also and they do not even have cannons. They just do the clerical work. I do not know where C is. Anyway the other night B Battery was firing and they made a mistake. They did not send a round or bomb far enough and it landed right on the runway at the Phu Loi airport. That just goes to show how messed up the National Guard can be. Luckily, no one was hurt.

I could never get out of this place soon enough. I am really fed up with all the crap going on around here. I still have not seen one good reason why the U.S. should be involved in this war. It is just ridiculous. All I can think of is being home with you and living with you again. I miss our son so much. He must be really changing fast by now.

ALMOST BACK

Thursday, October 17, 1968

Well the cannons just started firing and I jumped about two feet. I cannot take much more of this. When I get out of here I am going to make the biggest bonfire out of all the army clothes I have and I am just going to watch them burn.

Wednesday, October 23, 1968

I found out today we are going to be in this area, Thunder II for about four months. Then we will go back Phu Loi where B Battery is and they will come out here. After that we will probably go to where C Battery is and they will come out here. Of course this could all change. If these rotations take place then it will put us here for a year and I seriously doubt we will be here for an entire year.

Remember the night at the Nubble Lighthouse we looked at the stars for about four hours and we saw all those different things? Wasn't that just great? Now we are married and we cannot be together. We did so many together before all of this. I hope and pray that I get out of this mess so I can repay you in some way for all the hardship that you have been going through. Bren, I just love you so much.

I guess our son is just about four months old. I miss him so much and I really do not know him at all. I just get so depressed, you know how emotional I can get at times. I just want to be with you so much, at times, I think I am going to breakdown. My living is not complete without you. It is just a bare existence. You are the greatest thing that has ever happened to me. I could write all day and all night and still not express what I actually feel for you.

We will just have to catch up on a lot of living that we have lost because of this corrupt political situation that rules us.

Thursday, October 24, 1968

All this talk of stopping the bombing without really getting promises back from North Vietnam, really kind of has me worried. I know if we stopped bombing they would just re-supply their forces and come back even stronger than before. I'll tell you this war could be won in thirty days or less if they would bomb the places that count, instead of fooling around with these ridiculous places we are now. We know where the Vietcong are located, which villages etc., but we just do nothing about it. It's like giving them opportunity to come at us. It is just so stupid. If only the proper people knew what was going on here.

Sunday, October 27, 1968

Hi Hon,

Well another day just about finished and again a very wet one, the wettest I have ever seen. Last night when I wrote you there was a typhoon in the area and we were told we were going to get a few side affects from it like rain. Well believe me Hon, the "side effects" were just like a hurricane we get back home. Talk about rain, it poured and poured. It did not stop until about three this afternoon. The kitchen tent, the only tent in the area was blown away and all types of food was exposed to the rain. Of course this is nothing exceptional for this place.

Oh, and talk about being cold, I never thought I would see the day it was cold in this hole, but last night I really was. All you have here is a poncho liner to protect you and use as a blanket and this little bunker of sand bags does not give you much protection especially with the open entrance way. I put my poncho in front of the entrance way. The people I really feel sorry for, are the guys who were on the guns. They were just completely exposed, completely soaked and they were stuck in mud up to their knees. It is really a crying shame to see American people living under such conditions. For what? I do not think anyone really knows. I do not like to talk about it because I just get so upset.

ALMOST BACK

You asked me some things in your last letter I will try to answer now. There is no electricity to speak of here. We have a few generators which run radios and four lights for the entire area. There is one light in the kitchen, one light in the captain quarters, one where Nelson works (Fire Direction Center), and believe it or not, one where I sleep. Because I share a bunker with the mess sergeant and he has some pull around here, plus he has to do paper work in here. There is just nothing around this place at all, it is a big empty space. The good thing about though is it is a fairly safe place.

Thursday, October 31, 1968

I just do not know about all this talk about peace. My hopes are just getting up too high about getting out of this place soon and being with you again forever and ever never to end. This would be the greatest thing to happen to me. I just wish these people would do something. Alt this talk is driving me crazy.

I just found out today that we are going to have to move out of this bunker because it is unsafe, which is no surprise to me. We are supposed to move into one that is completely underground and sleeps thirty-five. It is pretty nice considering the conditions and the materials that are available to build.

Friday, November 1, 1968

I did a very foolish thing today, I went to Laikee. My intentions were good. I went for the simple reason to buy a tape recorder so I can play the tapes you have sent me. Of course, as is my luck, the P.X. was closed. I swear it will be the last time I go because the road is full of mines and today one truck hit a mine and blew up. Fortunately no one was hurt badly.

Today they stopped the bombing in the North and I really hope they stop it over here in the South soon. As it stands now there has been no change and it is just as noisy as ever. But I have a feeling it may stop within a few weeks. I hope so anyway, because if this would happen, I do not think it would be very long before we were together again. I just wish so much I could be with you and I pray that I will be soon. If there were anyway of leaving this place, I think I would do it no matter what the consequences. I get so disgusted, I just cannot help it.

As far as action over here at Thunder II, there has been none. There has been action all around us they (Vietcong), go for places with helicopters. They really have nothing to gain if they did attack us, for we have six cannons and that is nothing to them. If they did attack us they would first have to go through the minefield and infantry in front of us, plus Thunder I and Thunder III would support us. ENOUGH WAR TALK! Be sides the war is almost over and I will be home soon. Kiss our son for me and many to you Bren, you know how much I need you, your loving husband, Dick.

Saturday, November 2, 1968

Hi Bren,

So, how is the one person I love more than anything in the world, today? I hope fine and well. Today was just the hottest day I have seen in my lifetime. No one could believe how hot it is over here unless you actually spend a day here in it.

I just love you so much Bren and I hope that we can be together soon. I just cannot take much more of this place. I get so disgusted at times, like I am right now. I just cannot see what I am doing here. There is just no reason the U.S. is here and if they did make a mistake coming here, why don't they get out now before more damage is done? I hope so much that these peace talks move swiftly and with much progress. I just cannot see how I can be away from you much longer.

So how is our son today? I swear I will make sure he never has to go through anything like this in his lifetime. I do not know how I will do it yet, but there has to be a way.

I feel I have taken so much away from your life by being

here. I just hope I can make it all up to once I get out of here. I promise I'll try never to say anything that could ever make you cry, I'll just do everything to please you and never hurt you in anyway.l love you so much, you are just life to me. Let's just hope that I can get out of here soon and just forget this place. I never want to think back on this place once I get out. Even though I could have it much worse than I do, I never want to think about this place.

All I want is to live a normal happy life with our son and any other children we might have. Bren, no one could imagine how vast my love is for you.

Please do not send any Christmas presents to me. I honestly do not want anything from anybody. Tell everybody to give my presents to you and Dickie. As far as myself, I cannot send anything and I will not go to Laikee again because of the road. I am no hero and will not go on that road. I'll just stay right here in this filthy little hole.

I just have to get out of here soon. At least the chances are better now than ever before. It will be the happiest day of my life when I am with you again. I think of that day constantly. All my love forever, Dick.

Sunday, November 3, 1968

Well my feet really ache tonight and my back is not that great either. I guess I do a lot of complaining. I'm just not cut out for this sort of life. I could probably take it if I was younger and not married and if there was a purpose to this thing. There is no reason for the U.S. to be here.

I really miss our son. I noticed in the pictures you sent today how big he is in contrast to the first pictures you sent. He sure does smile a lot, but how could he not when he is with a person such as you.

Brenda received flowers from Dick on Monday, November 4, to commemorate their first wedding anniversary.

Friday, October 25 for Monday, November 4, 1968

Well again my love another very important date in our lives and we are separated. I promise you that this will be the last anniversary that we will be away from each other. We have both shared the unhappiness and misfortune of being separated the greater part of this year. We can look back on this past year of our marriage though and remember the days when we were together and how happy and joyous those days were, which can only lead to many more years of happiness once we are together again.

This past year has brought us a wonderful and beautiful son, who we are both so proud of. We can thank the good Lord above that everything went so well in bringing him forth .Do love you so much my darling and there could never be greater person in the entire world than you have been to me. Your loving husband, Dick. HAPPY ANNIVERSARY!

P. S. I realize this is not much of a card, but the thought and the love is within me.

Tuesday, November 5, 1968

We are leaving here, Thunder II, tomorrow morning at eight. We are moving seven miles down the road to Thunder III. Anything can happen in a day over here. You just do not know what to expect. This evening after supper we packed and still have plenty more to do before tomorrow morning. The army does the stupidest things, but I guess it is known for that.

Everyone is pretty discouraged about this move, especially after all the work we have done around here to try and make this place livable. Everything is just wasted effort, especially the big underground bunker. Some of the guys literally worked on that bunker day and night and now it is just a big waste. Like I have said many times before most things around here are a waste, just like the war. I refuse to put myself out for this army because it has made me so miserable and you never get any satisfaction when you do something for them.

Wednesday, November 6, 1968

Hi Hon,

This is one day that will be pretty hard to forget. We worked like damn fools and for what, I could search my mind for years and never figure it out. I hate to say this and you will probably find it hard to believe, but this place is actually worse than Thunder II. I would like to cry about it just to get it out of my system.

I have never been so dirty in my entire life. Imagine a little boy that has been playing in the dirt all day and I am about five times worse. The heat is getting worse by the day. I am really surprised that no one dropped from the heat today. Well enough of my problems I am sure that you will hear more of them in the days to come.

I have to laugh, some person just walked in here and said he is going to sleep outside in a truck because the rats have overtaken the bunker. You just have to make joke out of this place or you would go insane.

Thursday, November 7, 1968

Well the writing conditions have not improved, nor have the living conditions in the last twenty-four hours. So, if I have to live like a pig, then I just have to do and there is nothing I can do about it. Besides, the war will be over soon. Even though things are not going well at the peace table, I still feel something will break soon. I am almost positive now that we will not be here a year.

I really miss our son so very much. I get so upset when I think about it. I really do not know him, I have never spent any long period of time with him and I wasn't even there when he was born. All I wanted was to make you happy in life and look what happened. I feel so upset with myself when I think about it. I hope I can make it all up to you. I just love you so much and could not stand to see you suffer anymore than you have.

Friday, November 8, 1968

I do not agree with the guy who you talked to you and said anybody who comes over here is a hero. I think that anyone that comes over here to live like I am is a nut, especially when I cannot see any purpose in it. All we are, are a bunch of puppets, being forced by a government, a government that is so involved in everything, it does not know where it stands. A government that is too mixed up to know where to move next. I do not feel that anyone here owes, to this government, the misery they are in over here. Everything the government does give us back home, we pay for dearly in taxes.

And now, because of a decision made many years by a few people, they say we are obligated to this place. It is just ridiculous. I know they want us out of this place because they are losing too much face around the world, but they do not know how to get us out.

Tuesday, November 12, 1968

To think last year at this time we were in Acapulco, soaking up the rays and giant waves. And now, look at the position we are in. We should have stayed there and I should have sold baskets on the seashore or something.

Thursday, November 14, 1968

Last night as I finished writing you, it began to pour rain. Everything I own got completely soaked. Thank God all the pictures you sent me where in my white travel bag and they did not get wet. My cot was completely soaked. This bunker leaks like a sieve. Tomorrow the cooks have to start building our own new bunker. This will be a month or so project.

So, our son did not sleep so well the night of November 7th.

I get so upset when I think that I am not home, where I am supposed to be, helping you. I feel so bad when I think of you alone, with this child, with no husband by your side to help you. I will make you live like a queen when I get back Bren. I just want to help you so much, I just want to be with you. No one could ever know how much I love and need you, my body is bursting with love for you.

Friday, November 15, 1968

Believe it or not today they fired $4,200 worth of rounds of ammunition at six big cows. They did it because they knew that these animals belonged to the Vietcong. They could not get to the Vietcong, so they decided to kill their most precious possession, but they missed.

To make things clear for you, every target or I should say just about every target, we fire on, is picked out by an air observer. The radio observer flies around in a helicopter and once he has a target, he radios back to us. He gives us all the necessary information and then we fire on it. He stays in the area, high above the ground in his helicopter and checks to see what damage we have done. In the case of the cows he figured once the first round hit the ground they would run one way and then the rest of the rounds would kill them, they ran the other way. Pretty stupid, but when you fire on people it is a different story.

Saturday, November 16, 1968

I have been trying to start this letter for about thirty minutes but the cannons have been firing on one side of me and the tanks on the other. Today was one of those days that I was extremely homesick. I am homesick everyday, but it seems to hit more on Saturdays and Sundays.

Sunday, November 17, 1968

Today I heard that South Vietnam has finally agreed to go

to peace talks. If this is true, the delay sure was stupid. If they pull anymore stunts like that we should just pull out of this place. If these talks do go on I sure hope the progress is rapid.

The infantry has just started with their mortars. Tonight they are supposed to fire around this entire area to make sure nothing is around. They do this every once in awhile. This infantry unit with us now moved in today. They are the eleventh Calvary division. This is the third infantry unit that has been with us since we have been at this place.

They move the infantry around quite a bit. This unit that is with us has just come from nine days of combat. They are probably here for a rest, even though this place is in the middle of nowhere and it is not very restful. After nine days of combat though, I am sure it could be restful here. The thing about this place is the radar system we have makes things pretty safe. Anytime there is anyone outside the perimeter and the radar picks them up, they blast the entire area.

Tuesday, November 19, 1968

Received two letters today, one from Tommy and the one I live for, from you. I am convinced that we are ONE, Darling. In the letter I received today you mentioned exactly what I said three days ago, concerning you getting pregnant again and that when I get home we should just enjoy each other. It is really amazing how our minds do run the same way no matter if we are separated.

Thursday, November 21, 1968

Hi Hon,

I received two beautiful letters from you today. I do love you so much. I was upset to find out you are not receiving mail from me everyday as you should. I write everyday and if anything is missing you should be able to tell from the dates on the letters. It gets me so upset to think you are not getting my letters the way you should. Especially knowing you look forward to the mail as much as I do. I just live for your letters Hon. Like you said, it is just a piece of paper, but it is our only means of communication and we need it so badly. I just dream so much about the day we will be together again and how great it will be. No one could ever imagine how much I love you and miss you, how I need you. It is just so great, it could never be expressed or explained. I also miss our son very much. Realizing that he is getting bigger and stronger everyday and that I am not there with you to share these things, I get so discouraged. I do love him so much even though I have not seen him that much or spent that much time with him. It is because he is ours and we made him together. Together we made him, it's unreal when you really think about it.

Friday, November 22, 1968

Today you asked me to explain what a perimeter is. Well it is as far as the eye can see from where we are. We are all in a little area in what at one time was a forest or jungle. Then around the area of cleared jungle where we live, are the cannons. Also the infantry is there with their tanks and there is barb wire that surrounds the area. We do not go beyond that because even though the area is fairly clear, there are land mines. The land mines blow up if anyone steps on them. The area with the mines is about 200 hundred yards long and as with everything else is in a complete circle around us. After the land mine area, there are trees and you cannot see any further.

The main reason for the infantry is to protect us and our cannons. When our cannons fire they do a lot of damage. The damage is done about five to eight miles away from us because that is how far the rounds or explosive go when we fire them. So if the enemy ever decides to attack to destroy our cannons, the infantry is here to protect us from that. Enough war talk!

Last night I stayed up quite late listening to the tapes you sent. I listened to both of them three times. I almost cried; I would have if George P. had not been here with me. They came out great. I could here you and the baby very clearly.

Saturday, November 23, 1968

Last night was my first night in this bunker. There are rats in this one, but I do not think as many as the old one. Last night after everyone was asleep, I listened to the tapes you sent again. I love them, to hear your voice and the noises the baby make is just great.

I am fortunate for I do sleep in one little corner in a convex box. I do not know if you remember what a convex box is, but you may have seen one when we were in North Carolina. Anyway they are used to ship our things over here. There are two bunkers and I was lucky enough to be in this one with just five others, although it is still pretty crowded with six of us.

I don't remember if I told you or not, Mike Burns wrote to me a few days ago. It was a short letter. All he had to say was he had gone skiing at Sugarbush one weekend and O'Neil was living in Boston with Starr working for an insurance company and that the Stewarts were looking forward to graduation. He said he stopped in to see you awhile ago and both you and the baby looked great.

It just gets me so upset to think that all the people I used to hang around with are still home living normal lives. And here I am, married with a child, so deeply in love with my wife I could go out of my mind, for I love you so much and no one could ever make me happier than you have, I would do anything for you and I am here and you are so far away from me. It really upsets me.

I know this letter will not get to you until after Thanksgiving. As you know by now I did not send you anything. I feel very bad about it. There are no cards to be had around here. I did not send you roses and I should have, at least

I should have sent you something. Please forgive me Hon, for the stupidity on my part. My thoughts are constantly with you and you know how much I love and need you.

Monday, November 25, 1968

Now I am going to tell you what happened to George today. It is a long story so I hope I explain it so that you understand. When we were at Fort Bragg, George was a Forward Observer but decided to get out of this section because it could be a dangerous job in a war zone. A Forward Observer is a person that goes out and watches where our bombs land, but his primary duty is looking for the enemy. Since we have been here George has been asking and asking if he could again become part of the Forward Observer Team. The team consists of two people. They actually do nothing while they are here in camp, but when they go out in the jungle they more than make up for it. Anyway, today the captain walks up to George and asks him if he wants to go on about a ten day mission with the Forward Observers. So George gets all excited about the idea and says yes. I don't think he actually realized what he was getting himself into.

Regardless, at three this afternoon there was George with a pack on his back. You would not have believed the load he was carrying. He was with two other men in the team. They were airlifted by helicopter. I guess they are going quite a way up north as they will be out of the range of our (U.S.) cannons. They are supposed to join a battalion of Vietnamese soldiers but, of course, they will always be out in front of the Vietnamese because they will look for the enemy and then radio back that they have found them. A few rare people are cut out to do this sort of thing, I just hope he did not let his crazy talk get him into this.

George recounts leaving for the mission like this, "No one saw us off. We got our orders and waited two hours for the chopper to come. When we started to load up and go out, I turned around and there was Dick standing there shaking his head. It was like your mom standing there. He had his apron on from the kitchen and he was standing there shaking his head, with his hands on his hips. I can remember it like it was yesterday."

George could taste the disgust Dick's voice spoke as he prepared to board the helicopter, "George, what in the hell are you doing? Are you crazy? Are you crazy? Are you crazy?"

As George headed off to combat he was almost overwhelmed by Dick's concern for him. He could not believe that Dick had come running from the kitchen as soon as he had found out about the mission for which George had volunteered. He could not believe Dick insisted on seeing him off, and he would never forget how much it meant to him, that Dick cared enough to question his decision to go.

George's experience on this mission provided him with the realization that combat, especially combat in this war, was the antithesis of what he had envisioned. "We were way up North in Loc Nihn. It was bad place, it was at the end of the Ho Chi Mihn Trail. When we got there one guy asked us what we were doing there. He said there were North Vietnamese behind every tree. He told us when the shit hits the fan the South Vietnamese were going to leave us standing alone.

"The day the battle started they [the South Vietnamese] had to be implored to be pushed up to position, they would not come up. We left them back there and the Americans did the fighting that day.

"One night we had to maintain light and noise discipline because we had information that we were surrounded — in the jungle — by Vietcong. What light and noise discipline meant was no matches, no cigarette, no moving, no nothing! TOTAL QUIET! Well, about 50% of the North Vietnamese had tuberculosis. So they could not help but cough all the time. There we were, trying to be totally silent and all you could hear was this scattered, uncontrollable coughing. I realized then that we were dealing with a bunch of rank amateurs . . . I remember seeing afterward the carnage. I looked at the dead Vietcong and thought My God these are kids. Most of them were sixteen . . . We were not allowed to fire in the Michelin rubber tree plantation. It was a no fire zone because the U.S. government had to reimburse the South Vietnamese government for every rubber tree destroyed, of course the Vietcong were smart enough to hide there. So what that said to us was, the trees are more valuable than our lives. In other words, this concentrated effort we are making to 'win the hearts and minds' of these people only mattered when it did not cost the government too much money or it was not too inconvenient."

USARV Fact Sheet

You and the Bombing Halt
— What Does it Mean?

Being preoccupied with the daily matters of waging war against an evasive and determined enemy, you may at this point be wondering what the recent halt in the bombing of North Vietnam really means to the United States and you. Being in Vietnam, we must fully understand what it means.

First, let's review some of the events of the past few months to see what has been done by our country in an attempt to resolve the Vietnam conflict in a fast but honorable way.

To understand the United States' position with regard to the conflict in South Vietnam, we must examine the goals stated at the conclusion of the October 1966 Manila Conference. This conference was attended by our President, the Government of Vietnam, and representatives of all the Free World Military Assistance Forces fighting with us in South Vietnam. At that time, it was agreed that:

Allied forces shall be withdrawn, after close consultation with the Government of Vietnam and the other troop contributing nations, as the military and subversive forces of North Vietnam are withdrawn to the North.

Infiltration ceases; and

The level of violence thus subsides.

During the latter part of 1966, after the Manila Conference, and during 1967, the North Vietnamese continued building up their forces in South Vietnam and increased their subversive and terrorist activities. Because of this increased North Vietnamese Army activity in the South, the United States and its allies increased the forces committed to the defense of South Vietnam, while still seeking a peaceful settlement. In September 1967, President Johnson outlined a proposal which he hoped would lead to negotiations and peace. This proposal, referred to as the "San Antonio Formula," made clear that the United States would stop bombing North Vietnam when such action would lead to productive peace talks and not be used by the North Vietnamese for military advantage. This offer was rejected by Hanoi on 3 October 1967.

The communist offensives during 1968, commencing with the Tet offensive in late January 1968, proved to be a major turning point in the conflict. The enemy hoped for an uprising of the South Vietnamese people in his support. It did not occur. Not only was the enemy rebuffed in this political objective, but his military forces were soundly defeated. We have seized the initiative and kept it.

The enemy setbacks in 1968 took their toll in morale and combat effectiveness of the enemy — he realizes that he cannot win militarily in South Vietnam.

On 31 March 1968, President Johnson made yet another effort to bring the conflict to the negotiating table. He said at that time: "Tonight I renew the offer I made last August — to stop the bombardment of North Vietnam. . . . Tonight I have ordered our aircraft and our naval vessels to make no attacks on North Vietnam except in the area north of the Demilitarized Zone. . . . Even this very limited bombing of the North could come to an early and — if our restraint is matched by restraint in Hanoi." Bombing of North Vietnam above the 19th parallel was halted. This de-escalation was made as a test of the good faith of the North Vietnamese, and resulted in their willingness to meet with the United States in Paris for negotiations which we hoped would lead to peace.

The talks got underway on 10 May 1968 while fighting in South Vietnam continued. For quite a few months the discussions were nonproductive and appeared to be deadlocked. A few weeks ago, however, they entered a new, more hopeful phase.

In an announcement of the bombing halt on 31 October, the President stated: "We have reached the stage where productive talks can begin. We have made it clear to the other side that such talks cannot continue if they take military advantage of them."

We must understand that the bombing halt does not mean a halt in fighting in South Vietnam. The current negotiations will take more time, and hard fighting will continue to occur. Although the enemy has suffered severe reverses militarily, he still has the capability to continue his aggression in the South. Should he elect to continue fighting, he will be opposed by the combined allied forces, including the South Vietnamese Armed Forces, which grow daily in strength and effectiveness. Our military pressure has forced the enemy to agree to what we hope can be meaningful discussions in Paris leading to peace. This military pressure must continue unabated in South Vietnam to ensure that these discussions do lead to peace.

You can be certain that every possible step is being taken to be sure that the enemy does not take advantage of the bombing halt. Your commanders have been authorized and directed to take any and all actions necessary to defend your unit against attacks by the enemy anywhere in South Vietnam. The choices now are further de-escalation . . . or further destruction.

United States Army Vietnam Special Command Information Fact Sheet 3-69 (Nov. 68)

11) Hopeful Holidays

Thursday, November 28, 1968

Thanksgiving
Hi Hon,

Again no mail today. I guess the mail men took the day off to eat Thanksgiving dinner. We did have turkey dinner here today. Four turkeys about the size your mother would buy. But, it really makes no difference what day it is, I just get so homesick for you. If I were home tonight we would probably be at your parents house picking at the remains of a turkey, watching television and drinking beer.

I haven't told you yet that I love and miss you very much. My love and need for you grows greater every day. I have to be with you soon darling to hold you in my arms and get close to your beautiful body. I need you so much to live, without you I am not complete and never could be.

Have your parents decided where to ski this year? Is there snow on the ground now or has it melted? That was a ridiculous question, because by the time you receive this letter and answer the question, the snow situation will be completely different anyway.

I don't know how quite to say it but, I realize these holidays must be extremely hard on you Bren. I know it is hard living under the conditions you are. I swear this year will be the last time you will ever be in this position. I will never in my life leave you again. Once we are united again I will make the years we are together and all the events that happen in a year, the best and most perfect for you. When I do these things for you it will be great for me because whenever you are happy I cannot help but be the same. I love you so much and with you life is perfect.

It looks as though the peace talks are finally going to start. I hope they make some progress so we can all get out of this terrible place. I could never have imagined that people could live as we do. And to think that there are many Americans here who are living in much worse conditions than me. It just makes no sense, especially when you think of the purpose of why we are here. All I want to do is live my life with you. Each and every moment I have ever been with you, has just been happiness for me. I truly adore you.

Saturday, November 30, 1968

We had an accident here yesterday. It seems one of our cannons fired a round on Thunder II by mistake. There are people who got hurt at Thunder II as a result. One person was hurt pretty bad because he was evacuated by helicopter. It seems that the gun powder which is used to ignite the round was faulty, so it was really no ones fault. There is an investigation going on though. The people hurt were infantry just like we have around here. All they were doing was sitting on their tank and all of a sudden BOOM! Thank God no one was killed.

Morday, December 2, 1968

I am now listening to my fair lady on the tape you sent me and I heard you cough in the background. Do you have a cold? Even though it was a cough it sounded good to me because it was a sound from you and your body and I got to hear it.

Tuesday, December 3, 1968

Today the chaplain came for Mass and communion and I prayed so hard for you, the baby and for my quick return to you both, so that we can begin to live a normal life. Today again was a very hot day and a day that I am lonesome for you. I hate this life so much even though there are so many people over here living under much worse conditions than me.

Wednesday, December 4, 1968

Received word from George today. He is going to be out in the woods one more week. I packed some laundry for him, some clothes he needed. I imagine they are going to bring them out to him as well as clothes for the other people by helicopter.

A person over here received a clipping in a letter from the Union Leader concerning B Battery from Nashua. Well there are a lot of false statements in the article. For one thing, B Battery out of all the batteries from New Hampshire, has it the easiest. They have not yet even moved from Phu Loi, our base camp. Concerning the Union Leader* I heard today that A Battery will have a space allocated every week for an article and picture about the battery. I don't think you will see anything in the paper for a couple weeks.

I know the person who is going to write the articles and he has been told that everything he writes must be "good". Nothing he writes can be against the war or, radical and condemning of the war. Believe the article will not be the opinion of everyone in this battery. The funniest thing is that the person who was chosen to write these articles cuts the war and our presence here almost as much as me. I think he was chosen because he is one of the few people over that can write.

Oh Bren, how I would like to hold you in my arms and squeeze you. Just to be close to you and feel the warmth of your body. I don't like think of these wonderful things because I go crazy. I pray and hope so much that this will all be over soon and we are back together living a happy normal life.

---

*Manchester, New Hampshire's daily newspaper.

Thursday, December 5, 1968

Hi Hon,

Today was a banner day for me as far as mail goes. I received one letter from my parents, three from you along with some beautiful pictures and a package from Charlotte. The picture you sent of yourself is beautiful. I just adore it. I almost cry every time I look at it. You are so beautiful. I just have to get out of this place soon.

I don't know if I told you, but some people over here have received "Bond" fruit cakes from the Salvation Army. It really hit me hard to see the "Bond" cakes over here because last year at this time, I remember making out sales slips for these cakes at the bakery to sell to the Salvation Army.

Friday, December 6, 1968

Well you could never guess what I did after I wrote you last night. Myself, the rest of the cooks, the wire section and the F.D.C. section that was not on duty, basically all the sections who have nothing to do with the cannons were assigned to the cannons. I was with this kid Belanger and we carried ammunition to the guns. The rounds for these cannons weigh ninety-six pounds apiece, fortunately though Belanger and me only carried the powder which ignites these rounds and they do not weigh nearly as much. The reason we were all called out to the cannons to assist is because a village and a Vietnamese soldier camp was being attacked about three miles from here and we were giving them fire power to help support. They fired and we carried ammo until four-thirty or five this morning.

Today we found out that there were only ten Vietcong who were terrorizing the village we were supporting. You would not believe the amount of money we must have spent firing those rounds into the air. I am not telling you this to get you upset or worried because there is nothing to worry about. There is nothing to worry about, Hon and besides we will be together soon.

I just know it. We will live a happy life together. There are so many signs, nothing official yet, but so many people, just about everyone in the battery, says we will be going home soon. Sending the National Guard over here was an experiment to see what we could do and now they know.

I am thinking now maybe I should not have told you about last night because you are going to get worried. Please don't worry, it would be foolish. Remember any action we take part in is many miles away and we are well guarded from any trouble.

Brenda I just love you so much. Right now I wish I was brushing and playing with your hair. I just love to watch the expression on your face when I am doing this. You look like you are in another world, a world all your own. I can see it so clearly now.

Sunday, December 8, 1968

Today in one of your letters you asked me about R and R[1]. Today I found out I will be leaving January 29. Please wait two days before you make any arrangements. I still need to find out all the details. I was really lucky to get to go to Hawaii and in the entire battalion of over five hundred people from New Hampshire, I am one of only twelve getting to go in the month of January.

Well George made it back today and as I figured he had many stories to tell. He is even going to get a medal of valor, but like he said, they give medals for just about anything over here. However, I am sure he did a real good job out there.

I heard on the radio last night that all the National Guard that were activated and sent to Vietnam will be released almost as soon as we leave here. I pray and hope so much that these peace talks move along swiftly and they talk about de-escalation I don't even know when they are supposed to start, I surmise it will be pretty soon. I also heard on the radio that they figured

[1] Rest and Relaxation

out where they are going to sit and what door they are going to walk in etc. These are such stupid things to discuss! How can they settle a war when they get involved in such trivial things? I don't like to think about it because I get too upset about it. Once out of here, I NEVER want to have the slightest involvement with our government.

I don't think I will be able to leave you once R and R is over. I love and need you so much. As much as I love and want to see that dear son of ours I think it would be better if he stayed with your parents. I think he is too young to travel that far and I worry he may get sick, but if you think it is okay then please bring him.

Monday, December 9, 1968

Do you know my love for you grows greater every day? Did not receive any mail today, but did receive a beautiful package containing all the things I need and have asked for. It also contained Christmas presents which I have not opened because there was a note telling me not to open them until Christmas. I promise I will not open them until that day. You truly are the greatest wife in the whole world for sending me these things.

Tuesday, December 10, 1968

I received a Christmas card today from one of our friends. How anyone can wish me a Merry Christmas when I am away from my family, is beyond me. They must be nutty to think that I am going to have a Merry Christmas. I guess this is nasty for me to say and I guess people do the best they can considering the situation. I do appreciate the cards I receive. But again, how could I ever have a Merry Christmas? I don't even want to know what time of year it is. I just looked up and saw the empty box of Pampers you sent with all the things I asked for. Looking at the picture of the baby on the box just gets me so homesick and lonesome. I was pleased when you told me Dickie is growing hair. It will be good when I can see him in person and not have to see him in a picture, but in real life. I just have to be with you and our son soon. This useless war better be over soon.

Thursday, December 12, 1968

You will never guess where I am. I am back at Phu Loi Base Camp. I came back here on the convoy that brings supplies to Thunder III. They sent me here because I am supposed to go in front of the promotion board tomorrow morning, but the board is not meeting until Monday. So, I guess I will be here until Monday.

It is ridiculous sending me in front of the promotion board because it is impossible for me to get a promotion because I have not been a Spec 4 long enough. Also I do not know anything about a kitchen and I do not plan on learning. I try and do as little as possible for this army. All I want to do is get out of it. I think the reason they may have sent me here for a promotion because I did all the paper work when we did not have a mess sergeant. Regardless of the reason it is nice to be out of the field for a short time anyway.

Remember when I first got here to Phu Loi and how I said the living conditions were bad? Well, compared to Thunder II and Thunder III this place is pretty good. I actually have a pillow to sleep on tonight.

Sunday, December 15, 1968

Well I never thought I would see the day that I would enjoy an U.S.O., [United Services Organization] but today I certainly am. Last night when I had an idea that I might be able to call you, I was so nervous, I tossed and turned all night, hoping I might have the opportunity to call. Once here at the U.S.O. club I was so nervous and my heart was really going. Anyway I put my name on a list and it was a little over two and a half hour wait before they spelled out my name and told me to go to booth number one.

I picked up the receiver in booth number one and there was your beautiful voice. Speaking to you was the fastest five minutes I have ever experienced. I wanted to tell you how much I loved you, missed you and need you, but before I knew it, the time was up. Those five minutes of talking to you were the greatest and happiest I have had since I left you. I love you so much Brenda I think I am going out of my mind. If we are not together soon living a happy normal life, I think I will crack up. I only wish you could feel how great my love is for you when I write I love you.

After our short but great conversation, I went to the men's room, yes a real men's room, with urinals and sinks and even hot water and a real wall mirror that I just stared at for a few minutes. It was really a great touch of civilization. I must have washed my hands for about ten minutes along with checking myself out in the mirror. No, I am not conceited, I just wanted to take a look at myself since it was the first time I really got to look in a mirror since I left home.

Right now I am sitting in a leather chair, listening to some music and writing. The place is air conditioned and quite comfortable. Of course anything would be after living the way I have been for the past months in the field. I received your letter today mentioning that Dickie went to see Santa Claus. He must be getting to be quite the little man. I only wish I was there with you to share these moments.

Monday, December 16, 1968

Well today I faced the promotions board. I was nervous and I do not know why. It was actually kind of funny saluting and saying, "Yes, sir." They (the promotions board) all sit at this one long table, I walked in to report and then took a seat in front of them. They started asking me questions. They fired questions at me for about twenty-five minutes before they were finished. It was just like a scene you see in the movies. Even though the chances are slight I hope I do get the promotion, because it will mean more money for you.

Tomorrow morning I leave here for Thunder III. I sure am going to miss the pillow and all the little comforts that are available over here in Phu Loi. No one else would consider these little things comforts or luxuries, but after being in the field for so long, they are.

I heard today that Clifford[2] said that if the peace talks did not make progress because of Saigon, then there is nothing that says we cannot start sending troops home. I also heard that the first thing he wants discussed at the talks is de-escalation. If de-escalation does come about, I hope we are the ones they de-escalate. This is the most logical and sensible move, but you know this damn army and their decisions.

Tuesday, December 17, 1968

Well you will never guess what was waiting for me once I arrived here, (Thunder III). A Christmas Tree! I have not picked it up yet, but you are the greatest and most thoughtful person in the world for sending it to me. I also received a package from the American Tobacco Company that was sent to me by Budweiser, it contained five cartons of Pall Mall cigarettes.

Wednesday, December 18, 1968

This afternoon I set up the Christmas tree you sent me and it really is very nice. In the tape I got today your mother mentioned that when someone says to Dickie where is Da Da, he looks at the picture of me in the house. Every time you mention this I get misty eyed and today I really did. I love and miss that little boy so much. I just want to play with him and have him get to know me. We will have so much fun together.

[2] Secretary of Defense

Wednesday, December 25, 1968

Hi Hon,

You would never believe what I have been through the last twenty-four hours. It started yesterday afternoon about four-thirty when the mess sergeant told George and me that we were going to have to bake rolls and pies for Christmas dinner. Well George and I started at four-thirty and did not finish until quarter to eleven. Nice way to spend Christmas Eve, don't you think? Being in a warm kitchen tent making rolls and pies. Well anyway after that I came over to my bunker and started to write you a letter. Nelson came over and he had some Canadian Club so we had a few drinks to celebrate Christmas. After he left I figured I would finish the letter in the morning before the mail went out. I figured I would have time in the morning thinking that mess sergeant would not need me since I had worked until eleven that night. But he came for me at quarter past seven and I did not get to finish my letter to you yesterday which really gets me upset because I have to write you everyday. Anyway from seven-thirty this morning until five this afternoon I was in the kitchen, as were all the cooks. Now get this, after preparing the food Christmas Eve as well as today none of the cooks got to eat any of the food because it was all gone by the time we were done.

Many of the men remember their Christmas dinner at Thunder III as a bright spot in an otherwise bleak existence. The baking that Dick did was regarded with appreciation and gratitude. George tells of the feeling of the men: "He brought so much pleasure in such a horrible place just by all the extra goodies he made for us." Rocky Provencher vividly and fondly described the Christmas dinner that he largely credited to Dick in a letter to his wife, "as good or better than my mother had done." Of course Dick never mentioned to anyone but Brenda, that there was no food left for him and the other cooks.

When Brenda read the letter Dick wrote on Christmas the

dull ache that had come to reside in her heart since his departure, sharply and concisely turned to numbing pain. She had tried, rather successfully, to devote her energy to their son and her younger siblings during Christmas. But as she read Dick's Christmas letter to her and then the letter to their son she could not avoid the pain, loss and anger that pierced and crippled her spirit.

To My Wife on Christmas Day,

Well my love there is not much I can say on a day such as this, being in a situation such as this. But I wish you a Merry Christmas and Happiness throughout the New Year. I want to do so much for you, but do to these conditions I am unable to. You do have all my love and always will. Once we are together again, which I pray is soon, everyday will be Christmas for you. There could never be anything but happiness for us and our family throughout any year.

You are the greatest wife and mother in the entire world. You have all my love and always will. Once we together again there will never be a moment of unhappiness, our love is too great. MERRY CHRISTMAS. Your loving husband, Dick.

To My Son on Christmas Day,

Hi again Bren, I realize Dickie is too young to read and understand this or even this time of year, but what kind of father would I be if I did not make some kind of gesture to our son, who I love so much, on Christmas Day? I want to let him know I love him so much and wish him a Merry Christmas and a Happy New Year. I want him to know all of his years will be full of happiness knowing he has the finest mother in the entire world. We will see what I can do for him once I am with him again, which I pray is soon.

Wish Little Dickie a Merry Christmas for me and give him my love, as I know you do every day because you are the greatest mother in the world and he will realize this someday. I guess this note is mainly for you my love, knowing Dickie is too young to understand. You are the one that has made his first Christmas so wonderful as well as all his time in this world. I love you, Dick.

Thursday, December 26, 1968

Today we were visited by some senator from the South. What a fake show they put up for him. He even ate with some high ranking army officers. He came by helicopter of course. You should have seen the procedure that went on before the helicopter he was in landed. His helicopter stayed high in the air, while about six others came down low and circled around and around to make sure the place was safe for him to land. Once he was on the ground, it was sickening to see the way the officers who were with him, cater to his every need.

I don't even know what his purpose was in coming here, especially to this place, but whatever it was he must have gotten the wrong impression of the way things are. Everyone was trying to make everything look so nice and perfect for him. It is so ridiculous and disgusting. I am sure anyone with half a brain should be able to see through these army people.

Monday, December 30, 1968

I did make Spec. 5. I received orders today. I am happy about it mainly because it means more money for you. Spec. 5 is the same as sergeant except the title is Spec. 5. I don't know how I made it, but I did so that is all that counts. A few people resent the fact that I made it, especially since I have been in the National Guard a short time. It does not bother me though because you and Dickie are all I care about. Now I can give you a little more money. I realize money is just a material thing and we have something a lot deeper, our love for each other and that is the most important thing.

Tuesday, December 31, 1968

There is no cease fire this New Year's Eve, in fact the guns are supposed to start firing any moment now. I am really happy that there is no cease fire because you never know if the enemy is around you. It is dangerous because no one is really on guard.

I am just thinking of being with you January 29 (in Hawaii for R and R) so much. The thought is constantly on my mind. I cannot wait to see the pictures of Dickie with all his presents and the picture of him with Santa Claus.

I just have to get out of here soon. I pray and hope so much for peace or de-escalation. There is no reason why the U.S. should be here in the first place. I think the politicians realize this, but they do not know how to get out of the mess, they got us involved in. Nixon just better do something and fast. He actually has not said what he is going to do yet and that bothers me. He better come up some solution and very soon once he gets into office.

Brenda received flowers from Dick on New Years Day 1969. He again through the mail and in the middle of a war found a way to let his wife know he was always thinking of her.

I realize these flowers are not much in comparison to the vast amount of love I have for you. Once we are together again, I will do everything in my power to fulfill your and our families every little desire throughout the year.

Happy New Year Darling. Let us pray that early in this year peace does come about and we can make this year and all the other years the happiest in our lives. Which of course will be, because we will be together.

You have all my love Bren, and always will forever and ever, your loving husband, Dick.

Thursday, January 2, 1969

Here is another what you may consider a stupid question, how old are babies before they start to talk? I am always thinking of different things Dickie will be doing and how old he will be when he does do these things. I know I am going to enjoy him so much. I know I am going to enjoy playing with him and everything. I just love him so much.

Tuesday, January 7, 1969

So that man you talked to did not appreciate the fact that I do not like being over here and do not believe in this war. It is people like that who aggravate me so much. I don't care how much you read about this war or claim to know about it, you do not truly understand it until you participate in it. You could not understand unless you have been in a place like I am. I am quite sure I could tell him a few things that would change his views.

Nixon just better do something very, very soon after he gets into office, like getting complete peace or a large amount of de-escalation and then more de-escalation and more until there are no Americans left in this country.

Wednesday, January 8, 1969

Hi Hon,

How are you doing today, love? I hope well. I hope Dickie is behaving himself. You must really have to watch him, now that he can bomb around in his walker.

A new medic came up here today. The medics only stay out in the field for one month and then they go back to Phu Loi. They come from headquarters battery and rotate around to different batteries in the field. Anyway, today I went to see him because of my aching feet, and boy were they ever aching. Well, he is the first person in the army that I have talked to, who actually admitted I have real flat feet. He is going to have something sent up here to put in my boots to see if that will help. If that doesn't work they will make some special boots for me.

Only twenty-one more days and we will be together. I cannot wait. The time is going by so slowly because I am always thinking about being with you — to hold you in my arms and hold your body so close to mine.

This war has to be over soon, it just cannot go on. I read somewhere this war is starting its eighth year. Nixon just has to do something and soon. I don't think wanting to live with my wife and child is asking for too much.

As Dick wrote these wrote these words, Edgar, Fleurette, Brenda and especially Charlotte were preparing for Charlotte's marriage to William (Chick) Bowers. Edgar and Fleurette had wanted Charlotte to wait until Dick was home but Chick and Charlotte were young, very much in love, and eager to be married and to begin a life together as husband and wife. Wanting their only daughter's wedding to be an event for all to fondly remember, Edgar and Fleurette decided to support their daughter and future son-in-law 's decision.

With Brenda as one of her bridesmaids, Charlotte wed Chick in a simple but elegant ceremony at St. Catherine's church in Manchester. A reception followed the ceremony at The Manchester Country Club. It was a great celebration and party. However, a shadow of sorrow and lament sporadically eclipsed most everyone's spirit, as it was impossible to have a party of any kind (never mind one as significant and meaningful as his sister's wedding) without thinking of Dick. Undoubtedly, everyone at some moment or another thought of Dick and how a celebration was just not complete without him. They surely could not help but think of all the life, laughter and fun that always exuded from him and then infiltrated everyone whenever he was present.

Naturally no one was more aware of Dick's absence than Brenda. Her heart ached for him. And her soul cried for him, especially when she received his letter dated the day of the wedding.

Saturday, January 11, 1969

Today had been a real hectic day around here, one that I will never forget. Remember I told you the infantry leaves this place around seven or so every morning and goes out with their tanks etc. and checks the road for mines etc. before the open the road for traffic (U.S. trucks I should say)? Well any way they were about nine to ten miles from here and they got ambushed. Fourteen people were hurt and two were killed. So, you can see it was a real BAD day. I get so mad at the U.S. government subjecting Americans to this type of life. Why don't they mind their own business? I don't like to think about it because I get too angry.

Wednesday, January 15, 1969

How is Dickie doing today? Is he getting any fatter? Between his swing, walks and all his toys he should have enough things to keep himself busy for quite a long time. I imagine he still likes all the attention he can get from people. I know I am going to enjoy him very much. We just have to be living together soon. This war just has be over soon. I wish I knew what Nixon was planning on doing. He has not said a damn thing yet and that gets me a little worried.

Saturday, January 18, 1968

Today I read Johnson's State of The Union address in the army newspaper we sometimes get. Anyway his message really got me sick. I think I could spend about eight hours cutting up the points he stated. I just do not know how such a man could ever make it to be president or even a congressman. I have all my faith in Nixon. He better take action for the best, very soon after he gets in office.

I just have to be with you Bren. I live for you and just want to do so much for you. No one in the world could ever make me happier or enjoy life more than you have, my darling wife. I love you so very, very, very, much Brenda C. Genest. I adore you, I truly do. I live for you and always will. Dickie must really be getting heavy for you to handle, I wish so much I could help you.

I have to go outside now and take a "shower." You have to try and wash as often as possible in this place because you just get so filthy.

Kiss our son for me and many to you my love. You will get so many kisses all over your beautiful body in eleven days. We are just going to make so much love. Remember Bren you have all my love and always will forever and ever. Your loving husband, Dick.

Sunday, January 19, 1969

Thank God people can dream of wonderful things because if it were not for my dreaming of our being together, I would have cracked up by now.

This damn government of ours just better do something soon to end this ridiculous war that we have no business being involved in; at least not as much as we are. I just hope the U.S. has learned a lesson from this mess and will never forget it. I do not think the American people will ever let them forget.

Tuesday, January 21, 1969

We just have so many things to talk about in Hawaii. Mainly I want to know so much about Dickie and I can just talk to you about this war and tell you what I think. I was able to listen to part of Nixon's inaugural address and I guess he is going to concentrate on the war as one of his main objectives. I really have a lot of faith in him.

12) Ripped Apart

Dick and Brenda saw each other for the first time in close to five months on 29 January 1969. It had been an agonizing decision for Brenda not to bring Dickie, but she felt the long distance and extensive traveling would just be too much for a seven month old baby. She desperately wanted their son to see his father but she knew the risks of illness, fatigue, and general disruption of Dickie's little life outweighed the benefits of bringing him. It also served as an opportunity for Edgar and Fleurette to spend a substantial period of time with their sole grandchild. The practicality of not bringing Dickie in no way softened the blow of not being able to reunite her husband with his son.

Brenda arrived before Dick and checked into the room she had reserved at the Sheraton at Waikiki. Flying usually sapped Brenda of all her energy. She had never liked to fly and the twelve plus hours it took for her to get to Hawaii should have exhausted her. Much to her pleasure she found herself feeling energized and excited as she settled into the room and waited for Dick.

Dick was visibly shaking with anticipation as he was processed through the health, immigration and customs stations after exiting the plane that he had been confined to for twelve hours. He almost leaped from his seat and shouted, "ENOUGH ALREADY!", as he sat through the mindless, yet required, military dribble in the twenty minute R and R orientation and briefing.

Finally he was released for seven days of time that actually belonged to him. Seven days of another world, a world where time was not stuck in a quagmire of blood and bodies.

When Dick arrived at the hotel Brenda and Dick thrust and then molded into one another. Their arms intertwined around each other's torsos; willingly they each surrendered a shoulder to embrace and cradle each other's face. Together they became one. As much as Brenda wanted to look at him, kiss him and touch every part of him, she could not force herself to let go. She could not believe she actually was with him. She had been convinced when they said goodbye in Manchester that was to be the last time she would see him. Yet there he was. As they embraced one another, each breath she took became stronger and deeper, as if she were trying to inhale him.

It took every fiber of Dick's being to stop himself from sobbing. All the dreaming, expectation and anticipation he had done had not prepared him for the emotion that now raced through his body. Sheer joy and blinding rage alternately convulsed through him. Joy because he was at last holding on to and connecting with his reason and purpose for living. Rage because he now was face to face with the life he had been forced to surrender and abandon. Of course, there had not been one moment since he had left that he had not been painfully aware of what he had left behind, but holding Brenda at that moment, forced the reality of his despair to slam into his soul with the force of a sledgehammer smashing into tempered glass.

Dick took a deep breath and forcefully swallowed his pain. He would not let "them" ruin this time for him. He was determined to savor and relish every single second of this reprieve that he had been granted. He had been resolute in his decision to take the very first R&R that was available. Rocky had tried to talk him out of taking it so soon in their tour, Rocky remembers; "I said, 'Dick don't do it right away. If you take it so soon, it's gonna be a real hard tour.' But he said he wanted to go first because, 'I know I'm going to get killed. I know I am going to get zapped. I KNOW IT.'"

As they continued to hold and explore one another, Brenda finally allowed the shock and astonishment that had taken up residence inside her to be evicted by pure bliss and delight. She, too, had decided to cherish every moment that they were blessed to share together. At one point she longingly and lovingly ran her hand gently over Dick's body. "I did not think I was ever going to be able to do this again — when you left I thought it was the last time I was going to see you alive." Dick leaned over stroked Brenda's hair. "Well, it just goes to show you that I'm going to make it home soon."

Brenda and Dick naturally spent much of their time in their room passionately displaying and rediscovering their love, commitment, attraction to and necessity for one another. Really it is amazing that they ever left their room.

They spent time on the beach soaking up the sun, talking of their son. They spent time at the pool sipping tropical drinks, planning their future. When they dressed for dinner they discussed Dick's strong opposition to the war, the hypocrisy that accompanied the military life he was experiencing. They played in the Pacific Ocean and reminisced about all the times they played together in the Atlantic Ocean. Brenda shared with Dick the frustration of her living situation while they watched the sunset. When they walked hand in hand on the beach they recalled all the adventures they had shared and things they had done together. No matter where they were or what they were doing or what they were discussing their conversations always began with and reverted to their son and the bright future they were going to experience together.

And although they dared not talk to one another about it, neither one could ignore the dark shadow that mercilessly lurked around them. It was like an albatross on their souls. It was a presence that weighed so heavy that their heads actually dropped under the weight whenever they thought about it. No matter how hard they tried, neither could shake the feeling that they were on borrowed time that was going to demand remittance with compounded interest.

Brenda remembers a powerful moment, when on a rented sail boat with several other military couples, she looked around into all the faces of the men, and wondered almost aloud which one or how many would be dead before the end of the year. Although Brenda and Dick spent all seven days carefully dancing around the subject that eclipsed both of their hearts, they managed to renew a promise they had made to one another years before. They promised that if either one were to die, they would somehow, some way come back to the other.

Just as Dick and Brenda had begun to feel whole and alive, maybe even a little secure, their time was up. Of course Brenda and Dick clung to one another their final night and morning together, they had kept the shades drawn — as if not letting in the morning light would somehow fend off Dick's inevitable and involuntary departure.

Brenda sat deflated and mournful at the end of the bed. It was a sunny morning but the hotel room was tenebrous. Brenda and Dick had been awake for hours in a futile attempt to avoid the pain that the arrival of the day had brought. Brenda carefully absorbed each and every movement Dick made. He had very little to pack but what little he did have, he cautiously and deliberately placed into his small white leather bag. When he was done he carefully scanned the room over and over again. Nothing felt right about him leaving. He searched the room for something, anything that could provide him refuge. Maybe if he forgot something or maybe if he did not have the proper paper work or maybe if he lost track of time they would let him stay another day. He scanned the room again. He felt his heart sink into his stomach as his eyes locked on Brenda. Her tender brown eyes were foggy with bitter tears and her petite body crumpled with pain. Instinctively he went to her and cradled her. They held one another with every bit of love and strength their bodies possessed.

Reluctantly Dick stood up, bringing Brenda to her feet with him and said, "It's time for me to go." Brenda could not let go of him. She felt as if her arms were frozen around him. With every bit of will power Dick could muster he pulled away from Brenda and grabbed his bag off the unmade bed. "I love you, Sunshine. I'll be home soon and you and me and Dickie will have the greatest life. I promise."

Helplessly Brenda followed Dick to the door. They kissed. Dick opened the door and the bright, Pacific sun temporally blinded Brenda. She felt Dick slip through her hand and then the door shut with a hollow thud. She stood dumfounded. Confused she looked around the room. She felt her knees buckle. She reached for a chair and just as she sat down, the door flung open. She jumped up and Dick shot into her arms. His voice quivered, "I just can't do this. I can't leave you again Bren. I can't do it."

Again they held onto each other for what seemed like both an eternity and an instant. Three more times Dick would tear himself away and force himself to leave only to come back within seconds. Brenda stood waiting for the door to open again quite awhile before she realized that Dick was not coming back a fourth time. Weakly she staggered over to the bed she had shared with her husband the past week and wept.

At some point Brenda gathered her strength and began to pack and prepare for her trip home. As she walked around the hotel room touching and smelling everything she knew Dick had come in contact with, she could not help but wonder why instead of making love, laughing, and playing on the beach they had not just planned an escape. She became angry with herself as she replayed the events of the past week in her mind. Why had they not gone and bought wigs and disguises and got on the first plane off the island. Why had she been so selfish? Instead of only thinking of being with Dick, why hadn't she devised a plan to have him in Canada before the army even knew he was gone. Why hadn't she insisted they run away? The thoughts and regrets relentlessly stalked her as she prepared to leave. She felt as if she had let the only chance the only time in the past year when she could have had some control over her husband's destiny carelessly slip away.

Her feelings of guilt and regret only intensified as the day wore on. She could not shake the feeling that she had made the biggest mistake of her life by not insisting that Dick run away with her. By the time she reached the airport to catch her evening flight she felt like she had been in a fierce boxing match all day. Brenda wearily found her way to her gate and boarded the jet. She slumped into her window seat and let her forehead fall against the window. She watched the pavement scream underneath her as the plane began to take off. She rolled her head onto the head rest as the plane began its ascent. She wondered how far along Dick was in his journey back to Hell.

As she did every time she thought of Dick she reached her left hand over to her right wrist and began to feel every bit and piece on her gold charm bracelet. Without looking down, she could identify and see in her mind every detail of every charm Dick had given her. As her fingers carefully glided over each charm she began to visit everything the charm represented. She found herself in Dick's blue Mustang as she felt the heart shaped charm he had given Valentine's Day. She could almost feel the Acapulco sand sifting through her toes as the Aztec Calender passed through her thumb and forefinger. She could taste the steamers, lobster and laughter as her fingernails tapped against each tiny gold bar of the lobster trap charm. She felt the thrill and freedom of her high school graduation as she rubbed the oval charm with the cap and diploma. She was filled pure love, joy and pride as her she held the large round charm with tiny gold baby shoes.

The tender smile that had quietly climbed from her soul

suddenly twisted into a painful grimace as her fingers found their way to the charm Dick had surprised her with the day before. She felt as if she had been kicked in the stomach as she looked down at the gold and black coral coated pineapple. She had an almost uncontrollable urge to rip the charm off her beloved bracelet, break open the window next to her and chuck the coral back into the Pacific. As the pain in her stomach subsided ever so slightly, she suspiciously stared at what should have been a precious reminder of the time she and Dick had just shared. She was very confused by this strange and wicked feeling that had overcome her. How could she feel anything but affection for something Dick had given her?

A chill spiked down her spine. She did not know what it was, but there was something wrong — very wrong — with what the pineapple was going to represent for her and Dick.

13) Corrupt Confusion

Thursday, February 6, 1969

Hi Love,

    Well, as you can see, I made it back to this awful, terrible place. I just cannot say how much I hate this place. I also cannot tell you how great and wonderful it was to be with my darling wife, there are just no words. I love you Brenda and there could never be anything but happiness when we are together. I truly adore you Brenda C. Genest.

    When I left Hawaii in the morning the weather was really nice and sunny. I wonder how it was late in the day when you left. The flight left at eight a.m. and you would not have believed how quite everyone was. I bet you could have heard a pin drop on the carpet of the plane.

    Well anyway, we arrived in this friggin country about four-thirty on the fifth of February. I spent the night at the R&R center in Tan So Nute, and believe me the place is a real dump. I spent the night there because no one could pick me up since the roads close at six p.m.

    I hardly slept at all last night. Just thinking of how great it was being with you and how terrible it is without you. Anyway, they picked me up about eleven a.m. today and I am back in Phu Loi. I did catch a little cold, nothing too bad, but I feel really sick because I cannot stand being separated from you. I just have no ambition at all. All I can think of is being with you, Love. Living in our own home with our child, living a beautiful life. I want to tell you in different words how great and wonderful it was to be with you in Hawaii, but there are no words that could express how good it felt.

Sunday, February 9, 1969

Tomorrow I go back in the field, if you only knew how much I dread this. I heard today that we are going to be out in the field another three months. This does not sound probable, but this is the word going around. Personally I just cannot see how they can keep us out there another three months. People will just start going crazy, if that is so, and I will most likely be the first.

Monday, February 10, 1969

Well I am back in this desolate, terrible place called Thunder III. As usual the ride up here was dirty, dusty and hot. I did bring a little puppy with me from Phu Loi. The poor dog got car sick — actually I guess I should say truck sick. Fred and I are going to take care of him here.

Dick had returned to Vietnam just as an army program know as "Infusion" was about to begin. Infusion was the army's solution to preventing a significant number men from the same community being killed because of being stationed and/or placed together. Everyone in the National Guard were at the very least from the same state and most were from or lived by the same town or city. For example, in 'A' Battery most all of the men were from in and around Manchester. Therefore, to eliminate the risk of a large number of men from Manchester dying from a singular military action, say an attack or ambush at Thunder III, most of the one hundred and twenty-five men were infused into the different units within the regular army where the chance of them being with somebody from the same community was minimal. It has also been reported that the initial purpose for infusion was so the 3rd Battalion 197th Artillery would be employed in a tactical posture as well as serve as a means for the battalions original members to return to the U.S. after serving one year. Regardless of the reasons, most of the men were distressed over the prospects of infusion.

George Pavlidis remembers it like this: "We called it confusion — because that's what it was. There had been rumors floating around [while at Fort Bragg, North Carolina] that once we got to Vietnam, we were going into regular army units. We thought, 'Oh my God!' because regular army units could represent never coming out of the bush, always going out everyday, pounding the bushes and being in jeopardy every day. Anyway, while we were at a Fort Bragg, U. S. Senator McIntyre came down. We were told he was coming so that we could voice any concerns we had to him. We were told we could openly talk to him. So McIntyre says something like, 'Oh believe me. You people will be staying together.' That crap, that rhetoric that he just threw out at us. He placated everyone with his bull.

"Then we got there (Vietnam) and it started to happen. The word came down there was going to be a break up. After McIntyre assured us that we would not be separated, the word came down that we would be infused into other army units. We would be with total strangers. At least before you knew, I mean it had been a community of guys you had come over with.

"I think the motives on the military part were that hometown units is such, with such cohesiveness that they probably should not be in one spot at one time in case something happened."

Tuesday, February 11, 1969

Well today we had a formation and they told us about the infusion. I guess it is going to start pretty soon even though no one has left yet. Twelve people are supposed to leave this month, one cook will be one of the twelve. The captain is going to choose the people that are going to leave from this battery. I would not be worried if I knew for sure the captain was going to be the only one making the decision about who had to go, but I know the mess sergeant will have say as well. I think he may volunteer me.

Anyway, after the formation, the mess sergeant called a meeting of the cooks and asked for a volunteer. As you well know, I did not volunteer. I decided to go and speak to the mess officer to find out who was going to pick the cook who would be going. He told me the mess sergeant is not going to be the one who decides. While I was there I told the mess officer I did not want to get infused. (By the way I get along really great with the mess officer.) He told me I was definitely not going to get infused at this time or the next time. He said he would do everything in his power to keep me with this battery.

Oh, I forgot to mention, there has been a change in the infusion since I told you about it in Hawaii. Remember in Hawaii I told you infusion would include only about fifty percent of the people. Well it has been changed to eight-five to ninety percent. In fact all the people who work the cannons are guaranteed to be infused. I cannot believe that they are going to infuse as many people as they say. It just does not make any sense. I will keep you informed with all the news I can gather about this rotten infusion.

Wednesday, February 12, 1969

Well today without a doubt I had the biggest scare of my life. It was this afternoon about three o'clock when someone came over and told me the captain wanted to see me. I had no idea why, so I went over to the place where he sleeps, you might consider it his office. Anyway I walk into this place and he looks at me real solemn like and says, "I have bad news for you, something has happened at home." Well right about then I almost had heart failure, it felt as though my heart moved about a foot, plus I was shaking like a leaf in the breeze. All I could think was something happened to you or Dickie. I had never been so frightened in all my life. All these thoughts passed through my head in what must have been a split second, but it seemed like minutes, many minutes.

Well anyway I found out it was my grandmother's husband Eddy who the captain kept referring to as my grandfather. The captain asked me whether I was the only grandchild and if I was close to him. If it would have been my mother's father I would have tried to go home, but there was no chance considering my relationship to him.

Believe me hon, when the man said something has happened at home, I never had been so scared in my life. I was shaking so bad it was unreal. I had never experienced such fright in my life.

I received two letters from you today and I was relieved that you had no problem getting home with your connection and everything. As far as Dickie having eczema it is just one of those things and I am sure it can be cleared up with the proper ointments. One thing, I thought of though, is that, Harold had eczema when he was six years old or so and this kept him out of the army. So, Hon, make sure the doctors keep a record of Dickie having eczema. Like I have said before I'll do anything to prevent that child from going into the army.

Thursday, February 13, 1969

Today in "The Stars and Stripes", the army paper we get sometimes, it said that, Harriman, the man who used to head the talks in Paris for the U.S., said soon many troops will be leaving this country. I hope he is right and the time is very soon. I just heard on the radio that the peace talks are presently going on. I wonder if anything will get accomplished. Sometime at one of these meetings they are going to settle a major problem and the world is going to be shocked. This war has to end soon. It cannot go on forever. The Tet holiday begins February 17. The Tet time of year for the people of this country is supposed to signify peace. I sure hope it does this year.

Oh yeah, I have not told you I have been given a chance to go to Laikee to go to the dentist and get my teeth checked if I want to. I am not going to go because the road is dangerous and I do not like to travel on it.

Monday, February 17, 1969

Today I saw one helicopter that is called a crane drop another helicopter. The helicopter that is a called a crane was towing another helicopter and the cable snapped. Towing is not the correct word but anyway the one being "towed" came crashing down from the sky. What an explosion it was, once it hit the ground! It happened many miles from here but you could still see the explosion. The helicopter that exploded was worth half a million dollars.

Thursday, February 20, 1969

George has a new job. He is now on the water run. His job consists of driving the water truck to the water hole, filling the water trailers we have and filling the barrels people use as showers. The one bad thing about it is that he is on the road everyday because the water hole is seven miles from here. George told me he expects to get infused pretty soon. I tend to believe him because of the job they put him on and the entire thing about infusion seems like it is actually happening. I saw seven people leave for infusion from here, yesterday.

Friday, February 21, 1969

I just hate this army so much. Everything around here is getting on my nerves. But I'd rather, as much as I dislike it here, stay here than be infused. When you get infused you just do not know what you are getting into. You could easily end up in a lot worse place and conditions than here. Oh I am completely starved. I just get so hungry every night. I have these visions of eating all kinds of great foods. I probably could go to the kitchen, but I know there is really nothing edible there.

One of the many things that beat the men in Vietnam down everyday was the stagnant stifling heat. By mid-February the temperature was consistently over a hundreds degrees. George describes the heat like this: "I remember going to St. John Island in the Caribbean with mom after coming home from Vietnam, and my mother saying, 'Oh it is so hot here.' I said to her, 'No, this is not hot this is a cake walk.' And you know how hot it can get in the tropics. But nothing could compare to Vietnam. NOTHING can compare.

"Imagine it is so still at night with NO air movement at all and the temperature ALL day has been over a hundred. The humidity is unbearable. You are just lying there motionless and perspiration is keeping you awake. You are soaking in your own sweat. You are so tired and all you can think about is how you cannot endure staying awake. You just want the sweat to subside a little so you can fall asleep. Of course there are no showers or anything like that."

Saturday, February 22, 1969

Happy Washington's Birthday. I never pictured Washington's Birthday like this. I always thought of it as a sort of mild winter day with slush on the ground. A day like when I was in high school and we had no classes. I never pictured it like this with the temperature in the hundreds. It is just so hot over here.

Well this morning they officially changed captains. I did not go to formation because I was in the kitchen. I am glad because I cannot see standing out in the hot sun, watching idiotic military movements. You well realize I do not like anything about the army. Anyway, you will probably get to read about the entire ordeal, because Arcand wrote an article about that he will probably send to the Union Leader.

How is our little son today? I hope he is not creating too much work for you. It must be interesting and fun to see what he is going to do next. I really wish he would stop eating paper and cardboard, knocking pictures off the walls and bending so far over in his walker. I am really surprised he does not hurt himself more with all the crazy things he does. I just do not see where he gets all of his energy. But I do know we are going to have so much fun with him doing all sorts of different things. He is looking older and more lovable in every picture I receive of him. He looks so playful and a little mischievous in an innocent way.

Tuesday, February 25, 1969

Well today was a very bad day for me. I feel really depressed. I just cannot stand this place. This has to be over soon, so we can be together. I love you so much Bren and I cannot stand be separated from you. I live for you and have to be living with you soon. Life is nothing without you, but with you there is nothing but happiness.

I did manage to stick an ice pick in my hand in my hand today while I was chopping some ice. So as you can see I am still my old self. Today three more people were infused and they did not know a thing about it before it happened. This morning about eleven they simply told them to have their bags packed by two-thirty.

Also today we had an inspection, rifles in hand and the whole deal. An inspection in the field is completely unheard of. It just does not make sense with the conditions and everything. It is crazy.

Wednesday, February 26, 1969

Today I made the spaghetti and the sauce. Really all it was, was tomatoes and cheap hamburger. The meat the army uses is really cheap and I bet they pay a lot for it. Somebody, somewhere is making a lot of money because of this stupid worthless war.

Thursday, February 27, 1969

In one of the letters I received from you today you asked if the water we drink is converted salt water; it is not. The water we drink comes from a filthy little hole. There is a truck by the water hole with a flirtation system and the water goes through this system before we get it. Then the water is pumped into our water truck, but the tanks on this truck are not exactly clean. Anyway the water is not great and mostly we make Kool-aide simply to take away the bad taste.

Friday, February 28, 1969

The captain called a formation today and told us he does not like swearing or the use of bad language. We were told if you are caught swearing or mainly saying the word "fuck," you have to fill one hundred sand bags. I doubt he will carry this out but, can you imagine not being allowed to swear when you are forced to live in such a place as this?

Saturday, March 1, 1969

Again Bren, don't worry about me going anywhere, or on the roads because I never would, especially at this time of year. Anytime of year for that matter. I just wish they would take us out of the field.

Sunday, March 2, 1969

Two days ago a person that was in this battery but had been transferred to Headquarters Battery, died. Not because of combat or anything like that but because of a cerebral hemorrhage. A blood vessel burst in his head and it was a real sad thing because he was always complaining of migraine headaches.

Maybe if someone had given him a real good examination his trouble could have been discovered. I don't want to think or talk about it because I get sick, I really do. This government of ours just has to change its policies and quick or there is going to be a lot of trouble.

Monday, March 3, 1989

We found out yesterday that they have no plans to take us out of the field until May. You know how I feel about this. I just cannot see how they can leave us our here in the woods for such a long time. Some people are definitely going to crack up and I definitely may be one of the first.

Tuesday, March 4, 1969

I am exhausted and can hardly keep my eyes open because I had to work with a new cook. We started at four-thirty this morning and we did not finish until six-forty-five tonight. All and all it was a very hard day. But there is one consolation: tomorrow I have the entire day off. It will be the first time I have the entire day off since I have been in this terrible country. I plan on washing my clothes tomorrow.

Wednesday, March 5, 1969

Yesterday the battalion commander came over here and spoke to us about infusion. He said that all but thirty people in the battery were going to get infused. They just started firing and I must have jumped two feet off the ground at the first blast. There must be something happening because all the tanks that stay here during the day are leaving. I figure the huge supply convey that goes up here everyday must be getting ambushed somewhere along the road. It's probably the same place they always get it. It already happened once this week and if I am correct it is happening again.

I heard today it is supposed to get warmer over here which

is unbelievable, I just don't see how it can get any warmer.

Saturday, March 8, 1969

I was really sorry to hear that Tommy was on Social Probation. He should be careful, there is no excuse why he cannot drink in a safe place. He has so much to lose if he should ever get kicked out of school. We both know where he will end up if he does; over here and this place is really bad. If only he stays in school four years, then he would have a chance of not even coming to this place, maybe even a chance of not having to go in to the army at all. He is really stupid if he should get kicked out of school for drinking. I hope you told him he has everything to gain by staying in school. In fact I should write him a letter. Could you send me his address?

Tuesday, March 11, 1969

Yesterday about ten guys were out burning some tall grass where the wires surrounding this place are located because the infantry is going to put up new wire. So, we are burning the tall grass around the old wire. Anyway, they were burning and all of a sudden BANG! There was a hand grenade or something like one on the ground. It caught fire and exploded. Well this kid that just came back from R&R was hit by the exploding shrapnel right in the rear end. He wasn't hurt bad but they did take him out of here by helicopter. It is a good thing he was not facing the other way when it went off because he really would be in a world of hurt right now.

Isn't dumb to be out burning grass where there are all kinds of explosives. Of course it took an accident that never should have happened for the army to learn a lesson. Today they are using a sickle to cut the grass like they should have been doing all along. This army is so stupid. They always have to learn by misfortune.

Wednesday, March 12, 1969

It is really something to see all the new faces around here. It looks like they have brought more people in here than they have taken out. It looks to me as the infusion is going at a faster pace than it was supposed to be.

Monday, March 17, 1969

Again today I did receive a beautiful letter from darling, perfect wife. Your letters give me the strength to go on. I just love you so much Brenda C. Genest. I just have to be with you to live, for without you by my side I merely exist.

In some of my past letters I have I have told you how windy it gets here around six o'clock in the evening. Well today it happened again but, no exaggeration, it was twenty times worse than it has been. It lasted about twenty minutes and it was really bad. It actually blew the infantry mess tent down. We have a kitchen made of plywood and it blew the roof right off. I had to laugh watching the mess sergeant get all excited watching the roof he had nailed together blow away.

Tuesday, March 18, 1969

Today we found out where this kid Felch was infused. He was infused about a week ago and he was real nervous about where he was going to end up. Who wouldn't be though. Anyway he went to Thunder IV. It is about twelve miles north of here and it is not very safe at all. Like George he is in a 105 battery, which is not good because there is a large possibility of moving around quite a bit. The reason being is that the 105 cannons are smaller than our 155 cannons and are small enough to be lifted by helicopter, which they do quite frequently.

Now that I am talking about infusion, another person from Manchester got infused today. They say his being infused was a mistake for his name was never turned in. Anyway he is gone now. He was going straight to the Cambodian border, about thirty miles north of here and he too will be in a 105 battery.

I am almost positive this infusion is going faster than planned. This has to point to us getting out of here by July.

Wednesday, March 19, 1969

In the tape I received from you today, I was really happy to hear that your cold is just about gone. I get so worried when you are ill in any way. I cannot stand to see you suffer in anyway. God knows you have suffered enough bad times for the rest of your life in the past six or seven months. I thank God every night I was chosen to be your husband and I ask him to reunite us soon, Sso we can live a beautiful happy life together.

It seems like such a long time ago since we were together in Hawaii, but it has not been that long. But it does seem like an eternity (and it is) for a husband and wife to be separated for this long. It is so cruel for a government to separate a husband and a wife, especially for a place like this. A place where half the people are Viet Cong themselves. It is a civil war and we have NO business here. I don't even want to think about it because I get so upset. All I want to do is get out of here and live a beautiful life with you.

14) Almost There

After nine months of trying to maintain a home out of a bedroom in her parent's house the strain of her husband being away at war, raising a child, and living not only with her parents but also amid her five younger siblings, took a heavy toll on Brenda's well-being. In a letter to Dick dated March 15 she told him of a fight she had with her father regarding a call from Tommy. Really the squabble was one that many a daughter and father have had about the seemingly unfair treatment of the girls in the family as opposed to the boys. However, this particular confrontation nearly broke Brenda.

As Tom reprimanded her for not informing him that Tommy had been on the phone, Brenda became consumed by the contempt she harbored for the situation in which she found herself snared. It was unbelievable to her that her father was upset with her over a phone call. She could no longer accept all the little annoyances and inconveniences that went with living at her parents. After her father expressed his displeasure and disappointment in her, she told him that she did not need grief from him. She did not need someone angry with her over a stupid phone call, that if it was so important for him to talk to Tommy, he could call Tommy back, that she had a lot more to worry about than if he got to talk to Tommy, that her husband was at war, that she was trying to raise a child, that she did not need to be treated like a child, that she was not about to live like this any more.

Tom was, at the least, taken aback by Brenda and her reaction. He and Nancy had done everything in their power to help Brenda through this difficult time. They had opened their home to her and her child, they asked no money of her, and most of all if there had been something he thought he could do to bring her husband home, he probably would have. He was shocked and hurt by Brenda's attitude.

Brenda's frustration had been building for a few weeks and she had confided in Dick what a hard time she was having. Dick had encouraged her to move in with his parents. So when the tense situation arose with her father she called the Genest's and asked if she and Dickie could come live there for awhile.

Not only were Edgar and Fleurette thrilled to have Dickie in their home, but also they were pleased to be able to help Brenda while Dick was away. Just like at the Cavanaugh's, Brenda did not have to pay rent, but unlike her parent's house Brenda and Dickie each had their own room.

Although the Genests willingly and warmly opened their home and did all they could to make Brenda feel comfortable, she never really felt at ease. She could not help but feel she was a visitor who was imposing. Much to her surprise, moving out of her parent's home had done little to alleviate her frustration and pain. Almost immediately after moving into the Genest's, she "patched things up" with her parents. However, everyone agreed it would be best if she lived with the Edgar and Fleurette for awhile. While living at the Genest's she made sure to visit her family on a daily basis as Dickie had become so accustomed and attached to Tom, Nancy, Tommy, Jill, Mike, Nancy Lou and Jimmy that she did not want to disrupt his little world any more than it already was.

Saturday, March 22, 1969

Hi Bren,

Well this is the day after I received your letter of March 15. I did not write last night and I really feel bad about it. I did try,

I honestly did. In fact hon I had this pen and paper in my hand from six-thirty last night until eleven, but I just did know what to say. All I felt like doing was crying.

Again today I had my pen in from my hand from two-thirty this afternoon and now it is seven. It is going to be a short letter because I am going to make you a tape[1] in a very few minutes.

I want to go home so bad to see you Bren. In fact, last night I almost put my name in for infusion and I am still seriously thinking about it. I figure if I get infused I can probably tell the new unit I go to that I have not yet had R&R. I am sure they would not check it on it. I do not give a damn about the money or cost of it, I am just so worried about you.

You and I need to live together with Dickie and the hell with everyone else. I just get so upset if anyone hurts you in anyway. If people do not have enough sense to realize what you have gone through in the past ten and a half months, then they are idiots. Bren, I wish you would move out of your house and go live with my parents. It would be a change and by the time you get accustomed to it, I should be home.

Sunday, March 23, 1969

Today has been a bad day. The cannons have been firing non-stop since five and it is nine now. The reason they are firing so much is because a helicopter pilot was shot in the foot while flying about a mile from here. After he was shot he landed here and then was taken out of here by a medical evac helicopter. I did go over to see the helicopter that was hit. It really was a mess, bullet holes everywhere. I have just about had it with this place and all the needless suffering that is going on. All of this is happening because of a civil war that would have ended many years ago if other nations had not interfered.

---

[1] Besides writing to one another everyday, Brenda and Dick sent one another audio tapes twice a week.

Monday, March 24, 1969

    Well today Dickie is nine months old. He certainly is getting to be a little man. It is really hard to believe that he is already nine months old. I love that baby so much. Looking at the pictures you have sent of him. I know I am going to nave so much fun with him.

    You don't know how happy I was to hear that you moved in with my parents. I want you to stay there even though you are back on good terms with your parents. I know that the best situation would be if we were together in our own home, but I think it will be easier for you to live at my parents because you and Dickie will have more privacy and room to move around.

    I am going to re-read the letters I received from you today to see if there are any questions you might want me to answer. I would be re-reading them anyway because I always read your letters at LEAST three times.

    Brenda I do not want you to worry about me over here. Don't worry nothing will happen to me, okay. That is a promise, Hon.

    In one of your letters you mentioned that you were going to keep forty-eight dollars from the income tax refund to buy some new clothes. Hon, I want you to take one hundred dollars to spend on clothes and I mean this so much. Brenda what can you buy for forty-eight dollars? I will be very upset if you do not do this. Then you can send pictures of you and what you buy to me.

Thursday, March 25, 1969

    Today all the cooks had to start building a place for everyone to eat. A place that will protect everyone from the rain, once the rainy season starts. The off duty cooks shoveled sand all afternoon and myself and another kid joined them when we were done cooking. I don't know why the cooks are the ones building, it since it is for every ones benefit. You just cannot fight it, so you may as well go along with it.

Last night was a real bad night around here. I swear they are going to burn this entire country to nothing. You could see fires all around last night that were miles away. They were so huge. Also last night a person in the infantry got killed here. It was an accident, but it was a dumb, careless accident. seems that one kid was cleaning his rifle and his friend was sitting across from him. There was a bullet in the rifle and it went off right into his friends chest.

What a thing to happen. What a waste! For what? It is just so stupid and I don't even want to think about it.

Monday, March 31, 1969

Hi Love,

I love you baby and need you so very much. We did receive mail today and I received a beautiful letter from my darling wife and one from Nancy Lou. In your letter there was a picture of Dickie "standing" next to my picture. I could cry when I look at him next to my photo. I love and want to enjoy that child so much. The time is getting shorter from when we will all be together to live in happiness forever and ever.

Now for some news that I don't want you to get all excited about because it is really nothing. Tomorrow I leave to go to a place seven miles west of here known as Landing Zone Joe. They are going to air-lift with helicopters, three cannons from here and forty some odd men, of which I am one. The thing we are going on is called an operation and should last one week. So, it is likely by the time you get this letter I will already be back at Thunder III. We are supposed to leave here at seven a.m.

I don't want you to worry because believe me, any trouble that is happening around us is far away because the cannons we are going with are big and they fire a long distance (about eight miles). They would not send these cannons unless the trouble is far away because they would be of little use if the fighting was close.

ALMOST BACK

Wednesday, April 2, 1969

Well I am at this new area and have been here since yesterday. I did not write yesterday only because I did not have time. We worked setting this place up until three a.m. This place is not dangerous, but the living conditions are just unreal. We have been eating cold C-rations and I am completely filthy. But it will be over in a few days.

This may be hard to believe, but it is actually hotter in this place than at Thunder III. I really feel bad for the people on the guns. They are firing about all the time and it is amazing that some of them have not passed out because of the heat. At least I can get into the shade once in a while. I used to think Thunder III was bad, and it is, but looking at this place makes Thunder III look like paradise. I guess it is true that things can always be worse wherever you are. I am sorry this letter is so short, but the conditions are not very good. I will not miss another day of writing no matter how much work has to be done. After all it is only the damn army.

Kiss our dear son for me, that I love and many to you. Bren, you do have all my love and always will forever and ever, your loving husband, Dick.

Thursday, April 3, 1969

It just has to be warmer here than Thunder III. I am so dirty it is unbelievable, just filthy. A barrel with stagnant water to bathe in will look good after being here. My hair is so dirty. It is just one big mass all stuck together. I am not the only one like this though, everyone is and it will only last a few more days.

I am living in this hole about four and a half feet with a medic and a mechanic. Every time the cannons fire sand falls down onto us and the guns are about always firing. You can imagine what a mess it is. For a roof we have a pallet that the ammunition comes on. It does not cover the entire hole, but it is better than nothing.

I had a great dream last night. You and I and Dickie were at the beach swimming and needless to say, I was quite upset when I woke up and found myself here.

Easter Sunday, April 6, 1969

I have really had it with this place. I hate this place and this army so much. All I want to do is live a good peaceful life with you and our children.

Saturday, April 12, 1969

Well I am back at Thunder III. I got back here yesterday afternoon about four o'clock and I did not write you yesterday because as soon as we got back I just collapsed on my cot and did not wake up until two this morning. I received and read six of your letters today. The picture you sent of you and Dickie, the picture of Dickie by the Easter lily and the one of Dickie in his playpen out by the pool are just great. I agree that Dickie is starting to look older. He is so cute. And you my darling wife, you looked so beautiful, you are so beautiful. We just have to be together to give each other the great amount of love we have for each other. This day has to come soon. They have to give me a chance to make you happy, they cannot keep us separated much longer, they just cannot.

When I got back here some people said that they heard there was a good possibility of withdrawing fifty-thousand troops out of here in the next sixty days. I hope and pray so much it is true and that we are included. We should be, for there are only eight or nine thousand National Guard and reserves here. If it should happen that we are not included (which I doubt we wouldn't) write senators and congressmen and everything. Everybody's wife is going to do this.

I enjoyed the article you sent me from the New York Times. These peace demonstrations will put a lot of pressure on Nixon and he going have to act accordingly. If he does not, it is just going to get out of hand and I am sure he realizes this.

Monday, April 14, 1969

In one of the letters I received from you today you said you were trying to reach me with mind waves and tell me to call you. Well I guess I did get your message because I was planning on calling you before I received that letter. Also in the letter you mentioned when you tried to get Dickie to say "Dada," on the new tape you sent, he would not. Then after the tape was done that is all he would say. What a little rascal.

Thursday, April 17, 1969

Well I am in Saigon and I have just spoken to you. I just cannot express how great it was to hear your voice and talk to you. After I spoke to you we were at the door of the U.S.O. getting ready to leave and a M. P., a military policeman, stopped us and asked us where we were going. We told him we were going back to Phu Loi and he said it was getting late and the road would be closing very soon. He took us to the M.P. station and said we could spend the night here. It is so nice here. We had a steak dinner and now I am sitting in a recreation room in a big leather chair. They have a pool table and a big television here. They have flush toilets here as well as showers with cold AND warm water. And someone just came in here and offered me a cold beer.

Sunday, April 20, 1969

Well I am back at Thunder III. What a place, but I guess I should be thankful for it is a safe place. As usual it was a very dusty, dirty ride back here. I was really amazed to see all the new faces here. The infusion is really going on quite rapidly. I found out when I got here that an officer from the New Hampshire National Guard was killed the other night. It really hit the people over here hard, including me.

This man was with us at Landing Zone Joe. I guess he left L.Z.J. a few days ago and went to Fire Support Base Dot where he ended up getting killed. It is so sad and what a waste of human life, it is just unreal.

There also was a person from Laconia, New Hampshire who was killed in Phu Loi. I found out his death was an accident, if that is what you could call it. He was killed by an American — a drunk American — that had thrown a hand grenade out to scare some people. Anyway, this person from Laconia happened to be innocently walking by. He got killed and seven others got injured. That damn person who threw the hand grenade is in jail for manslaughter. It's a real shame. Like I say I don't even want to think about it because it gets me so upset.

I was not back here at Thunder II more than thirty minutes before I was put to work. Before the battery was split up it was not too bad, but now we have to work everyday and many, many hours. To think I am working like this for the army just makes me sick.

Monday, April 28, 1969

The convoy that goes by here about every other day got ambushed about ten miles from here today. I was really surprised because it hadn't been ambushed in a long time. I guess the two helicopters were shot down and four tanks destroyed. It must have been a big ambush.

You asked if I ever go on the roads. No, I don't. I never have a reason to. The only time I have been on the road is when I went to Phu Loi to call you.

There are hardly any of the old or original people here at this place. Mostly all the people that are here now are new and came here because of the infusion. All the original people are still out at the super field, Landing Zone Joe. I hope that operation ends soon.

Dick was sent back to Landing Zone Joe on Thursday, May 1. And although the conditions had dramatically improved there, it was still a far more dangerous and crude place than Thunder III. Rocky describes L.Z.J as, "A very, very bad place. It was hell. We were in the middle of the Michelin Rubber Plantation and twenty thousand N.V.A. [North Vietnamese Army] were around us just waiting to get us. We slept in a culvert with a piece of metal over us. It was a bad place."

Sunday, May 4, 1969

I did try and write this afternoon, but there is no sense because it is so warm. All you do is sweat and the paper gets all messy. You would not believe how hot it is over here. All you do is drink liquid and then sweat them out. It just gets so hot in the afternoon that you have to sit down and hardly move at all. If you tried to work in the afternoon, you would probably faint.

Oh, I hate this army so much. It is just ridiculous to see all the money that is wasted over here. It makes no sense at all and I NEVER want to have ANYTHING to do with this government at all, once out of here. This damn army is just ridiculous. Well Nelson just came over to this bunker where I sleep and Provencher should be coming by any minute now. I don't know why but everyone seems to congregate over here at night.

Tuesday, May 6, 1969

Last night I saw my first bit of action and I'll never forget it as long as I live. It started about three in the morning. I awoke immediately when we got what they call a mortar attack. I swear I have never been more scared in my life. It lasted for about two hours, but seemed like a lifetime. All you could hear were these big bombs landing outside and the balls of fire after they exploded. Anyway four people were killed in the mortar platoon (a group that is here with us). One of the mortars landed in the place where they sleep. One person was hurt in our group and had to be taken out by helicopter.

Today we spent filling sand bags and putting them around the bunkers for protection but I doubt anything will happen again. Bren, I do not want you to worry. Nothing is going to happen to me. Everything I have told you has been very truthful and I always will be truthful with you. So don't you worry because I will be home with you in July.

Wednesday, May 7, 1969

We do not have to worry about any more trouble around here because they brought in about seven hundred infantry people with tanks and the like. We are now completely surrounded by the infantry. They arrived here this afternoon and have already killed one person who they think was V.C. They assumed he was (and he must have been) because he was around the area of the perimeter and he had no business being in that area.

Dick returned to Thunder III on Thursday, May 8.

Monday, May 12, 1969

Well last night the super field (L.Z.J.) got another mortar attack, but it was not nearly as a bad as the other one. No one was hurt and none of the mortars landed around where people slept. The mortars landed on the airstrip and they counted only forty mortars. From what I understand every year about this time there is a little offensive by the Viet Cong for Ho Chi Mihn's birthday which is on May 19th. This place, Thunder III, is completely surrounded with tanks and everything. More infantry people came in today plus two more cannons, which is really good.

Tuesday, May 13, 1969

Today was another normal day, but it did mark one year

that I have been in this rotten stinking army. I get so mad when I think that I have been in it for one year. A year lost for both you and I. Hon, I promise we will make sure we make up for it because there is not a man on earth that has ever loved a woman as I do you Bren.

Wednesday, May 14, 1969

Well tomorrow morning at ten Nixon is supposed to talk about Vietnam. I am really anxious to hear what he has to say. It is supposed to be broadcast live on the radio. I hope that he has something good and definite to say, for a change.

It really is raining hard outside now. I cannot believe how hard it can rain over here. It is just unbelievable. I never thought such a terrible place existed. I hate this place so much.

Saturday, May 17, 1969

Well another day gone by and what a wet one. It just rained so much today. This place is completely surrounded by water. There is water everywhere. The bunker I live in did leak a little more than usual, but luckily where I sleep stayed dry. If the rain does not stop, the cannons we have will be completely useless. The reason the cannons are useless in the rainy season is because every time they fire, they sink into the mud. That makes them ineffective because they can only fire once and then they have to be pulled out of the mud and reset. At L.Z.J. they are just about completely useless. But, here at Thunder III they are set up a little better for the rainy season than L.Z.J. is because they have been preparing for this the last six months.

I really enjoyed the pictures I received from you today. Dickie looks good as usual. So he is saying words like Dada, Mama and car. Does he associate what he is saying with a particular object? I am going to have so much fun with that dear child. Chick sure did have a wild outfit on. I guess the styles have really changed since I left. I guess I will have some things to get used to once I get home.

Monday, May 19, 1969

I agree with you, that they build up the news about this place in the U.S. news reports. But, I do not want you to worry about me dying over here because there is no way that is going to happen. I AM NO HERO and never will be. I will be home soon and this all will be in the past.

Wednesday, May 21, 1969

It is raining again and the wind is strong. What a place this is. For a few months it is so hot and you never see a cloud. Then all of the sudden it just rains and rains, and even right after it rains gets really hot.

I guess all the offensives are over for awhile. I think the last one was on Ho Chi Mihn's birthday on the 19th.

Toward the end of May Brenda, along with one other wife whose husband was serving in the 197th, began circulating a petition to bring the National Guard home. It was a very bold move by these young women as they were definitely the minority in Manchester in regard to opposing the United States involvement in Vietnam. When they did not run into resistance or out and out opposition, they were faced with people who agreed with them but were either too intimidated to put their names on the petition or who felt their efforts were in vain. Brenda remembers going to Bill Starr's house (Dick's best friend growing up), and his mother answering the door. "She looked at me with such pity and sadness and said, 'Brenda, honey, I will sign this but it's not going to do any good.'"

Friday, May 30, 1969

Well this will be the third Memorial Day weekend I have spent in the army. One while I was in basic, one at Fort Bragg, and one in this place. In the letter I received from you today you mentioned how some people did not want to sign the petition. I guess that is only normal, some people just do not want to get involved. They do not realize that there is nothing wrong with it. All the petition is doing is making a request or pointing out certain facts to a man that is supposed to be your federal representative. I was upset but not surprised that a wife of a guy over here would not sign the petition because she thought it might get the senator mad. It is as if she believes for some reason he does not want to see us come home. If we come home in July it will benefit him. You would think that most people would realize it is for their sons and husbands. I really don't know what to say, other than some people do not realize why they put men in higher office.

 I would really like to call you soon, but I do not like the idea of going down the road to Phu Loi. Actually I never like the idea of going down that road. The only time I want to go down it is when I leave this place for good. I will never take any unnecessary chances because part of me is waiting for me with you at home. I wish they would give a date when we are going to get the hell out of here.

Thursday, June 5, 1969

 I feel even more sure now in saying that I will not get infused. There are very few left to be infused and if I was one of them, I am almost positive they would have told me by now.

 In the letter I received from you today you asked me about the rockets that came into camp here. Well, first you can hear them whistle in the air, and then they explode. They can be fired from as far as five miles from here whereas mortars have to fired from close by. The difference between a rocket and mortar is that a rocket is bigger than a mortar and rockets are not as accurate as mortars.

Friday, June 6, 1969

It is ten at night and I had planned on writing you earlier but about seven-thirty tonight about twelve mortars were fired at this place. Only two landed inside. It really was nothing. The reason for the mortar coming in here was probably because there were only two tracks of infantry (about 15 men) around us at the time. Whereas usually there are about twenty tracks and tanks (about a hundred men) around here.

The reason there were so few infantry around, is because, the convoy that goes by here everyday, got ambushed again about five miles from here. So most of the infantry was up the road helping the convoy. I am sure nothing would have happened and the infantry could have been here fast because it is flat and open around here and someone firing mortar can be easily spotted. Another reason they may have fired mortars here is because our cannons were firing in the general area of where the ambush was. So, the V.C. probably figured they could distract us (which it did) by firing in here.

Monday, June 9, 1969

Well today Nixon did announce that he is going to withdraw twenty-five thousand troops from this place within thirty days and a total of forty-five thousand by the first of September. I imagine they will announce within a few days who they are going to take out. Needless to say, I pray that we are among the ones who get to go. I found out today that when the mess sergeant leaves I will take charge of the kitchen. I don't think he is leaving for awhile but the way he talks he will be leaving soon. So who knows.

By June of 1969 Dick and the others who had not been infused had been in the field without a break for nine months. Being in the field meant they had no electricity, no running water, they slept on cots in sand bunkers (a lucky few had pillows). Basically, they were camping in the middle of a war zone. They had been scheduled to be rotated out of the field every three — four at the most — months.

One of the men to whom Dick was close recalls the circumstances and his reaction to being in the field without a break for so long. "The captain would get up in front of us and take a vote about the unit going back to base camp. He would say things like, 'Look if we go back to base camp it is going to be like being stateside, formations and inspections everyday.' And while he was saying that I was saying, 'Bull shit,' because I had been hurt a couple times and I had been sent to base camp. I would tell everybody, 'Hey I have been there and you get milk two or three times a day, you get your mail, a nice bed and a girl to clean up your bunk.' I was trying to tell them the longer we stay out here the more dangerous it becomes.

"Well everybody fell for the bull shit and we ended up with a whole tour there. It should have never have happened. We were told if we stayed in the field we would have it made. That we were almost built up and then we would have it made. But the work never stopped. We worked all the time and went all over the place and it just never stopped."

Thursday, June 12, 1969

It did rain quite a bit today and believe me this place is nothing but a mud hole. It just sticks to your boots and it feels like you are walking around with ten pound weights on your feet. They are presently firing those damn cannons again. The noise still gets on my nerves and I still jump every time they go off.

It will be so great to get away from all of this. I don't see how people could take it in World War II. Living like this for four and five years. I cannot see how they did it. We have a new first sergeant and he is regular army. He was in Korea and he is just amazed that we have been out in the field for nine months without a break. He said he has never seen it before and that no one stays out in the field that long without a break.

Saturday, June 14, 1969

We found out this morning, on the news, some of the units that would be leaving this place. I was really disappointed, disappointed by no means is the word, to find out that we were not one of them. But, I still do have hopes, for they do have nine thousand more people to go.

We received mail today and I did receive a beautiful letter from you my love, plus a fathers' day card. Enclosed in the card was a description of what a father is and it was beautiful. I do appreciate you sending it to me. I love you so much Brenda. You are the greatest and most thoughtful wife in the world. I also received, from Dickie, a book of poems all about fathers. I am going to keep the book, always, along with the description you sent. I treasure them both and always will.

Friday, June 20, 1969

This morning about six a.m., seven mortars were fired into this place. I never thought they would fire a mortar INTO this place. I still maintain they could not fire too many into this place because they would be spotted. With the superior fire power we have it would be all over for them if they tried to fire more than a few. One of the mortars landed close to the kitchen and the two cooks had to take cover in the F.D.C bunker.

The Eleventh Cavalry infantry unit is here with us at the present time and that is very good. They think nothing of destroying anything that moves toward us. They have been known to destroy villages. I hate to say it, but I wish they would destroy the village about two miles south of here because it is completely loaded with V.C. The U.S. government knows it is overrun with V.C. but does nothing about it.

One of the problems is you don't know who is a Viet Cong

and who is not. One day they may be fighting with the Americans and the next with the Viet Cong. It is just not worth the unnecessary death and suffering of American people. America just has to get out of this war.

The convoy that goes by here everyday got ambushed again today. It was even being escorted by the tracks and tanks and still was ambushed about five miles from here. At the present time you can see jets dropping bombs on the area and helicopters are flying around the area.

I get so upset sometimes when I think about everybody I know back home. It seems that everyone from my old neighborhood was able to stay out of the army or avoid the draft one way or another. At least I know once out of here I will have a happier life than most of them because I have a beautiful wife and son who love me as much as I love them.

Saturday, June 21, 1969

We found out today that three cannons are definitely coming back here tomorrow. That is good because they have been gone a very long time. I wish once the cannons arrive they would say, "Okay, all the National Guard personnel, pack up your bags. You're all going to Phu Loi and then you are going home." I think we would know by now if we were part of the withdrawal.

The ones they pulled out were not even combat troops. They have a lot of balls not taking us out since only combat troops were supposed to go and we are one of only two combat National Guard units over here. Also we were one of the first reserve forces over here. And now the ones that got here after us, had better living conditions, will be leaving before us. I do not think they will leave much before us, but it is the principle of it that gets me so mad.

This army and everything will soon be in our past and it is going to take a hell of a lot for them to get me to another foolish National Guard meeting. I will really fight it. They are going to have to have a lot of nerve to tell us we have to go to meetings. But I have, in the past year, learned they do have a lot of nerve.

Three more days and Dickie will be one year old. It is hard for me to believe. I remember so clearly when you were carrying him. I remember how I used to make you stand in front of the mirror sideways so you could see yourself and your belly.

A whole year later and I don't even know him. I am kind of in the dumps and feeling a little blue today. I miss you so much Bren. Once we are reunited nothing in this universe could ever separate us again. Right now I just have to remember that I have a lot of things to be thankful for, if I only stop to think. I could have ended up in a lot worse unit than this and in a much worse place. And besides, I have the most perfect and beautiful wife waiting for me and the beautiful son she gave me.

Thursday, June 26, 1969

The battalion doctor came up here today and inspected the kitchen etc., and said everything is okay. I asked him when they were going to take the rest of the National Guard out of the field. He said if he would have had his way we would not have been out here for more than six months. Anyway I told him I was about to go nutty because I have been out here so long. So, he said if I wanted to spend a few days in Phu Loi, all I had to do was tell the medic I wanted to see the doctor and he would cover for me.

I will not take the opportunity because I refuse to go down that road. The only time I will go on that road is when I leave Thunder III for good.

Sunday, June 29, 1969

I found out what is taking so long for us to get the date when we will be withdrawn. They have not yet decided how we are going home. They haven't decided whether they are going to have us regroup (because the battalions have been broken up by infusion), or not. I don't give a damn how we get home as long as we do get home. I also found out on July 6 some congressman from New Hampshire is coming over here. I cannot see why he is coming. I guess for the show of it, just like all the other politicians. Besides, we are all split up now and there are only twenty-five people in each battery from New Hampshire. I hope I have the opportunity to say a few words to him. I am sure I would make his hair straight on end — if he has any. I can picture it now, he will be completely surrounded by high ranking military people, shaking hands with us and not giving any one a chance to speak. Just a big show to benefit him back home.

The infusion ends July 3rd or so. Remember when the infusion first started and I was most likely scheduled to be one of the first to go? Then I went and talked to this lieutenant and here I am now and most everybody I hung around with is gone. It really does not matter now because in seventy some odd days I will be free of the army. It is a good feeling. Especially since I have been thinking about the army or the war almost every day since I was eighteen and now, it will finally be over.

Wednesday, July 2, 1969

Well another wet, rainy, muddy day, but at least it is one less that I have to be here. I received two beautiful letters and a tape from you today. I already listened to your tape and it was just great to hear your voice. So, according to what you told me in the tape McSwiney says we are going to be at Fort Devens on September 5. I can't believe they have not told us that yet. I am happy for that news because it brings the count down by ten days. Also, I am glad you found out we will be released from any further service in the National Guard. What a relief not to have to go to drills, meetings, summer camp, etc.

I just checked a calendar to see when Labor Day is and it is on the first. I never thought it came that early. Robichaud just came in and in the mail he got a clipping from the Union Leader that said we are going home September 5. I don't know why they have not told us yet. I guess maybe they don't even know yet or they have not received official word.

I just cannot wait to make a big bon fire out of all the army clothes I have.

Thursday, July 3, 1969

Only sixty-three more days of this army crap. I swear Dickie will never see the army or any of the different services. I am pretty sure though, by that time he is old enough, everything will be on a volunteer basis. Even if it is not, I will do anything in my power so that he never has to see the service. But, like I said, I am pretty sure it will be volunteer by then.

Well last night this battery really messed up. Every night we fire what you call deaf-cons on Thunder II. Deaf-cons are when we fire around Thunder II. We fire about three rounds around their perimeter. No shrapnel or anything ever goes into the area. The reason we do this is in case there is any enemy around Thunder II. Likewise Thunder II fires these deaf cons at Thunder III. It is just self protection and usually a good thing. Anyway last night we fired the deaf cons on Thunder II, one of the cannons was not adjusted right and we dropped a round right into Thunder II. It destroyed the mess hall. Luckily no one was hurt. There is a big inspection up here today because of it. Since the infusion there has been a lot of inexperienced people on the cannons and in the battery.

Friday, July 4, 1969

Well another holiday gone by that was spent without my love. Only one more to go and then we will be together forever and ever.

ALMOST BACK

Saturday, July 5, 1969

Well they are really going crazy here because that congressman is coming here tomorrow. I knew they were going to put on a big show, but they are really going all out. It is so hypocritical to try and make everything look so good for the congressman. I don't know why they won't let the man see things as they are, even though the only reason he is coming here is for show.

I hope it rains all day tomorrow so it is muddy and sloppy as usual. So that with every step that you take, you sink six inches into the mud. In case it does rain, they have built a little broad walk from where the helicopter will land to the track that goes around this place, so the congressman does not have to walk in the mud like the rest of us. I hope I get to say a few words to him. The captain has to introduce me to the congressman because I am in charge of the kitchen. The captain will probably try to rush him away from me because the captain knows how I feel and he will not want me to embarrass him.

Sunday, July 6, 1969

The congressman did come today and the big show went off pretty much like I expected. After I met him I showed him around the kitchen. I did talk to him for a few minutes, but I could not really tell him what I thought of the situation because the captain and all the other high up military people were right on our heels and watching every move I made. The congressman did get a little muddy, which made me happy. He was here for about an hour, had lunch and then left.

Not more than forty-five minutes after Congressman Cleveland left, the group food supervisors popped on. Group is higher than battalion. In other words, group is battalions boss. Anyway the food supervisor came up to me and said he wanted to look at all the kitchen paper work. He started reviewing it at one this afternoon and did not finish it until four. He found a few mistakes, so his helicopter did not come to get him until six-thirty and I had to spend the whole time with him hearing about my mistakes.

Monday, July 7, 1969

Today I had to correct all the mistakes the food supervisor found yesterday and we found out on the twenty-ninth of July we are going to have what they call an I.G. (Inspector General) inspection. It makes no sense to have an inspection like that in a place like this. It is unheard of in a place like this. I will have to do all kinds of foolish things. I just cannot stand the army and their stupid way of doing thing. Fifty-nine more days of this BULL SHIT.

When you come to get me on September fourth, make sure you bring some of my regular clothes. I just cannot wait to get out of these army clothes.

Wednesday, July 16, 1969

A guy that used to work at the bakery was on what they call, gate guard duty today. Let me explain what gate guard duty entails. This place is surrounded with wire and they open a small area by the road during daylight hours so that trucks and tanks can go in and out of here. Everyday they have someone stand by the opening — a gate guard. The reason they have someone stationed there is because there is always a whole mess of Vietnamese kids that are out there in the road who like to come in here and look in the garbage cans, etc. Also many of the kids congregate around here because across the road we have what you could call a dump and the kids are always going through the junk before we burn it. Well, the army does not like to have the kids in here because you cannot trust them.

Anyway back to the original story, this guy who used to work at the bakery, was on duty when some kids were trying to get in the camp and a few even threw some rocks at him. One kid started to come in and just would not listen to the gate guard telling him not to. Well the guy who used to work at the bakery shot his rifle to scare him away, but he shot too low and he hit the kid right in the leg. They do not know if the bullet hit the kid directly or if the bullet ricocheted off something and then hit the kid. The bullet went right through the kid's leg. He is going to be all right.

The guy who used to work at the bakery is really shook up about the whole thing. He is a real nice and honest guy. It's sad because he was only doing his job and they would have given him hell if the kid had gotten in. I remember at Landing Zone Joe they caught a little Vietnamese kid right outside the wire drawing maps of the place.

In your letter today you showed me the correct way to address my letters to you in York Beach. Well let me tell you why I write York Beach, York Beach, Maine. I write York Beach twice because I want to distinguish my mail from the rest of the mail that goes to York Beach. I figure by now, who ever handles the mail there, automatically knows one of your letters when they see it because it is addressed differently. And because it is different, they probably know who it is for just by looking at the envelope. That way they put it right where it belongs or where they can get to it easily and then it gets to you faster.

I just thought, tonight at nine or a little later after, they are supposed to be blasting off to the moon. It just sounds unreal. All they have been saying around here for two weeks is how they have arranged for us to hear it on the radio and of course tonight the generator is broke down.

Saturday, July 19, 1969

Remember in a past letter I told you about the I.G. inspection we are supposed to have here on the twenty-ninth? Well get this, all the cooks must have a food handlers permit. So, to get these permits we have to have a blood test, a chest x-ray, and some kind of shot. Of course we were supposed to have the food handlers permit as soon as we got here. See how stupid this army is? They wait until we have some sort of inspection a month before we are going home before they decide we need the permits.

Sunday, July 20, 1969

I am in Phu Loi. I am here to get the food handlers permit. I left Thunder III this afternoon and came here by helicopter which was pretty good — a lot better than going by road.

Brenda received the following letter August 8, 1969 — Dick's twenty-fourth birthday; the third birthday he would "celebrate" in the army.

Monday, July 21, 1969

I found out that the advance party (of the 197th) that got to Vietnam on September seventh, has received their orders to go home, to leave on August 26. Since they got here just seven days before us, it is only logical that we will get our orders in the next four or five days, but you never know what the army is going to do.

When I get home I am personally going to write the Congress and I feel justified in doing so, because they are supposed to give you orders saying when you are going home about 90-120 days before you leave this place.

I also found out most of the people at Thunder III said they wanted to process out in California instead of Devens. That is good because they are equipped to do it in California and it will take about six hours. Whereas, at Devens, they are not equipped to process us out and who knows how long it would take. Also if we process out in California then when we get to Devens, we would be all finished and could just walk away. I just wish they would make up their mind as to what they are going to do to us, so we would know what was going on. This army is so disorganized.

Wednesday, July 23, 1969

Well I am back here at Thunder III and I did come back here by way of road. I left Phu Loi about twelve-thirty this afternoon. Last night I did try to call you, but there was too much interference. Needless to say, that did get me upset, as I really did plan on speaking with you and I really thought I would because the other two times I called you I was successful. Anyway in forty-four days we will be together.

I really did not enjoy the ride up here today on the road. I just hate that road so much and I refuse to go on it. I hope that maybe when we leave here, that they get a Shinook type helicopter to bring us to Phu Loi, so we do not have to go by road.

Thursday, July 24, 1969

They are really making a big deal out of this inspection we are going to have on the twenty-ninth. They are trying to get everything so perfect. The things they are doing now should have been done a long time ago.

I still have my mustache. I just know when we get out of here they are going to make me trim it down to nothing. I hope they do not make me get a real short haircut, but they probably will. They let you live like a pig out here, but when it comes time to go home they make you look neat and proper.

I will be so happy when all of this is in the past.

Friday, July 25, 1969

I found out today that the infusion program they had was a big waste. When we leave here this battalion is no longer going to exist. All the people that were infused into it are now going to be placed into other battalions. Just goes to show you how screwed this army is.

Friday, August 17, 1969

I heard today that we are going to at Fort Devens on the thirteenth of September. If that is true I will be really mad. My heart is so set on being home on the fifth of September to be with you and Dickie. It would be just like the army, since they have already screwed us an entire year over and if the patterns follows, they will screw us to the end. Forty-three more days instead of thirty-six left here, if what I heard is true. It is only seven more days than I thought but, those seven days mean so much to me. This damn army. I hate it so much, I just cannot stand it. Once I am out of it, they can shove it. This will be the last time this army will screw me.

7:00 p.m. — We just had a formation of the National Guard left in this battery and they told us we are definitely going home on the thirteenth of September. So, forty-three more days of this bull shit.

Sunday, August 3, 1969

Five more Sundays without you and then never another one apart. I made you a tape today, but I still haven't put film in the camera to take some pictures around here. I am glad you have not been nearly as bad as me about taking pictures. You just will not believe all the pictures you have sent me. You are really going to be surprised when you see them all together.

Oh Brenda, I just cannot wait until we get our own house and to make a home.

Monday, August 4, 1969

The battalion commander of the 197th was here tonight. He said we would be home or at Pease by the thirteenth. He said we could leave here anytime between the fifth and thirteenth. Hon, let's plan on the thirteenth so we will not be disappointed. Thirty-nine more days at the most.

There is a good possibility that the battery may be split

again, like it was when they had three guns out at L.Z.J. It is really stupid if they do because the guns are really ineffective in the rainy season.

Thursday, August 7, 1969 — Dick's Twenty-fourth birthday
Hi Love,
    Another day just about over and believe me this one is really dragging. The ration truck has not yet arrived. I hope when it does come that the mail is on it. I look so forward to your letters, you just cannot imagine how much. Thirty-six more days at the most and twenty-eight at the least. That does not sound like many when you say it, but it seems like they are never going to pass by. I miss you so much hon. All I want is be with you, because when I am with you everything is perfect. You are my life and without you I have nothing.
    A group of engineers moved into this place today. It seems they want to tar the road that goes by here. They have already tarred the part from Phu Loi to Laikhe. The engineers are going to work on it from here (Thunder III) to some place north of here. It will be good once they get it tarred because, then most likely, there will not be so many mines on it. Just a point of interest I thought you might like to know.
    How is that dear little son of ours doing today? Is he being an angel? A monster? Or a little of both? Has he got any new tricks? I am sure he does. I cannot wait to see him and play with him and do things with him, make him laugh. Finally to see our son and get to know him. The three of us finally together forever and ever. I can hardly wait to see what he does when he realizes I am going to be around all the time. I wonder how long it will take before he knows me well.
    It will be REALLY GOOD to put on some regular clothes, instead of these junky green things! When I finally get out of here and am home with you we are just going to relax, take it easy, eat, drink and make love.

I know my letters are getting pretty bad because I just repeat myself day after day, but all I think about day after day, is being with you and Dickie.

Friday, August 8, 1969

The guns that were sent to the super field two days ago are coming back here tomorrow. It just proves the army does not know what it is doing. They probably did not even get set up at the new location and whatever they might have built while there, they probably had to tear down. I'd bet just air lifting the stiff there cost a hundred thousand dollars. I know the helicopter they lift the cannons with cost one thousand dollars an hour to operate. They probably realized we were going home soon and that they need all the equipment and people back over here. I swear, I have never seen anything as disorganized as the army, in my entire life. I doubt there is anything as disorganized because no type of organization could operate for any length of time as the army does.

Sunday, August 10, 1969

Four more Sundays at the most without you. With a little bit of luck it will only be three more Sundays and we will be together forever. I am constantly visualizing how great and perfect it is going to be once we are reunited. Soon you will know how great my love is for you because you will be surrounded by it every minute of every day. I cannot wait to kiss your lips. I am getting kind of tired of kissing a piece of paper every night.

Monday, August 11, 1969

Well you could never guess what happened; the three guns that came back here yesterday are going to move out again. So, I spent most of today getting stuff ready for them. Of course most of the stuff I had to get out for them was stuff I put away yesterday from when they returned on Saturday. This army is so messed up they may not even go anywhere. I don't even try to figure things out any more.

Now get ready for a laugh, today they told me to get ready to go to Phu Loi because in three days I am going to go in front of the promotion board to become a sergeant E-6. Well you know what my answer is going to be. I want no part of it. All I want to do is get out of this rotten army.

Tuesday, August 12, 1969

Hi My Darling Love,

I love you Brenda and have to be with you. You are my life and I cannot be happy without you. You are the world to me Bren. You are perfect in all ways and I do mean this very much. I adore you, I truly do my love.

Well last night about one a.m. the shit hit the fan here. The village down the road was attacked. About eight mortars did come into the place which is no big thing, but since it has been so quiet, it was a change. This afternoon four more mortars were dropped into this place and again it was no big thing. You would not believe all the protection we now have. There are so many people tanks and tracks around this place I'm sure the action is all over.

Wednesday, August 13, 1969

Well things are back to normal around here. Yesterday the road that goes by this place was closed. We had a real hard time getting water. Everything had to be flown in. You should have seen the air cover we had the night that the village down the road got hit. There were so many helicopter gun ships in the air that just about al night it looked like complete day light. Last night they had some flying around here, but like I said, things are back to normal now.

Well I did tell them today that I wanted no part of being sergeant E-6. They tried a little to talk me into it, but of course, they did not get anywhere and have given up. Like I say it is so crazy thinking that I would want it. They know I have no interest in this disorganized thing they call the army. All I want to do is get out of it and for good. That great day just cannot get here fast enough.

Thursday, August 14, 1969

Another day just about over and one closer to the day we will be together. The days, as slow as they seem, are none the less going by. Again today there was a little action around here. The convoy got hit about a mile and a half away from here. There were some mortars fired at this place but only one landed inside. Mortars really are not a big thing at all. Just about all the bunkers in this place are mortar proof. The one I am in is definitely mortar proof. The only reason they fire them at this place is to keep our cannons from firing. Like today when they hit the convoy and the other night when they attacked the village.

Anyway today they (the U.S. army) completely bombarded the entire area around this place. They used jets and everything. After that nothing could be around here anymore. So, don't worry hon, because I assure you there is nothing to worry about. We have so much protection around us it would be foolish to worry. We have the best protection here than we have ever had, right now. I will be in your arms, at the most, in twenty-nine days.

Saturday, August 16, 1969

Well the third of September is the day! Finally a little bit of luck did come our way. The first good news we have had in such a long time. From now on everything will be good news. I cannot wait to get my arms around you. To squeeze you, feel your warm beautiful body pressing against mine, to be naked and feel our flesh touching. And finally to be able to see our son. It is really hard for me to believe he is over a year old and I am finally going to see him. I know I am going to be amazed when I see him and all things he can do.

We are going home in jungle fatigues, so have some clothes ready for me, okay hon.

Wednesday, August 20, 1969

Thirteen more days before you are completely surrounded by my love. I received a bit of disappointing news today. We found out that the twenty or so National Guard from A Battery that are left here at Thunder III will be the last to go to Long Bihn. We are going to leave on the twenty-sixth, spend the night in Phu Loi and then go to Long Bihn on the twenty-seventh. The other batteries have already started to go to Long Bihn and many of the people who were infused are already there.

Thursday, August 21, 1969

Twelve more long days and it will be all over. After a year of waiting and existing for that great day, the remaining days just cannot go by fast enough. We found out today we are definitely leaving here on the twenty-sixth. On the twenty-seventh we ship home the stuff we want to, the twenty-eighth we do some out processing, the twenty-ninth we practice for the ceremony that takes place at Long Bihn on the thirtieth. The ceremony is the change of command for the battalion. The next day we will probably get paid, do more out processing and then just wait to go home.

Write your last letter on the twenty-sixth. There is no sense in writing any after that as I am sure I will not receive them.

I wish they would tell us we are leaving tomorrow. Every one here is just useless and I am the most useless of all. I am just in a dream world constantly thinking about being with you and Dickie. You asked me how much I thought we were going to spend on a house. Really, hon, I have no idea. It is just going to be great to live in our home, live the way we want, do the things we want and with no one to bother us.

Saturday, August 23, 1969

Well another day coming to an end and believe me it did pass by slowly. Ten more days and I will be in your arms. Two more full days in this place and then I will be out of this hell hole and that will be good. Maybe once in Long Bihn the time will go by faster.

I do not remember if I told you, yesterday a Shinook type helicopter blew up in the sky about a mile from here. It was not shot down or anything. No one thinks so anyway. There must have been some sort of malfunction. It just came crashing down. Later in the afternoon we saw another Shinook helicopter pick up the pieces of it and then there was nothing left.

I'll be so happy to get out of this place and away from these sorts of things. It just gets me sick. I just want to make you so happy and make your life so perfect and beautiful. As long as we are together we will never have anything but happiness. We are just made for each other and finally after this miserable nightmare of a year we are going to be together.

Sunday, August 24, 1969

Another long day just about over and I swear this month has been the longest month of my life. One more full day in this place and I will be out of this miserable little place. I imagine Long Bihn will not be much better. I will not be happy until I am in your arms, home and with Dickie.

Today was another real hot day. I cannot figure out why it is so warm all of the sudden; we are still in the rainy season. It is hardly raining at all and it is getting warmer and warmer all the time.

We had a steak dinner and free beer this afternoon. I guess they are going to have free beer until ten-thirty tonight and it is going to be free tomorrow night also. The money they are using to buy the beer for us, is the profit they made from selling it to us, for the past year.

One more day and two more nights in this place. It is hard to believe. I will be really glad to Phu Loi because once there it will mean that we have gone down that road and going down that road is going to be the worst part of the trip home. I hate that road so much, just like everyone else. I wish we could leave here by helicopter to Phu Loi, but no such luck we are going by truck.

Monday, August 25, 1969

Hi My Darling, Darling, Love,

Well another day just about gone by, eight more and I will be with you forever and ever. This is my last night at Thunder III. We leave here tomorrow at one in the afternoon.

Today was just about the same as any other day. I did paper work and we were inspected by the group commander. Since I am in charge of the kitchen I had to show him around. He was a really nice person. He talked to me about going home and the place we were going to stay while we are in Long Bihn. He was about the nicest person I have ever met. The convoy that came here today from Phu Loi forgot the mail bag. Now I have to wait until tomorrow before I get your letters.

I just cannot believe that tomorrow I am finally leaving this place. In eight days I will be in your arms and home. We will never be separated again. I just love you my darling wife. You know my love will completely surround you, constantly every minute of every, day. I adore you Bren. You're my life. I need to be with you. You do give me more happiness than I could ever possibly want or desire. You are perfect Bren. The most perfect wife in the entire world. I do mean this so very, very much, my darling.

Tonight I am going to get all my stuff ready to leave. I do not have that much, but I do have a lot of stiff to get ready to turn in. I guess I will wait until tomorrow morning to take the pictures down. You are really going to be amazed when you see them all and how Dickie has changed in the pictures. I just cannot wait to see that dear little boy and play with him. It is going to be so great. We are going to live the most perfect and beautiful life ever lived by any two people. Our love for each other will never cease to grow. We were made for each other and just have to be together always. We will my darling.

9:00 p.m.

Hi again hon

Everyone is kidding me right now because they say I will be home before my letter gets there, but I still would rather write. I love you Bren I just love, love love you. I cannot wait to wrap my arms around you and be so close to you. You are my life and I just want to make you so happy. I am going to make your life so perfect. You do know how much I love you and live for you and adore you.

Kiss Dickie for me and always remember that you have all my love and always will, forever and ever and ever. Many kisses to you son. Soon our life will be together as our bodies. I adore you hon, your husband that loves you, needs you, lives for you and always will, Dick.

Many kisses here for you hon	I love you, I miss you, I adore you, I live for you, I need you, I just love, love, love, love, love you, so very, very	Dickie

much my darling wife. Love you, love you so very much, love you, love you.

15) Kindred Summer

Brenda and Dickie spent the summer of 1969 in York Beach, Maine at the Cavanaugh family beach house. Nancy had taken all her children to Maine for the summer and Tom would join them every weekend. Now matter how tired or drained Tom felt, every Friday he headed to the beach to be with his family. Tom's grandparents had purchased the summer home for their family in 1898 and the house quickly and continually became a lifeline for all the Cavanaughs. For anyone who knew Tom, it was of no great surprise that the hour drive from Manchester to York Beach invigorated him. He and Nancy treasured every minute they spent with their children, but the time at the beach always seemed particularly special. And having Brenda and Dickie there with them made it even more enjoyable.

During the summer the classic Victorian home was surrounded and filled with activity. Its location was prime for every event and enterprise available in York Beach. To go the beach known as Short Sands (hardly an apt description considering the beach stretches almost a mile), it required only walking down the ten steps from the porch of the house to the sidewalk and crossing the narrow, unhurried road appropriately named Ocean Avenue. To visit any one of the many candy stores, the bowling alley, the arcade known as Fun-O-Rama, the movie theater, restaurants, it was less than two minutes walk. To sit on the expansive, inviting porch of the Cavanaugh house was to feel the pulse of the much visited seaside hamlet.

Inside the house four generations shared and reveled in one

another's space and company. From Tom's Uncle Harrison, 80, the patriarch, to the baby, Dickie, just a year old, Tommy, 19, Nancy Lou, 10, Mike, 12, Jill 16, Jimmy 8, Tom 44, and back around again, everyone enjoyed, explored and cherished this time together.

Despite all the love, activity and company that embraced Brenda, she could not shake the loneliness, terror and sadness that had snatched her spirit and gripped her soul from the moment Dick had been forced to leave.

Brenda dealt with the emptiness by filling the days with Dickie. She and Dickie shared a bedroom. In her front corner room that faced the ocean, Brenda would wake every morning as the sun crept through the east windows and the sound of the sea brushed against the house. And for a brief, fleeting moment, before she really was awake, a slice of peace would wedge itself beside her. And then as quickly as it came, it would disappear. She would open her eyes and know that while the ocean was soothing her, guns, heat, noise and destruction were goading her husband. Then, without fail, as if he felt his parents' distress, Dickie would loudly and defiantly awake.

Brenda would rise from her double bed, gently hold and rock her son. Once Dickie was calmed she would change, wash, and dress him. She would dress herself and they would go downstairs. (The second floor of the beach house consisted of six bedrooms and one bathroom with two staircases to the main floor — one to the front hall and one to the kitchen.) Brenda and Dickie would greet whoever might be in the kitchen as Brenda placed Dickie in the highchair that had loyally served five generations of Cavanaughs. After breakfast she and Dickie would go for a bike ride. With Dickie in his little seat that was perched on the back of her three speed bike as if to try to pedal away her pain, she would ride up and down Ocean Avenue. Of course Dickie being an adventurous and happy child, loved every minute of their morning rides.

Brenda and Dickie were a known and welcome sight those summer mornings in York Beach. Brenda such a young and beautiful mother. Dickie such a vibrant, active one year-old who looked and acted as if he were the crown prince of York Beach.

Once Brenda had managed to delight her son and temporarily stifle the emptiness that filled her soul, she and Dickie would head back to the beach house. While Dickie played with Nancy Lou and Jimmy, Brenda would fill the minutes before the post office opened talking with her mother. Ten minutes before it would be open, Brenda would place Dickie in his stroller and briskly walk to the post office.

Of course, once there, Brenda experienced the best and worst parts of her day all slammed into one moment: the best because once she entered the compact building she was within inches of touching a piece of her husband, the worst because she was so close, to only a piece. The postmistress set her watch by Brenda and always had Dick's letters ready for her . She walked back to the beach house clutching Dick's letters close to her heart with one hand, as she pushed the stroller with other. She would imagine she could feel the beat of Dick's heart against hers.

Carefully she would carry Dickie and the letters into the enclosed sunroom of the beach house. She would set Dickie down on his favorite blanket, surround him with his favorite toys and once she was sure he was content, she would begin to read Dick's letter the first of several times. After two readings she would grab the writing tablet she always had nearby and answer any questions Dick had asked in his letter. If Dickie was still entertained by his toys she would once again read the letter, silently kiss Dick, telling him she would talk to him later and would put his letter away until after Dickie was put down to sleep for the night.

She would then pack a lunch for herself, Dickie and anyone else in the family that might be joining them for the afternoon at the beach. Dickie would play in the sand, run after dogs, splash in the water. Brenda remembers, "I loved taking Dickie to the beach and he just loved being there. It was the one place I did not constantly worry about him. It was so safe there. He could just run around with no real restrictions. He had so much freedom and that made him so happy."

Those afternoons on the beach probably salvaged Brenda's sanity while Dick was gone. Being a new mother she was constantly, if not overly, concerned about Dickie's well-being and so to see Dickie having so much fun in safe surroundings warmed her war hardened heart. It was while watching Dickie literally scream with joy as he played on the beach that Brenda was able to believe that soon everything might actually work out. It had been eight months since she had seen Dick in Hawaii and the more time that passed, the harder it seemed to get. But during those lazy afternoons she tried to be thankful that each new day brought a letter from him and not a telegram from the government. She would tell herself that with each day that passed his chances of survival increased. She would anxiously watch the sun creep across the sky and silently celebrate as it disappeared. She felt triumphant, as the days of their forced separation became shorter.

When Dickie had covered what seemed to be every inch of the beach and back again, Brenda would walk her son across the street and put him down for a nap. In the early evening Dickie would awake and join the rest of the Cavanaugh brood on the porch. He would play with the other children as the adults settled into what came to be known as "cocktail hour." Nancy would prepare dinner and the entire family would sit down in the west facing kitchen, watch the setting sun, eat, laugh and always delight in Dickie's antics. Dickie was comfortable in his role as Prince of the beach house and everyone in the family adored him.

After dinner Brenda would once again leave the house. It

was not as if she did not love her family and the house. She just had to stay in motion, because if she stopped to think for too long, she felt surely she would go mad. So, every night she would take Dickie for a short walk to Fun-O-Rama or to the outside picture window of the salt water taffy store where they could watch all the taffy being made for the next day or to the play ground for a swish down the slide or a push on the swing. Jill, Jimmy, Nancy Lou or Mike were always close by and frequently demanded their "turn" with Dickie. They each had their own unique relationship with their nephew and Dickie thrived on their attention. It was almost always after 9:00 p.m. before Dickie had thoroughly exhausted himself and Brenda was able to put him to bed. However once in his little bed it rarely took longer than a few moments for him to fall into a deep restful sleep.

Dick's absence and Brenda's sorrow affected all the Cavanaugh children deeply. However, having Dickie around them helped them greatly. With Dickie there it felt as though Dick was surely coming back, because the world they knew could not be cruel enough to rob that little boy of his father. They just were sure that nothing could keep Dick from coming home to his family. They were convinced that Dickie was going to have the greatest life. That Dick would surely play with his son even more than he had played with them. That Dick would make Dickie laugh until his stomach hurt as he did with them. That no matter what was happening around him, he would always have time for his son, because he always was there for them. They were convinced that nothing could or would happen to Dick because the world they knew and trusted could not possibly deny Dick at least the chance to be the father and husband he longed to be. As the summer in York Beach began to skulk to an end, the usual sadness and dread that precipitated the Cavanaughs' return to Manchester was replaced with nervous excitement. Dick was going to be home in less than a month and finally everything would be normal; finally everything would be okay.

Wednesday, August 20, 1969 11:00 p.m. — York Beach
Hi Hon

The reason why I am writing so late is because I went to the movies with my mother. Today has been quite a day! Tommy (he has been working at the dealership) was at my parents' house in Manchester and he called to tell me I had received a letter from the National Guard. So I told him to open it and read it to me. As you may know by now, or at least by the time you receive this letter, you are landing at Pease, Thursday, September 4. After brief ceremonies, the army is going to be very generous and understanding as usual, and they are going to allow us to be together for an hour. Then they are taking you to Devens. They advise the families not to go along because there are not many facilities at Devens. Then on Friday at 5:00 p.m. you will be issued a weekend pass. You will have to go back on Monday the 8th to finish the processing and hopefully they will finish with you that day or Tuesday at the latest. I am going to call McSwiney tomorrow to see if I can drive you to Devens and to see if you can leave Pease, Thursday night.

I am really at a loss for what to do. The army just likes to make things as complicated as possible for people, but I am so very thankful that I am going to see you on the 4th and not the 13th. It is really like a dream come true. I only wish I could talk to you right now to see what I should do.

Charlotte and your mother came up here this afternoon around two and stayed for supper. They left around eight. Today was beautiful beach day. I went on the beach from eleven to twelve and then again with everyone this afternoon from two-thirty to four. Your mother brought Dickie a xylophone that he can pull around and that makes noise. He really liked it. No mail from my little hon today. I am hoping for some tomorrow, telling me that you finally know that you are coming home on the 4th. I still can't believe it. I won't believe it until I see you and touch you and kiss you and hug you.

The advance party will be home Sunday! I could not believe the article in the Union Leader (about the advance party coming home); it was about an inch wide and two and a half inches long, on page 34 out of 45 pages! But, a few days ago on the front page they had a huge article on the National Guard going to summer camp on Friday — it's just sickening! One consolation though, is you will be home before those guys going to summer camp!

It was quite cold last night and is like that again tonight. It has not been this cold at night for a long time. It's sort of fall-like now at night. I love you so very much and your body and your whole being. As you are reading this letter you'll probably have less than a week left over there.

Well hon, time for bed. Don't forget for a moment that you are constantly in my thoughts. Please be careful — very careful and take good care of yourself — we are so close.

All my love, Bren

Saturday, August 23, 1969 — 8:00 p.m.

I did get a letter from you today. I was the one written last Saturday. After this letter only four more and my letter writing career will be over and my loving career will be starting again.l I do love you so very much my darling.

I talked to someone at McSwiney's office and they said it is up to your commanding officer whether or not you can leave Fort Devens Thursday night. They said the C.O. will probably let you go but to start working on it now. I really don't see what they could do if you just left on Thursday night and came back on time on Friday. The most they would do is make you a Spec. 4. I mean if they gave you a dishonorable discharge after you served a whole year over there — well it would be rotten. I am anxious to hear what you have to say once you find out your schedule.

Today, again, was a perfect day. I went on the beach with Dickie for an hour this morning and then from 12:30 to 3:30. When I was watching Dickie play on the beach today, I thought to myself, "You are really and truly going to have a father. Finally!" Tomorrow he is going to be 14 months old and just think when you see him he is going to be 14 months old. I bet you just don't believe it.

Oh my darling, I just cannot wait to be with you and kiss you and hold you. I just want to spend Thursday night and every night with you once I see you.

Well Hon, another exciting day done and only 11 more to go without you. Do please take care of yourself, my little hon — until I can take care of you — be very, very careful. You are constantly in my thoughts and in my heart and always will be. All my love eternally,

Bren

Sunday, August 24, 1969 — 11:30 p.m.

Hello My Darling,

The reason I am writing so late is because I went to Wallis Sands to visit a friend. I took Dickie and we got there around 8:00 and got back around 10:00. Dickie fell asleep in the car on the way home. When we got home I put his pajamas on him and he did not even wake up! But, after about fifteen minutes he woke up and he just now went back to sleep.

I love you Dick and I still can't believe I am going to see you in ten more days! I don't think that I am going to really and truly believe it until you are in my sight. I just cannot wait and I do hope we can stay together Thursday night. I did go to 10:30 Mass today to thank God for keeping you safe and for sending you home 10 days early.

Today was an unbelievable day, after the cool dry days we

have been having. Today was absolutely sweltering and quite unexpected. Poor Dickie, I put him to bed with his blanket sleeper and during the night it got really warm. I hope the weather is half as nice as this for us when you get home.

I just love you. We're going to be so, so happy. I just can't wait! Three more letters after this one! It doesn't seem possible at all, at all. After this time they are finally going to allow us to live together. Just to feel your body against mine will make me happier than I could ever say.

Well hon, it's late so I am going to close now and go to bed. Do take good care of yourself hon and be very careful. You are constantly in my thoughts. All my love forever,

Bren

Monday, August 25, 1969 — 9:30 p.m.
Hello My Darling Precious Love,

I love you and will eternally. You are my whole life and I just can't believe that I am going to be with you in nine days. I just think of it all the time and all the things we are going to do. I know Dickie is going to adore you as I do and always will. I just can't wait to love you and I think of it all the time.

Today was another beautiful, hot, sunny day with huge waves. My tan hasn't been this good since the beginning of summer. I just hope we can have nice weather like this, but if we can't it won't matter anyway because we will have each other, finally forever.

Today I was on the beach from 10 to 4 except for lunchtime. It was low tide and Dickie really amuses himself well in the puddles at low tide. Your mother called today. I told her my plans unless I hear different from you. I told her Thursday night after seeing you, I'll drop Dickie off with her and then we'll pick him up on Friday when you get your pass. I told her we will stay at my parents house because they should be going to the beach that weekend. I told her this could change once I talk to you. Your mother got a job at the College Shop — one day a week arranging the window.

Only two more letters after this one and that is just great because I can never think of things to say except for repeating myself.

Again, today on the beach as I was lying in the sun all I could think of was meeting you and being alone with you and Dickie. And to think that it is going to be forever! Oh how I love you and always have from the very first date. Every second with you has been precious to me and fun and every second with you when you come back will be the same way — I'm sure.

Oh hon, I'm sorry for these short letters lately but now the time is getting shorter and so are my letters. I just can't seem to think of anything to say that I haven't already said a few hundred times. So my love I am going to close. Do please take care and be careful until you are with me. You are constantly in my thoughts and heart. My body is yearning for you.

All my love eternally, Brenda

Tuesday, August 26, 1969 — 10:30 p.m.
Hello My Darling,

This is going to be my last letter to you because it's going to be mailed tomorrow and it usually takes a week and so you should get it next Tuesday. I am now in Manchester. I got home about 1 p.m. and came home to get your clothes. My mother also came home to get the kids school clothes. I went to Bradlees to get Dickie some papers and some dungarees and to Bon Ton to get him some new shoes. He was so good all the way home from the beach and all the time we spent shopping.

When we got home I had him down in the cellar with me while I was putting clothes in the washing machine. Well he went into the bathroom and apparently in the shower and coming out of the shower he tripped and fell. I went in when I heard him and he was bleeding a lot from his mouth, so I brought him upstairs and put wet cloths in his mouth. There was so much blood I could not tell where he was hurt and was afraid he knocked out a tooth. The bleeding wouldn't stop and I still could not see where it was coming from. I called my father at the garage (I was here alone) and he came home right away but by that time it had finally started to slow down. There was blood all over Dickie's shirt, my shirt, the kitchen floor, the shelves and the telephone. I was shaking like crazy. When it finally stopped, I saw where he got hurt. His bottom lip was cut in two places and right between his two top teeth there was a scab. He cut a bad cut there and that must have really, really hurt. Oh boy I don't know how I'm ever going to survive through all these little tragedies.

I took Dickie to your parents' house for a little while after supper. He was awful fussy because of his injuries, and then he bumped his mouth again and it started bleeding again, only a few drops though, thank God.

Your mother is going to take care of him tomorrow while I do errands. One thing I am going to do is call Roycraft and see if they have any new houses and for how much and maybe look at them. Also in the afternoon I am going to look for something for your parents anniversary with Charlotte.

I am writing so late tonight because Dickie didn't go to bed until about nine and then I washed and set my hair — the last time I will wash my hair until it is for you my precious darling. I still cannot believe it, but you must know, as you are reading this, because you must be about to board the plane to come home.

I don't believe the weather around here (the weather report was just on t.v.) Today was 22 degrees cooler than yesterday — today the high was 71. I'll bet we will get a hurricane up here this fall. They have already had five in the South and one really, really bad one as you probably know. 120 people were killed in Mississippi.

I'm going to have your body again — I just cannot wait. In the shower tonight I was thinking of the past year and what a waste it was. I don't know how I ever made it; not to mention how you ever made it, living in such utter desolation and grossness and heat and without love. I love you baby and will always, always. You just can't imagine how I've missed you and want to sleep with you Thursday night and every night there after. I adore you, Dick. You are just so perfect my little hon. Within 24–48 hours after reading this our bodies will be touching.

Do please take care of yourself and don't forget I still thinking of you constantly, more than ever now.

All my love eternally, Bren

P.S. This is my last kissing of paper. I can't wait to get your sweet, soft lips on mine. I truly love and adore you.

16) Coming Up for Air

*"Your joy is your sorrow unmasked.
And the selfsame well from which your
Laughter rises was oftentimes filled with your tears.
And how else can it be?"*
Kahill Gibran — The Prophet

Brenda woke up early on the morning of the 27th. For the first time in over a year she felt like she could breathe. She was amazed that she actually felt like it was safe for her to take a deep, long breath. The heavy, stifling, pressing pressure that had defiantly resided within her had finally retreated. For the first time since Dick had left she felt safe. For the first time in a year she did not feel her heart plunge into her stomach every time the phone rang. For the first time in a long time she did not start to tremble as the morning newscast came over her clock radio. The only morning in months that she did not fear what news the day might bring. As she sat up in bed she wanted to scream, "AT LAST!!, WE MADE IT!!"

By now he surely had left that pit known as Thunder III and was at least in Phu Loi, and most likely enjoying all the comforts (running water, covered buildings, etc.) of Long Bihn, Brenda thought as she rose from bed. She looked down at her son who was resting soundly in his crib. She smiled and whispered, "Finally your daddy is safe. Soon he will be home with us and you will be able to get know your father. You will finally have your daddy home." Brenda got dressed and was amazed at how light and free she felt. She felt as if she was floating around the house as she prepared herself and Dickie for what promised to be a big day.

Brenda's enthusiasm and obvious relief was contagious. Everyone in the Cavanaugh house felt excited and positively nervous. Beautiful butterflies danced in everyone's stomach. When Brenda arrived at the Genest home, Fleurette, Charlotte and she could barely contain their anticipation of the great things that would surely follow Dick's homecoming. As Dick's mother, sister and wife chatted about all the things they were going to do with Dick once he was home, they could not suppress the smiles that had burst through their souls and had confidently conquered their faces.

Fleurette watched Brenda and Charlotte as they hopped into Dick's blue convertible Mustang. They looked so happy and carefree as they sped down the street, their hair blowing in the wind and smiles as big a slice of watermelon. Fleurette was glad for the company of her daughter and daughter-in-law and probably could have spent the whole day talking with them about Dick's return, but she was also excited to spend some time alone with her grandson. She reveled in her grandson's presence. Dickie not only reminded her of her dear son when he was a boy, but also Dickie was the continuation of her family, as well as the glorious promise of their future.

The excitement of the day and things to come in the next few days filled Fleurette with joy. As she played with and pampered Dickie she thought how hard this past year had been on everyone. She watched her grandson switch from toy to toy and instead of the usual subtle tension that had eclipsed everything joyous she had witnessed and experienced in the past year, she felt a soothing peace and calmness. Soon, very soon, her son would be home and everyone, especially him, could begin living again.

As Brenda and Charlotte darted around town, Brenda marveled at the day. It was perfect — not a cloud in the sky, the sun warm and bright, she giggled to herself and thought, 'What a perfect day to be freed from the bounds of war.'

Charlotte scanned the certain sky and thought of her brother. She found herself imagining her husband Chick and Dick hanging out together. She visualized herself and Brenda cooking dinner, and the four of them, along with little Dickie, spending a laughter-filled evening together. She could hardly wait to spend Thanksgiving or Christmas or a birthday or whatever with her parents, her brother, her husband, her nephew and her sister-in-law.

Once Brenda and Charlotte completed their errands, they went to Roycraft Builder (a developer of homes in Manchester) and got a list of new houses on the market. They spent the remainder of the afternoon looking at potential homes for Dick and Brenda. It surprised Brenda and Charlotte that with each house they looked at, they both became more and more eager to have Dick home. They were shocked to discover that as full to the brim with anticipation as they felt, that somehow more and more excitement and expectation managed to comfortably cram itself within them.

The afternoon quickly passed. There were a few houses they had not seen when they realized they needed to head back to the Genest's. Edgar and Fleurette were going out to dinner to celebrate their 25th wedding anniversary that night and Brenda wanted to pick up Dickie so Fleurette would have plenty of time to get ready for this very special evening. As Brenda drove toward the North End of Manchester she was not the least bit disappointed that she and Charlotte had not seen all the houses on the list. Just more houses that Dick and I can look at together, she thought to herself.

When Brenda and Charlotte arrived at the Genest home, Fleurette did not want to see Dickie go, but she needed to get ready for what promised to be an unforgettable night with Edgar. Brenda and Charlotte told Fleurette to enjoy herself and to give Edgar their love. They loaded Dickie up in the car and headed over to the Cavanaugh house.

17) Last Out

"And knows that yesterday is but today's memory and tomorrow is today's dream."

"And let today embrace the past with remembrance and the future with longing."
Kahill Gibran — The Prophet

Dick was having a hard time believing it was really happening — they were finally leaving. He had waited so long for this moment. He had been ready to leave this shit-hole from the minute he had arrived and now, at last, he really was leaving. He and the others all but ran to the convoy trucks that were there to carry them out of the field that had held them hostage the past year. The dull, dirty green pick-ups with canvas canopies probably looked like grand, golden, chariots about to embark on the greatest race of all time to Dick. Because to the twenty-five remaining men of A Battery who had not been infused, who had spent an entire year in the field, those trucks were both their ticket and their ride out of the area of hell they had called home. Because the air at Thunder III was saturated with magnificence, royalty, danger and anticipation. And because as much as the men would have rather have been flown out, those trucks, at that moment, were the most glorious vehicles they had seen in a year.

It seemed every man there wanted to be in the first vehicle

to leave the place they had grown to hate and resent. But, it did not take long for the men to realize that it made little difference what truck they were in, as long as they were in a truck headed out. After rushing to be in one of the first trucks, Dick stepped back. He realized that he had waited over a year for this moment and it would not kill him to wait a few minutes more.

Dick and four others, Gaetan Beaudoin, Guy Blanchette, Richard Raymond, and Roger Robichaud all patiently waited to load themselves into the last of the transport trucks. It has been said that Gaetan Beaudoin wanted to drive the truck out. He was very familiar with the road and all its hazards because he had driven the road almost daily to pick up supplies in Phu Loi and Laikee. It has been reported that Beaudoin approached the drivers of the truck — who were new "in country"— and told them he wanted to drive because he knew the road and all its dangers. The two drivers refused his request because they had signed the truck out and therefore, army protocol dictated they were the ones who would be held responsible for it. Not without some hesitation and concern did Beaudoin acquiesce to the drivers insistence that they be the ones to operate the truck.

Dick, Roger, Guy, Richard all would have preferred for Gaetan to drive them out. But by then really all any one cared about was getting the hell out of there. They willingly put aside their preference and climbed into the back of the truck. Roger quickly joined them. Dick sat down on one of the beaten wooden benches and cautiously situated himself so his back was against the cab of the truck. He put his small white travel bag that contained all the precious photos Brenda had sent him on his lap and prepared to travel the road that he hated and that had haunted him the past year.

The truck took its place at the end of the convoy. As the truck lurched forward Dick could not get rid of the uneasy feeling that had parked itself in the pit of his stomach. He leaned back and thought, "God, I can hardly wait to get down this damn road." The convoy of five trucks proceeded down the dusty and squalid road.

The road, "Highway" 13, was also known as Thunder Road. It was commonly referred to as Thunder Road because of the nightly placing of land mines by the Viet Cong. Every day, before any "regular" army vehicles were allowed to travel on the road, U.S. service men were sent out in tanks or track vehicles to sweep (clear by unearthing or running over) the road of any and all mines that had been placed there during the night. Sometimes the road had to be swept several times during the day — depending on enemy activity — and even then, there were no guarantees that all land mines had been removed.

It is unlikely that there was anyone else who was more aware of the dangers of Thunder Road than the remaining original members of A Battery. Those men had spent a whole year at the mercy of that road. As Dick mentions in his letters, it was not unusual for ambushes or other calamities to be a daily occurrence on the road that was the only connection Thunder I, II, III and beyond had to the "outside world." Dick and the others surely could not help but feel a bit anxious and nervous as they began their journey down the road one last time.

Each truck moved at its own grievous pace managing, even with the dust, to keep one another in sight. The further they made it down the road, the more excited everyone became. They were so close to having this nightmare of a year over.

Dick looked up from his lap when he felt the truck stop. He knew that even as much as he wanted to believe it that they had not been traveling long enough to be at Phu Loi. Quickly the truck began to move again but it obviously was taking some sort of detour. He could sense they were maneuvering around something. Again the truck slumped to a stop. This time Dick felt the rear tires of the truck urgently and hopelessly spinning.

18) Shattered

"This young man was sent away
To serve his country; so they say,
But he himself did not want to go,
He hated war and killing so.

At war he was; this man of peace
He hoped this crazy war would cease . . ."
     Franklin P. Frye

It happened so fast, and with such force, that the sky screamed as the ground ruptured.

One of the spinning rear wheels had struck a land mine. The careless wheel had unearthed and awakened not the usual anti-personnel land mine that was most commonly found on the road, but a much stronger, anti-vehicle mine, that was meant to disable (if not destroy) armored tanks.

The force of the mine severed the back of the five-ton truck from the cab. The drivers' heads reverberated with the deafening shatter. They sat stunned and dumfounded as the pieces of the truck bed and ALL its contents hailed down and upon them.

Instantaneously the ground was strewn with blood, bodies and baby photos.

19) Fall Out

"The reality of the national psychic cost, is better understood when you consider that government statistics show that 43 million Americans are connected (family related) to the 58,000 names on the Vietnam Veterans Memorial in Washington, D.C."
Ed Henry — *Forgive & Forget and Then Move On*

The news that five of Manchester's sons had been killed quickly became a wail of sorrow that resonated up every street, through every home, down every alley and within each citizen of the Queen City.

Of course, the shock and sadness that entrenched and then anchored itself in the city as word of the disaster spread, seemed pale, weak even, when compared to the grief and misery that family and friends were forced to endure. Disbelief and indescribable pain invaded and then mercilessly conquered them. Everyone felt a torment so deep and unforgiving, that no one in the Cavanaugh or the Genest family remembers exactly how he or she found out or what precisely happened when he or she found out, in the same way. However, everyone unequivocally remembers that Wednesday, August 27, 1969 was the most painful and heart wrenching day of their lives.

Brenda: "I remember I walked into my parents' house, I was holding Dickie and Charlotte and I were laughing about something. I walked into the den and the kids (Nancy Lou, Mike, and Jimmy) were all just sitting there and Jimmy said to me, 'Why are you laughing? WHY ARE YOU LAUGHING?' and I just looked at him. I could not figure what his problem was. He seemed so angry with me. I was still laughing a little and I said, 'What's the matter with you.' And crying he said, 'YOU KNOW, YOU KNOW.' At that point I wasn't really paying much attention to him, I just thought he was being a brat. He said, 'Dick's dead.' I was getting really annoyed with him by then but I lightheartedly said, 'No, he's not. He's coming home in a couple days.' I turned and started to walk away from him because he was really starting to make me mad. He started crying really hard and then he yelled, 'DICK'S DEAD.'

"My knees just buckled beneath me and I screamed for Charlotte to take Dickie because I could not support my own weight and the whole room was spinning and I felt like the whole world had just crashed down upon me. So I think Charlotte grabbed Dickie and then I grabbed Jimmy and shook him. I grabbed his little shoulders and shook him, and I said, *'Don't say that. DON'T YOU SAY THAT. DICK IS COMING HOME IN A COUPLE DAYS. DON'T YOU EVER SAY THAT.'*

"And then one of those men from the army came into the house and I ran up to him and started screaming, *'Do you like your job? Do you like this job? What kind of person has this for a job? Do you like doing this? Do you like ruining people's lives? What's the matter with you? Do you like this job?* I was in his face just screaming as hard and then all I could say was, *'Do you. Do you? Huh, do you?'* I was so angry truly the only thing I could see was red. And then my father and mother grabbed me and held me and tried to calm me down."

The news of Dick's death ripped and tore through Brenda's soul as violently as the bomb that had severed and slaughtered Dick.

Nancy: "I'm not sure where I was at the time, but for some reason Jimmy answered the door when the man from the army came. All he said to Jimmy was, 'Is your mother home? Tell your mother Dick is dead.' And of course this ruined Jimmy — he had loved Dick, he idolized him. Then Brenda came home and Jimmy told her that Dick was dead and she slapped him across the face and said, 'Don't you say that. Don't you say that. Dick will be home in a few days. Don't you EVER say that.' I don't remember much else. It was just a horrible day. It was just awful. Just terrible, terrible."

Nancy Lou: "They came to the door on Tory Road. They pulled up in a military car. It was like my mother knew it was not going to be good news and they asked for Brenda. I don't remember her coming home or anything. It's just so foggy. I know we were in the family room crying. I remember when they came to the door and told us he was killed. (Begins to cry) It's so hard — even now — I never lost anybody like that. I've lost people that I loved, but for some reason, he is just different.

"When I first heard, I had this felling in my stomach and I can't describe it. It was like awful. It was like this horrible scream went off inside me. I have never had that feeling again. It was almost like being punched really hard in the stomach. It was physical, like the wind totally being knocked out of you. I mean you are physically there but there is a big hole in your heart. Oh God, it was awful."

Jimmy: "I was down at the dealership for some reason. Just hanging out or whatever and the man came to talk to my father. I knew something was wrong. Anyway my dad put me in the car and I know we drove home really fast. On the ride home my dad told me what had happened."

Charlotte: "I remember we had been out looking at houses

and we were going to drop Dickie off at Brenda's parents. We turned down Tory Road and we see the cars. There were like three cars there. Two or three army cars. The minute she saw those cars she knew right away. It's a dead give away when you see those army cars. She spazzed out . . . So, the minute she walked in the door and one of them (men from the army) was there she just like pushed him away. And her parents were like, 'Brenda, Brenda,' but the minute she saw their faces she knew.

"So then we had to call my parents and tell them just to come to the Cavanaughs'. So they thought something had happened to Brenda or me or Dickie. You know they never dreamed, you know, because he was on his way home."

Tom: "What I remember is, it seems they came to the house and told Jimmy, who was just a baby. Imagine this guy telling a kid like that! I am sure Jimmy was the first one they told. And I know the guy had been drinking. Anyway, some how I got a call (he was at work at the car dealership) from the house and when I got home the guy had come back. I don't know how that clown came back again — he was half in the bag — but I was there then and it was official that time.

"Edgar and Fleurette were down at a restaurant in Milford, so I called Edgar and said, 'You better come home. It's important and I don't want to tell you this on the phone. Come right to my house.' I remember this part real well: They drove up and they parked at the foot of the driveway. The guy from the army tried to walk out there with me and I said, 'No, you are not going to go near them. Understand?' There was no way I was going to let this clown tell them. There is no question in my mind this guy was drunk.

"And then he said, 'I have to do this.'

"So I grabbed his arm and said, 'Now listen here buddy, they are going to here it from me — not you,' and I walked up to them. I said, 'Edgar I gotta talk to you. I gotta tell you right off — Dick has been killed.'

"Fleurette started screaming. She was sitting in the car and we were standing behind it. She started screaming. I'll never forget it. I'll never forget that."

George Pavlidis: "All of us who had been infused had received orders to report to our original C.O. We all (all the men of the 3rd Howitzer Battalion, 197th Field Artillery who were in Vietnam), were being sent to Long Bihn — the staging area — so everyone in the original unit would be going to go home together.

"So when I got there I walked into the barracks and went down to the end of the hall. I stood there and thought, 'Geez, I am going to see Dick soon,' and so I took the last two bunks. I took one and I left the last one on the end for Dick. I took the mattress of the bunk on the end and folded it over so no one would take it. That afternoon a couple of guys tried to get the bunk but I said, 'No, no, I'm saving that for Dick.' So, in walks a 1st lieutenant and he walks down the hall. I did not think anything about it at the time. Well one of the guys, who had not yet arrived at Long Bihn, brother was sitting at the end of the hall on a bunk and the 1st lieutenant walks up to him and says he has some news he has to tell him.

"That's pretty much when I knew something was up. I mean I did not know what was going on. The two of them turn their backs to and sat on a cot. Then I see the guy with his hands over his face and with his elbows on his knees, sobbing. The 1st lieutenant has his arm around the guy. Then the 1st Lieutenant turns to get up and I am looking at him thinking, 'What in the hell is this about.' And my heart sunk and I thought, 'My God this is not good.' So, I look at the 1st lieutenant's face and he had tears and he could not look at me. And that was it. You know I remember it like it happened yesterday, like yesterday. Anyway he (the 1st lieutenant) starts to leave and I stopped him.

I said, 'WHAT HAPPENED?!!" and he just shook his head. And I just kept saying, 'WHAT HAPPENED, WHAT HAPPENED??!!!'

"And he shook his head and said, 'It's not good. His brother just got killed.'

"Then almost instinctively I thought — my God — just tell me that Dick is all right. That's all I said to him. I said, 'Just tell me that Dick is all right.' And he just shook his head. I grabbed him by the shirt, it was like, 'Don't do this! Don't say that!' He was just as devastated as everyone else and he had to be the harbinger of bad news.

That moment is etched in my mind forever."

Richard Murphy: "I had seen the Genests' (Edgar and Fleurette) the day before. We talked about how Dick was on his way home I had told them maybe with the international dateline and all, he was already on his way home right then. Then I think it was the very next morning and I was standing in my house brushing my teeth, and on the radio this announcement comes on, five service men killed in Vietnam, five National Guardsmen. And they say the names. I remember how the toothpaste tasted and I remember how I looked in the mirror, I can see myself doing it now, I remember listening to the names — all French names — and they said Richard Genest. All I remember then is walking over to Starr's. I was in a daze and told them what I had heard. I remember Starr's mother saying, 'I have known more people killed in Vietnam than I did in World War II.'

Bill Starr: "I remember going over to Murph's house and just sitting there in a total daze."

Roland Provencher: "I had come home (from Vietnam) before the others because my wife had broken her arm and I was allowed to come home and take of her and our son. Anyway I got a call about 11:00 p.m. from somebody at headquarters who was home on emergency leave. Well he told me about four, but he did not want to tell me about Dick. He left it for last and then finally he told me Dick had been killed too. I DID NOT BELIEVE IT. I thought it was like a bad dream."

Jill: "I was working at the Goldenrod in York Beach. I was working in the candy department. My mother had taken all the kids home because it was getting close to Labor Day and school always started the day after Labor Day. I was able to stay in York Beach because I had my own car and I had to work Labor Day weekend at the Goldenrod.

"Anyway I was working and I saw my father come in and he had that look on his face. It was in the morning and I knew he was supposed to be at work in Manchester. He had the same look on his face as he had had when my grandfather had died. And I remember thinking, 'Oh my god, I just hope it is Grammy.'

"Because my grandmother was in a nursing home and she had been sick. And I was thinking, 'Oh God, please just let it be Grammy.' But the look my father had was so bad that I knew that it had to be worse than that. He had already asked Mrs. Wagner if he could talk to me and he was going to wait until he could take me outside but I would not let him because I just had to know what was wrong — why he had that look on his face. So when he walked up to me I said, 'It's Grammy, it's Grammy.' And he said 'No, Dick got killed. Dick got killed.' He told that right there in the Goldenrod. And then I just remember walking out by the big candy table they have there and I doubled over. I just started crying, 'NO, IT CAN'T BE DICK, IT CAN'T BE DICK.'

"My father had his car parked across the street from the Goldenrod and he made me go get in his car because I was like hysterical. So then he drove me over to the beach house (a block away) and he said, 'We have to go. We have to go to Manchester. Can you drive?' And I said, 'Yeah I can drive.' So on the drive home I followed him in my Fiat. I was just going down the road thinking this HAS GOT TO BE a nightmare. This can't be true.

"When I got home I thought, well you know, maybe this was a mistake. It just couldn't be true. I walked into the house and it was so sad. Brenda was in the living room and you could not even talk to her (starts to cry). You just could not even talk to her. All you could do is cry. Everybody was crying. It was like you had no way to communicate with her because you felt so sad but you knew you were not hurting half as much as her. My mother was so sad, I mean she had all this to deal with plus all the kids and we had no food in the house because she had just come back home after being at the beach for the summer. So my mother asked me if I could go grocery shopping and I said yes because I could not handle being there. I mean there was nothing I could do to help and I just could not sit there.

"So I went grocery shopping and I bought all these goodies. Once I got out of the house I was kind of all right but it is the weirdest feeling. You feel like the whole word should stop. I was in the grocery store and I was looking around and I was like how can these people keep going on with their life? Don't they know what's happened? Don't they know? How can they keep being so normal? I just felt like I was on t.v. or something and these people were actors and they did not know what was going. And I was the only one who knew what was going on. Like I was going through the motions and they are just acting like everything is normal. It was like they did not know the world had stopped."

Brenda remembers fragments of the first night her life became as shattered as her husband's body. "I think the doctor came and gave me a tranquilizer that night. I was so angry and hurt and I was just totally consumed with grief. I just could not believe after surviving a whole year he was killed on his way home. I just could not believe it. I think Father Kenney, who had married us, and who was very close to my father, came over. It was like I was there, but then I wasn't. It was like I was not part of my body. Like there was no way this could be happening and I was watching it happen to someone else or something. Like the pain I was feeling would for sure kill me if I stayed in my body."

Fleurette: "I remember sitting in bed that night and I just sobbed and sobbed. I kept hearing this dull thud over and over again, and although my head was throbbing with pain, I knew the constant thump, thump was not in my head. At some point I realized I was crying and convulsing so hard that my sobbing was causing the headboard of the bed to slam back and forth against the wall."

Charlotte: "I remember my father standing on the balcony that was off my parents' bedroom. I remember him standing there and he was just devastated and he would take a drink from a glass and then fling it off the balcony. And then he would get another glass and he did that over and over again."

20) All Over Town

SP 5 Richard E. Genest
197th Artillery — National Guard

All municipal flags are being flown at half-staff in honor of
SP 5 Richard E. Genest.
I wish to express to you my deepest sympathy.

John C. Mongan, Mayor

By the next morning, Thursday, August 28, news of the tragedy began to saturate and at the same time absorb all of New England and most of the United States. The mayor of Manchester, John C. Mongan, made this statement: "The news that five Manchester boys were killed in Vietnam from the same cause is shocking. With the peace talks in session, the bombing halt, partial troop withdrawals and with these men due to arrive home within a week with their unit, it is very, very difficult to accept this tragedy."

The catastrophe that had befallen Manchester seemed unbelievable to everyone who heard. How could five men from the same town be killed on the eve of their return? How much longer could this war go on? When was the United States really going to go "in there" and win? How many more husbands, fathers and sons had to die before we could claim victory? Why did the United States have to win? Why had so many died

236 ALMOST BACK

already? When was enough going to be ENOUGH?

As communities throughout the United States mourned for and sympathized with the families of the fallen men, the dreaded and morbid telegrams began to arrive at the Cavanaugh home.

WUE141 CTC101 WW SNA040 LG GOVT PDB
SN WASHINGTON DC 28 1224 EDT
MRS BRENDA C GENEST, DLY 75
373 TORY RD MANCHESTER NHAMP
I WAS PROFOUNDLY SHOCKED AND DISMAYED AT THE ANNOUNCEMENT THIS MORNING OF YOUR HUSBAND'S TRAGIC DEATH. YOUR SACRIFICE TO THE NATION IS BEYOND MEASURE. YOUR HUSBAND'S CONTRIBUTION IN HEROISM AND DEDICATION TO DUTY WAS ENORMOUS. ALLOW ME TO SHARE IN SOME SMALL WAY YOUR GRIEF AND TO EXPRESS MY DEEP PERSONAL SYMPATHY AT THIS MOST SORROWFUL TIME. MY PRAYERS AND THOUGHTS ARE WITH YOU
THOMAS J MCINTYRE U S SENATOR
(1237).
117P EDT AUG 28 69

WUE258 B WA089 XV PDB 4 EXTRA
FAX WASHINGTON DC 28 356 P EDT
MRS BRENDA C GENEST, DON'T PHONE, CHECK DLY CHGS ABOVE 75 CTS
373 TORY RD MANCHESTER NHAMP
REMAINS YOUR HUSBAND RICHARD E. WILL BE CONSIGNED TO GOODWIN FUNERAL HOME, 607 CHESTNUT ST., MANCHESTER, NEW HAMPSHIRE. PLEASE DO NOT SET DATE OF FUNERAL UNTIL PORT AUTHORITIES NOTIFY YOU AND FUNERAL

DIRECTOR DATE AND SCHEDULED TIME OF ARRIVAL DESTINATION
DISPOSITION BRANCH MEMORIAL DIVN DEPT OF THE ARMY WUX MB
(401).
453P EDT AUG 28 69

MRS BRENDA C GENEST, DON'T PHONE, CK DLY CHGS ABOVE 75 CTS
373 TORY RD MANCHESTER NHAMP
THIS CONCERNS YOUR HUSBAND, SP5 RICHARD E. GENEST. THE ARMY WILL RETURN YOUR LOVED ONE TO A PORT IN THE UNITED STATES BY FIRST AVAILABLE MILITARY AIRCRAFT. AT THE PORT REMAINS WILL BE PLACED IN A METAL CASKET AND DELIVERED (ACCOMPANIED BY A MILITARY ESCORT) BY MOST EXPEDITIOUS MEANS TO ANY FUNERAL DIRECTOR DESIGNATED BY THE NEXT OF KIN OR TO ANY NATIONAL CEMETERY IN WHICH THERE IS AVAILABLE GRAVE SPACE. YOU WILL BE ADVISED BY THE UNITED STATES PORT CONCERNING THE MOVEMENT AND ARRIVAL TIME AT DESTINATION.
FORMS ON WHICH TO CLAIM AUTHORIZED INTERMENT ALLOWANCE WILL ACCOMPANY REMAINS. THIS ALLOWANCE MAY NOT EXCEED $75 IF CONSIGNMENT IS MADE DIRECTLY TO THE SUPERINTENDENT OF A NATIONAL CEMETERY. WHEN CONSIGNMENT IS MADE TO A FUNERAL DIRECTOR PRIOR TO INTERMENT IN A NATIONAL CEMETERY, THE MAXIMUM ALLOWANCE IS $250; IF BURIAL TAKES PLACE IN A CIVILIAN CEMETERY, THE MAXIMUM ALLOWANCE IS $500.
REQUEST NEXT OF KIN ADVISE BY COLLECT

TELEGRAM ADDRESSED: DISPOSITION BRANCH, MEMORIAL DIVISION, DEPARTMENT OF THE ARMY WUX MB, WASHINGTON, D. C., NAME AND ADDRESS OF FUNRAL DIRECTOR OR NAME OF NATIONAL CEMETERY SELECTED.

IF ADDITIONAL INFORMATION CONCERNING RETURN OF REMAINS IS DESIRED YOU MAY INCLUDE YOUR INQUIRY IN THE REPLY TO THIS MESSAGE. PLEASE DO NOT SET DATE OF FUNERAL UNTIL PORT AUTHORITIES NOTIFY YOU DATE AND SCHEDULED TIME OF ARRIVAL DESTINATION. PLEASE FURNISH AREA CODE AND TELEPHONE NUMBER OF FUNERAL DIRECTOR SELECTED

DISPOSITON BRANCH MEMORIAL DIV DEPT OF ARMY WUX MB (948).

21) Disillusioned

"No healing, no apologies, no memorials, nothing can possibly compensate for the damage done and the pain inflicted . . . The only thing we can possibly do twenty years too late is try and tell the truth."
Eric Bergerud — *Red Thunder, Tropical Lighting*

To everyone in the Genest and Cavanaugh family Labor Day weekend of 1969 is a glaring and painful blur. Brenda recalls, "It was very hot, unusually warm for that time of year and I think I went with Charlotte to go shop for clothes. I mean I was twenty and it was not like a black dress and veil was part of my wardrobe. I remember the only proper dresses we could find were long sleeved and heavy black wool. I was so weak and in a daze and drained. I felt like I was going to just collapse and then to put on that heavy hot dress — well it just took everything out of me. And then I was supposed to plan a funeral. I was twenty. What the hell did I know about making funeral arrangements? It was all just so terrible. And then the worst part was we had to wait for the body. It was a horrible nightmare that just got worse and worse."

Charlotte: "I remember the worst thing was we had to wait for the body to come."

While Dick's family and friends in New Hampshire

attempted to wade through the quagmire of sorrow that had engulfed them, close to five hundred men of the 197th, still in Vietnam were also grieving and in great pain.

George Pavlidis: "Right after I found out, I went and got drunk. Now normally I did not drink at all, but that night I got so drunk that I sat in the gutter in the middle of that base and just bawled and cried. I did that for the next two days, then I got defiant.

"About the time I started to sober up a 2nd lieutenant arrived at the base and he really started giving everyone a real hard time. Well I had gotten so drunk the two days before that I had developed a real bad cold in my throat and I decided I just was going spend the day in my bunk. So anyway this lieutenant comes over to my bunk and tells me to get up and make formation. So I got up and said, 'Do you understand what has happened here?!? Do you understand that playing this stupid game is over for me?!!? I DON'T GIVE A FUCK IF THIS WHOLE PLACE BLOWS UP AND THIS WHOLE GODDAMN EFFORT OVER HERE IS LOST!!! What was it all for? So you can walk around in your spit-shined boots and pull rank on everybody?'

"Then he says, 'YOU can't talk to me like that.'

"I just could not take it anymore and I said, 'You have pulled rank on everybody around here and I have had enough of that shit. I'll throw you right the hell out of here. I'll throw you right out the window! DO YOU UNDERSTAND WHAT KIND OF LOSS WE HAVE HAD?'

"He started to walk out and then he turned around and he looked like a deranged maniac and he screamed, 'I'LL HAVE YOU COURT MARTIALED FOR THIS!!!'

"He went right to the colonel and he tried to put an administrative leave on me in order to keep me in the country for sixty more days pending a court marshal. But I mean really, what more trauma could he cause? I mean everybody in that place was so upset. You could cut the air with a knife.

"So after he went to the colonel I got word from a sergeant major that what I had done was wrong but that a lot of the guys respected what I had done and the word from the colonel was, 'Humor the bastard,' meaning that nothing was going to happen to me. To make it look right, they gave me and some other guy 'extra duty.' We had to paint a review stand. I left that God-forsaken hole with such bitterness. With such hatred for what it meant to be in that system. I was not proud of anything by the time we left."

22) Five Flags

After much unnecessary confusion and flawed communication from the army, the families of the five dead men were notified that the bodies of Dick, Guy, Gaetan, Roger and Richard would arrive at Grenier Field at the Manchester airport on Saturday, August 30. As if the trauma of losing these men had not been enough, the families were forced to endure many painful obstacles before they could actually see the remains of their loved ones. It was maddening, to say the least, to know that the army still, even in death, controlled their loved ones' destiny. Most everyone agrees that being given conflicting information about what had happened, being given several different times and places as to the arrival of the bodies and that having to wait three days for the bodies was almost unbearable. It seemed so unfair and cruel. How could an army that was supposed to be organizing, successfully fighting and winning a war not know when or how they were going to get these five men home? It was disconcerting and hurtful to all who just wanted to put their loved ones to rest.

However, despite the lack of information (no specific time was given for the arrival of the bodies on Saturday), and the confusion generated by the army, by mid-morning Saturday, family members and over two thousand somber and solemn people had descended upon the airport and spilled into Grenier Field. The men, women and children of Manchester huddled together and reluctantly witnessed the beginning of what had been termed, "The Saddest Day in the City's History."

Spectators filled the airport's sky deck and overflowed into the waiting rooms of the usually quiet and prosaic airport. Government, religious and military officials from all over New Hampshire and New England came to express their sympathy and sorrow. As members of each of the five devastated families arrived, hushed cries could be heard. The family members wearily waded through the crowds and took their place at the edge of the runway.

Brenda clutched Dickie and held him close to her heart as she was escorted by her father through the throng of people. Every face in the crowd seemed focused on her. As she walked she felt as if she was seeing the same thing over and over again. Every person and every face looked just like the last. All she could see was a sea of pity and sorrow. And with each look of sympathy, sadness and compassion that was projected toward her, Brenda could only feel rage and disappointment. She wanted to scream, "Damn you! Where were you when I needed you?" "Where were you when I was trying to find out if they were going to have to go?"

"Where were you when everyone told me not to worry; that they would never actually go."

"Where were you when I tried to keep them home?" "Where were you when I was trying to bring these boys home ALIVE?"

"Where were you when I knocked on your door and asked you to sign a petition to bring them home?"

"Why did you send me away and tell me what I was doing would do no good?"

"Where were you when I cried for help?" "WHERE WERE YOU THEN?"

Brenda was jolted from her mental rampage by Edgar's brother, Roland Genest. He touched her arm and said, "Brenda, look, here is Senator McIntyre." There, right in front of Brenda, was the one man who truly had had the power to help a year ago. There — not more than four feet in front of her — was the man who had ushered her hysterically crying away from his office, claiming he was powerless. And now he stood before her, chest puffed out, basking in pomp and power. With an overwhelming feeling of venom disgust Brenda turned away. Roland once again gently touched her arm, with obvious surprise in his voice he said, "Brenda, THAT'S SENATOR MCINTYRE." Brenda whipped her head around, sharply narrowed her eyes upon the Senator, pausing long enough to let her gaze puncture his calloused soul. Then looking as if she might vomit she said, "I know EXACTLY who he is." Quickly she turned her back to him and for an instant, the Senator was completely deflated.

The sound of the chartered DC-9 containing the bodies barreled down on the crowd. The brightness of the early afternoon sun caused Brenda to squint as she searched the sky. The pounding anguish that raged inside Brenda marched forcefully through her hundred pound body — almost overtaking her as the plane slowly came into view. She pulled Dickie close to her and gently rocked him. Near by, Charlotte was held by her father and Chick as she shook and cried. The plane made a long, low pass over the field.

As the plane taxied down the runway Charlotte waited for the announcement to come that there had been some mistake. That they had been wrong and her brother would be home next week with everyone else. She felt that everyone had suffered enough already and that after waiting all this time for her brother, that there was just no way possible they would send him home in a coffin. This just had to be a mistake.

The sun throbbed with blistering heat as one-by-one the steel, flag-draped coffins were wheeled off the airplane. There was only one way to distinguish which coffin contained the body of which man — a small, white cardboard tag that was hardly visible from where the families were forced to stand. Despite the overwhelming heat, members of all five families huddled together forming a large, black mass as the first of the five coffins was pushed on a steel cart toward them. A drum roll began as the first casket attended by color guardsmen was wheeled toward the families. For a moment absolute silence followed the cart down the runway. Then as that first casket took its place in front of the families, the air became saturated with moans, wails, and guttural sobs. Like falling dominoes, the cries of pain passed through and collapsed upon the entire crowd.

The next casket was wheeled toward the families. Dickie, who was in his mother's arms, tossed his arms up toward his face and called out, "Da." As the casket drew closer another wave of pain crashed down upon the crowd. Women trembled and doubled over in pain. Men felt their knees buckle. Children sobbed and shook. War hardened reporters and photographers became obviously choked up. Although a drum roll was supposed to escort each casket the drummers were given a high sign to stop. It had become obvious that the ominous beat of the drums only served to amplify the severity of sorrow.

The remaining three caskets were placed in front of the families without the resounding of the drums. But it was too late; the drums had burst the dam of grief and a flood of devastated emotion surged with the arrival of each casket.

A Catholic bishop flanked by two priests approached the families and the line of flag draped caskets. The bishop's bright purple robe flapped lifelessly in the hot breeze. As the bishop sprinkled holy water on each casket he spoke, "Oh, God, the source of all holy desires and just works, grant unto all nations that peace which the world cannot give, even when young men like these give their lives for it." He stepped slightly back from the caskets and then as if to make sure the words he was about to say would surely embrace the dead men he took a deep, calculated breath, "The lord be with you."

"And with your spirit," several voices replied. The bishop continued, his voice still strong and poignant, "Let us pray.

Lord, listen to our prayers as we ask for your mercy on the souls of your servants, Roger Robichaud, Richard Genest, Richard Raymond, Guy Blanchette, Gaetan Beaudoin, whom you have summoned to leave this mortal life. Let them into a place of peace and light and make them one in the company of your faith through Christ our Lord. Amen."

Brenda's arms felt like lead balloons. She felt as if the world and ground was spinning around her. It was all she could do to keep herself from collapsing. She set Dickie down for a moment. He stood holding on to her leg for a brief moment and then he turned toward the five coffins. He took several little steps toward them before Brenda reached out her arm to stop him. He stretched out from his mother's arm lunging toward one of the caskets his arms open and his tiny fingers extended as he called out, "Da-da."

The military band began to play "Abide with Me," while each casket was loaded into its own hearse. An unknown distinct and powerful voice bellowed, "Present Arms!" The slap of men's hands grasping their guns, the rumble of men's boots forcefully clapping against one another and the rap of men's fingers brushing against hats briefly transcended the plaintive sobs that drenched the crowd.

The door of the fifth hearse was closed with painful finality and the morbid procession began its journey into Manchester. The motorcade was escorted from the field of the airport by the New Hampshire State Police. Along with the hearses the procession included vehicles containing family members, as well as the mayor and aldermen of Manchester, military vehicles whose passengers ranged in rank from color guardsmen to generals, limousines whose passengers included the governor of New Hampshire and U.S. Congressmen.

All along the seven-mile drive from the airport into Manchester citizens lined the road and streets, trying in some way to show their support and shared grief. The city was eerily silent as each hearse broke away, each headed to a separate funeral home. People from all walks of life paused and felt the sorrow of a family and a city, a nation even, pass through them and trample over them as the vehicles moaned down the city streets.

23) Conviction

"If only I had the courage to do things before, maybe this never would have happened . . .
I will never be afraid to act or stand by my convictions again."
Brenda C. Genest — 1969

The Cavanaughs and the Genests pulled into the small tree-lined parking lot of Goodwin's Funeral Home. No one could believe that there was still more pain and anguish to endure — that the ceremony at the airport had been the beginning of what promised to be a tortuous journey. It was inconceivable that now the real pain and mourning was to begin. Charlotte remembers that everyone waited outside while Roland Genest went into to check the condition of Dick's body. The army had wanted to have a closed casket and no one, including the members of the stateside military, knew the condition of Dick's body. And of course, everyone held out the hope that Roland would come out of the steady and ominous brick building shouting. "It's not Dick! It's not Dick! They were wrong! There's some sort of mistake! It's not Dick!" When Roland came out from viewing Dick's body, it was not necessary for him to speak. The look on his face spoke to the family in volumes.

Brenda remembers clutching the hand rail with one hand and holding Dickie against her hip with her other arm as she ascended the six, cold granite stairs that led to the foyer of Goodwin's. Her legs became weaker and her feet heavier with each step. She felt as though someone had poured cement into her shoes and every time she moved forward more cement was added.

She passed by five members of the honor guard who were sitting, heads down, and silent in a small room. The next thing she saw was the metal box that contained her husband. Around the casket were men in military uniforms quietly talking. They became silent as Brenda approached. They stepped aside and drenched her with looks of pity. Brenda wanted to turn and yell, "How dare you pretend to feel bad for me or anyone else! You did this to him!" At that moment, she wished she could repel their pitiful expressions the way a wet dog rids itself of water. She walked toward the closed, flag-draped coffin. Quietly, she told no one in particular to take the flag off and open the casket. Brenda heard murmuring and felt the hesitation in the room before the flag was removed and the casket opened.

She then walked over to Dick. Her knees almost buckled. The only reason she did not collapse is because she had Dickie in her arms. The casket was now open but it was covered with a large thick piece of glass and underneath the glass was someone who resembled Dick but certainly it was not the Dick she had known. The young man in the sealed coffin had straight hair that was slicked back. His mustache was manicured and contrived. His body was stiff and tense, adorned in a meticulous military uniform.

The room began to spin around her. She felt all breath and life defeatedly leaving her body. With one hand she grasped the side of the coffin in an effort to try and steady herself. Her head pounded, "This CAN NOT be happening! What have they done to him?" Her Dick never combed his hair back. His soft loose curls always playfully rested on his forehead. When the mood struck him to grow a mustache, he never concentrated on it. He preferred to let it be its own work in progress. His body had always been relaxed and inviting. The clothes he usually wore were always comfortable and casual. Her eyes frantically scanned the casket for some piece, some shred of the man she loved. When she could not find him, it was as if she had been violently slapped in the face. Her pain and confusion turned to anger and rage.

She whipped her head around to the military personal and the funeral director. "TAKE THE GLASS OFF!," she commanded. They were only able to look at her with surprise and shock. She repeated herself slowly and forcefully, "I SAID, TAKE THE GLASS OFF!"

The funeral director, military men, and even her family stood wide-eyed and still; it was as if her words had knocked them senseless. They were overwhelmed by the power that this wounded young mother now commanded.

She moved Dickie, who had become noticeably concerned for his mother, up from her hip and pulled him close to her breast and heart. She comforted him by gently rubbing her cheek against his. She refused to release the men from her controlled, commanding gaze. David Goodwin, the funeral director who was no stranger to grief, cautiously stepped toward her and said, "Brenda, I am sorry but we cannot take off the glass because of diseases that may have come from Vietnam."

Brenda fixed her eyes onto him with an intensity that burned right through him. "YOU CAN TAKE OFF THE GLASS OR I'LL BREAK THE GOD DAMN GLASS. I DON'T CARE HOW IT COMES OFF. JUST TAKE IT OFF, NOW!"

Tom cautiously moved toward his daughter who was not about to release Mr. Goodwin from her unrelenting and severe gaze. The room had become thick with tormented tension. Edgar touched Mr. Goodwin's arm and said, "I think you better take off the glass."

Mr. Goodwin looked to the military men for support. They only looked down and ineptly shook their heads no.

Tom moved closer to his daughter. He wanted to comfort her, try and calm her. But he like everyone else knew from her tone and intensity that there was nothing they could do to placate her but remove the glass.

Brenda felt her father's presence. Deep inside she wanted to run into his arms and have him hold her and protect her from anymore pain. But even deeper inside, her soul screamed for her to honor her husband. Her mind mandated that NOTHING MORE be taken from him. They had taken his happiness, his youth, his innocence and most preciously his life. Her spirit roared, "NO MORE!" She could not and would not allow them to take anymore. She was not about to have her husband spend eternity in the uniform he despised. The uniform that he told her he could not wait to burn once he got home. There was no way he would be buried with token medals from a war he did not believe in. He would not be made to look as THEY saw fit. They may have dictated the terms of his subservient existence that was the last year and a half of his life, they may have delivered him to death, but enough was enough.

"EITHER YOU TAKE THE GLASS OFF OR I AM GOING TO GET A BASEBALL BAT AND BREAK IT. DO YOU HEAR ME?!"

Tom looked at Mr. Goodwin. His face contorted with a mix of sternness, concern and pleading. Brenda recalls, "I don't remember exactly how the glass came off but somehow it came off. We might have been told to leave the room so they could discuss it — I don't remember them doing it in front of us, anyway finally the glass came off."

Brenda reached for Dick's hand as her heart hammered against her soul. Her eyes saw the lifeless stiff body of Dick before her, but her heart refused to trust her eyes. With every ounce of its will and might, her heart tried to beat all its power and vigor through her hand into his. She had waited so long to once again hold his warm, loving hand and she refused to believe that she had waited in vain. There was just no way that life could have been taken out of the warmest loving and most alive being she had ever met. She squeezed his hand and silently pleaded, "Come to me, my love. Please come back to us. There is no way I can live without you. I need you. Dickie needs you. Please, please come back to us."

Dick's hand and body remained stiff, cold and lifeless. She gently began to place his hand back at his side. As she reluctantly released Dick's hand reality bitterly smacked her in the face. And then again she realized her husband was dressed in the uniform he thoroughly had despised. Her mind became flooded with images and words from his letters. *Bren... Make sure you bring some of my regular clothes . . . It will be good to put on some regular clothes, instead of these green junky things . . . I can't wait to build a big bon fire and burn all my army clothes . . . I hate this army so much . . . I never want to have anything to do with this government at all once I get out of here . . . I told them I wanted no part of being sergeant E-6 . . . They know I have no interest in this disorganized thing they call the army . . . All I want to do is get out of it and for good!*

"GET HIM OUT OF THOSE CLOTHES."

Mr. Goodwin was still reeling from the impact of Brenda's last demand. He beleagueredly looked to her. Brenda again pierced him with her eyes and tone. "HE WILL NOT BE BURIED IN THE UNIFORM HE HATED. I WANT HIM OUT OF THESE CLOTHES, NOW!" Feebly Mr. Goodwin searched the room for support. The military men stood utterly dumfounded. They had never heard such an outrageous demand in all their lives. Surely someone was going to stop this crazy woman before she completely lost it. Tom and Edgar's posture and faces tacitly expressed their support for Brenda.

Brenda was not sure what was happening to her, but for the

first time in eighteen months, for the first time since they had found out Dick had been activated, she felt like she had some control. For the first time in almost two years she was not crippled by fear. She realized they had absolutely no power over her because they had made her worst fear, her worst nightmare a bitter reality. There was nothing to stop her now — what in hell made them think she had anything but distrust and disgust for them and their procedures.

Brenda quickly swept past everyone and went into the tiny room where the five members of the color guard were waiting. They all looked up at her as she walked in and stood over them. She took a deep breath and with virtually no trace of the boiling anger that was raging inside her, she said, "Did any of you know Dick?" The men's eyes became transfixed on her. No one had ever commanded their attention like this. Quietly Brenda repeated herself, "I said, did any of you know Dick?" She looked intently at each man. One by one they shook their heads, no. With genuine concern and relative calm, she continued, "Isn't there something else you would rather be doing on Labor Day weekend? Wouldn't you rather be outside enjoying the sunshine? Where would you rather be; with your friends and family, enjoying this holiday weekend or here, carrying the coffin of a man you never knew."

They sat motionless, scared to even breathe. Brenda then said with absolute resolve and authority, "GET OUT OF HERE, NOW."

Brenda does not remember leaving Goodwin's Saturday afternoon. Since the moment she had heard the news, it was as if relentless waves of pain mercilessly and continually washed over her, each time knocking her down a little harder than the last. She felt as if she barely had time to get up before the next swell crashed down on her.

Brenda was not alone in feeling battered, bruised and wounded. The news of their son's death had shattered Edgar and

Fleurette's world. Each day seemed to get harder as their life became more and more fragmented. Everything that they saw, did, and experienced was so unconformable, so unnatural. There was nothing right about burying their child. There was no comfort to be found. The world had betrayed them in the cruelest way.

Edgar, as he always did, tried to take care of everyone. Brenda remembers that Edgar went and got Dick's favorite suit at her request. When Fleurette or Charlotte looked as if they might collapse under the weight of the sorrow, Edgar held them up. When David Goodwin needed direction on family's wishes, Edgar instructed him. But no matter how much he did, Edgar could not help but feel incomplete. His son was dead and both he and Fleurette felt as if a trench had been jaggedly dug through their souls.

Tom and Nancy also felt as if their world was spinning out of control. They had loved Dick. Their children had adored Dick. They found themselves frantically trying to hold their family together. It was all so overwhelming. They felt frustrated, confused and helpless as they watched their first born being pulverized by pain. Their hearts ached many times over as they tried to comfort Tommy, Jill, Mike, Nancy Lou and Jimmy. They prayed to God for strength. They searched their souls for answers to their children's questions. *"Mom, why did God do this to Dick?"* . . . *"Dad, I don't understand, why did this happen?".* . . *"Who will be Dickie's dad now?"* . . .

24) Never Okay

Sunday morning spitefully roused the Cavanaugh and Genest households the same way: with dread and sorrow. It was impossible for anyone in the either family to believe that their "official" and "public" mourning was just beginning. They felt like it had been a hellish eternity since they had heard the news. It seemed like a lifetime since they had first seen Dick and the others splattered on the front page of the newspaper. It felt like years since they had gone to the airport. And yet still the nightmare continued. They began yet another day of ceremony and mourning.

Tom drove Brenda and Dickie to Goodwin's for Dick's wake around 10:00 a.m. As much as she dreaded it, Brenda knew she would be spending the whole day at the funeral parlor because Dick's funeral was the next day and there were many people who wanted to attend the wake. Brenda had not intentionally bucked a traditional two-day wake. It was just that she truly felt she could not endure two days of receiving condolences, survive two days of known and unknown people weeping at the sight of her husband or bear two days of sitting next to the body of the man to whom she had committed her life. She felt she could barely take one more minute of it all, never mind another day.

When Tom, Brenda and Dickie arrived at Goodwin's they were met by a large group of reporters. The word of the five men's deaths had snatched a piece of the nation's heart. Even though the country had become accustomed and hardened to the dead and wounded count that crept onto their television screens while they ate dinner and watched morbid flashes of the war, the news of five dead from Manchester had managed to capture the nations attention.

A large contingent of the reporters had been dispatched to Dick's wake for a multitude of reasons: the Genests and the Cavanaughs were both well-known and established families in Manchester, he was the only father of the five, his funeral was the first. However, these considerations were minor when compared to knowledge that for the first time in memory, a military funeral and everything that went along with it, was being rebuffed and refused (refused is hardly an apt word when it is taken into consideration the lengths to which Brenda had to go), by the widow of a fallen war soldier. And, although none of the reporters had direct knowledge that a non-military service was going to take place, word that it was a possibility had began to circulate Saturday night.

Brenda paid little, if any, attention to the cameras and questions that bombarded her on her way into Goodwin's. Once inside she went immediately to Dick. She precariously grasped the relief that swept over her spirit. She almost smiled as she looked at him — he actually looked like Dick. His hair was no longer slicked back. The wax had been removed from his mustache. He was in his favorite green suit; the one that always seemed to make his eyes the bluest of blue, the one that fit his 120 pound body perfectly, the one that made women stare and men say, "Cool suit."

Just as swiftly as it had come, the slight bit of solace Brenda had experienced looking at Dick in his "regular clothes," bitterly exited. No matter how much he looked like himself or how much better he looked than he did the day before, Dick was still dead. Brenda looked up at her father who had been watching her from across the room. Tom tenderly approached her. He wrapped his arms around her and Dickie. He held her as she wept. He held his daughter and prayed that God would give him the wisdom and courage to help his daughter get through this.

Suddenly, Brenda stepped back from her father. It was as if Dick was whispering in her ear. *I never want to have anything to do with this government at all once I get out of here.* Brenda's eyes filled with rage, "Get that flag out of here."

Over Tom's shoulder Brenda had seen the flag that had adorned Dick's coffin neatly folded and resting on the table by the entrance of the room where Dick's body lay. Tom turned to the man who had been dispatched by the army — the Survival Assistance Officer and said, "Sir you heard her, please remove that flag from here." The S.A.O. was obviously mortified by what he heard. He knew that Brenda was totally irrational, unpatriotic and possibly insane (he would later call her among other things, "hostile," "hippie," and "beatnik"), but he could not believe a man whose family had served in the U.S. military since the Civil War, a man who had served in the South Pacific during WWII, was supporting this obvious Communist. He stared at Tom with incredulous disdain.

Tom walked over to him, grabbed him by the elbow and led him from the room. Once in the hallway Tom let go of the man's elbow. He then stared the man straight in the eyes, put his index finger against the man's chest and slowly, forcefully and clearly said, "I don't care what you do with it, you can keep it somewhere else, you can give it to the Genests. I don't give a damn. My daughter wants that flag out of here and you will take it out of here. Do you understand me?" The man would not look Tom in the eyes. He opened his mouth, but before any words came out Tom looked at him with eyes that were as black and bright red as burning coal, a glare so sharp it shredded the S.A.O.'s words silent.

While Tom had been attending to the S.A.O., members of Dick's family had begun to arrive. Jill remembers: "I remember it just did not look like him the day before and I just had to see him again because I just could not believe it. Anyway I go over to the casket and Fleurette is just crying and crying. My heart just ached for her so much. She was so sad. I remember I put my hand on her shoulder and said, 'It will be okay. It will be okay.' I mean I was just sixteen and I did not know what to say. I did not know what to do. Anyway she turned to me, her eyes swollen and full of tears and she said, 'NO! It will never be okay.'"

Throughout the rest of the day hundreds of people came to pay their respects and express their grief. Dick's friends from school came. People he knew from the bakery came. People who knew him from his bread route came. All his friends from the neighborhood came. Men who had been in Vietnam with him came. People he never knew came. Citizens from all over the state came. They all came and they all felt the loss of a father, a son, a husband, a brother and a friend.

25) Affirmation of Life

Sunday, like every day since they had been notified, ended with agony that was cruelly mixed with grim relief. While bitter relief escorted every nightfall with the awareness that another day had been survived, agony accompanied the darkness with the knowledge that tomorrow would surely bring more ceremony and sorrow. True to the unwelcome pattern, Monday, September 1, 1969 — Labor Day, was the day they buried Dick.

No one, especially Brenda, really recalls how all the details of Dick's funeral came to be worked out. Maybe because Brenda was so sure of what Dick would have wanted — the untraditional, precise and poignant arrangements she made came instinctively to her. Instinct coupled with strong yet tender determination and devotion consumed Brenda. She knew what she HAD to do to put Dick to rest and everyone in the Genest and Cavanaugh family followed her lead.

And lead is exactly what Brenda did. She asked Charlotte's husband, Chick, to find out who among Dick's friends would be willing to be pallbearers. She asked her sister Jill, Dick's cousin, Tina Genest and Dick's high school friend, Tom Bartlett to sing the music for the service. She enlisted the younger children of her family and the Genest family for offertory procession. She bravely and eloquently asked Monsignor Philip Kenney, the pastor who had presided over her and Dick's wedding and also had baptized Dickie, to go against church protocol and make Dick's service an affirmation of life and a rejection of anything that violated life.

By Monday morning news of the young Vietnam War widow who had demanded her husband be taken out of his military uniform had spread across the entire country. No one could recall such a bold and blatant move being made by a war widow in U.S. history. Practically every news agency in the country sent a representative to cover what was sure to be a controversial and emotionally-charged service. Television crews and reporters from all over the United States and throughout the world were waiting outside St. Catherine Church as Dick's family and friends arrived to say their final good-byes to Dick.

Over 400 hundred people made their way into the peaceful, white brick building that less than two years previously had been filled with bliss and joy as Brenda and Dick married. The church that barely more than a year before had been overflowing with anticipation, hope and promise, as Dick, Brenda their families and friends celebrated Dickie's baptism. Bill Starr, remembers the somber irony, "I was his best man at his wedding and then a year later I was a pallbearer at his funeral."

Conditional silence rocked the church as Dick was carried into the building. With deference and grace Dick's childhood companions placed the steel casket containing their friend in front of the altar that was decorated with two simple flower arrangements. Jill, Tina and Tom tearfully sang, "Where Have All the Flowers Gone?" There could not have been an eye without a tear, a heart without an ache or a soul without sorrow as the three sang, "Where have all the husbands gone? Gone to be soldiers everywhere. Where are all the soldiers gone? Gone to graveyards everyone. When will they ever learn, when will they ever learn?"

When they finished singing Monsignor Kenney spoke.

"... *Nothing seems as final as a casket. Nothing seems so terminal as a burial* ...

"... *Here in this church today there are many young adults in whom this multiple tragedy in our city engendered a feeling of frustration, a sense of futility. Many of us of the generation ahead of you share your feelings. In every institution, whether industry, the academic community or the church, those who make up the honorable have a choice to make. Either they remain within the structure and fight for what they think is right, or they cop out . . .*

"*To meet the challenge of this hour requires enormous human effort. And, if at times, the struggle is beyond our human resources, this Mass reminds us that we share life-to-death-to-life experience of Christ. And in both its agony and its triumph, we share His love, His grace, His strength.*"

When Monsignor Kenney was done speaking some of the youngest in the Genest and Cavanaugh families proceeded to the altar for the offertory procession. Six children — not one older than twelve — that included Nancy Lou and Mike Cavanaugh came to the altar each carrying something different. To the sacrifice table they not only brought the bread, water, and wine, but also they brought Dick's baseball bat, his baseball glove, and one of his textbooks from school. As Monsignor Kenney had just said, "objects . . . which symbolize the range of young peoples lives. The obvious meaning: this is an affirmation of life and a rejection of whatever violates life . . ."

The boldness and poignancy of Monsignor Kenney's words and the children's participation echoed throughout the church.

Mourners began to line up to receive communion. Jill, Tina and Tom began to sing again. At first the words from "Blowing in the Wind" came softly. Then with little warning but with great impact and significance, Tina's voice rose as people filed past her to receive communion. "How many times must the cannonballs fly before they're forever banned? How many ears must one man have before he can hear people cry? The answer my friend is blowing in the wind. The answer is blowing in the wind."

Once communion had been completed, Jill, Tina and Tom sang one last song, "Abraham, Martin and John." The words defiantly hung in the air as Dick's coffin was carried out of the church. "Has anybody here seen my old friend Abraham?

"Can you tell me where he has gone? He freed a lot of people but it seems only the good die young . . ."

26) Forever Removed

"The memory of that song,
'Where Have All the Flowers Gone?'
at the Mass is more moving to me than the drumbeat
at the John Kennedy funeral and the singing of 'Glory Hallelujah'
at the Robert Kennedy funeral."
(The deaths of the five boys) were, ". . . what put me into the
view that other people had . . .
of the futility of the war. At that Mass I could understand."
John C. Mongan — 1989

"Man-child of eighteen as you face your final agony now
Eyes that are beginning to cloud ask me one last question, 'Why?'
Please child, don't ask me why you die like this in mud and slime.
Why you will never again awake to a spring morning.
Why you will never see a child grow in your likeness.
Why you will never again feel wonder as you lift your eyes to a
star-filled night.
What drummed up frenzy of false patriotism sent to inflict and
receive suffering
in my name as an American?
Child, child
What can I possibly give you in return for what was so brutally
taken from you
A sliver star that is already tarnished
An unfeeling cold bronze medal
That piece of land you gave your life for will soon be no longer

ALMOST BACK

> *strategically important*
> *I weep for you and the ones who sent you."*
>
> Dorothy Dean Magee — October 1969

Although there were no more reporters outside the church than when they had entered, almost everyone who exited the church after the service looked shocked and bewildered by the volume of people outside. The media had formed a mass around the front of the church and had spilled out onto the street. As Dick's family and friends made their way toward the vehicles that would be taking them to the cemetery they were bombarded with questions and cameras.

As Brenda walked toward the street she felt like she was watching a silent movie in slow motion. She saw peoples lips moving but she heard no words. She saw microphones being slowly thrust at her. She saw what seemed like hundreds of different cameras and their lens moving toward her. Behind Brenda, Edgar held Dickie close to him. Fleurette stayed close to Edgar . Fleurette recalls, "It was just so awful and then it seemed to get worse with all those reporters. It was hard enough, but then to have all those cameras in our face, well it was just terrible, terrible."

At least seventy-five cars slowly made their way through Manchester toward the cemetery. The city was eerily still. Defeated and dejected the Queen City bowed her head as Dick's hearse passed the four funeral homes where the bodies of Guy, Richard, Gaetan and Roger lay. The convoy solemnly moved toward Mt. Calvary Mausoleum, its graveyard already the final address for 10 of Manchester's 26 sons killed in Vietnam.

The parking lot for the cemetery could not accommodate all the mourners and reporters. All around the cemetery streets were jammed with cars and people. Just like the church service, there was an overwhelming overflow of sorrow and a sea of people in and around the mausoleum.

Family members subtly infiltrated by a few reporters made their way through the crowd and into the stone building. Dick's casket was in the center of the marble-floored room. Almost instantly the open and large room seemed small and confining as the mourners gathered around Dick. Brenda and Charlotte stood against the smooth white and tan marble wall that would soon entomb Dick. The wall was dissected by large rectangular slabs of marble. Each rectangle identified first by a family name and then beneath it the names of those interred. Each space had room for two. With all her might, as if to make it disappear or to hide it, Brenda closed her eyes and pressed her back against the space that read

___ GENEST ___

___ RICHARD E___   ___ BRENDA C ___
1945   1969   1948

She hoped beyond all hope that this was the moment she was going to wake up from this horrible nightmare. She carefully opened her eyes. And the nightmare callously continued. She looked at the single bouquet flowers that sat on the center of Dick's coffin. She wondered if Dick was still holding the photo she had placed in his hand before the funeral service. It had been her favorite and most cherished picture of Dick. A photo of him cradling a newborn Dickie, their faces reflecting in one another's eyes. A photo that seemed to capture Dick's tenderness, his joy, his playfulness, and his unparalleled capacity for love.

Reluctantly Brenda became aware that Monsignor Kenney had finished. She felt numb and confused. How could this be it? How could this be all there was? Why now did she feel more alone and more empty than ever before? She had thought if she could make it through this, that somehow she would be able to make it through anything. But much to her horror, she found herself weaker, sadder and more afraid than ever before. She wondered how in the world she was going to be able to carry on now that she knew how it ended.

27) A Call to Peace

Richard Genest Jr. will be 18 months old on Christmas Day. There may be presents under the tree. But there will be no father to help him open them. Richard Genest Sr. is dead. He died in Vietnam. He and 4 other Manchester, New Hampshire boys were blown apart by a land mine nine days before they were expected home. There was no military funeral for Army Specialist 5 Richard Genest — no honor guard, no flag-draped casket, no bugles blown. His 21-year-old wife, dignified but determined, refused. She would have no part of these, for they were hateful to her Richard . . . as hateful as the war in which he found himself. Nor were there flowers at his Catholic Mass. Brenda Genest asked that contributions be sent instead to Another Mother for Peace. These would be a fitting tribute to a man who was no soldier at heart. These are her words in her letter to us: "He was the most honest, generous, patient, and loving person I've ever known . . . or feel I will ever know."
— From *Another Mother for Peace* Newsletter, December 1969

The hours and days following the funeral seemed surreal to Brenda and her family. When they went home their front yard was filled with reporters and cameras. When they went in the house and turned on the television they were on every channel. Their phone constantly rang and always on the other end was someone who wanted a quote or an interview. It seemed as though the whole world was peering at them through a towering magnifying glass.

The backlash that followed Dick's funeral was swift and severe, especially in Manchester. People from all walks of life found themselves horrified by Brenda's actions. They could not believe that such a person existed. It was inconceivable that she had had the nerve to dishonor a "war hero." The majority of Manchester's citizens thought Brenda was nothing short of despicable. People boycotted Genest Bakery and Cavanaugh Bros. Motors. Publicly she was called hippie, beatnik, traitor, and commie. One can only imagine what was said privately. Her brothers and sisters were taunted at school. When she walked down the street people would jeer at her and say things like, "You deserve a good kick in the ass," or "How dare you?" Some people demanded that she be put in jail and tried for treason. On Moratorium Day, just six weeks after Dick's death, the largest newspaper in New Hampshire, the Manchester Union Leader, posted a sixty foot banner (obviously "inspired" by Brenda's actions) that read *AMERICA* love it or leave it! VICTORY IN VIETNAM. The also ran the following headline that surely was directed toward Brenda and anyone that supported the end of the war, "ATTENTION all peace-marchers, hippies, yippies, beatniks, peaceniks, yellow-bellies, traitors, commies, and their agents and dupes: help keep our city clean just by staying out of it. Signed, The Editors."

Although they were not as vocal, there were those who praised her. Her actions gave many people the courage to speak out against the war that was taking a hefty toll on the soul of the country. Everyday she received letters from all over the country from people expressing their sympathy and commending her courage. Countless poems and tributes were written about the five men from Manchester, but especially about Dick.

There was one young Canadian man, Peter Franklin, who in front of the U.S. Embassy in Ottawa, Canada, marched and fasted while carrying a cardboard sign that on one side had a Life magazine photo of a bloodied American G.I. lying dead on a cot with lines from the then outdated story that had accompanied the photo that said, "So far, 130 Americans have been killed in the Vietnam war." On the other side of the handmade picket, Peter wrote in red pen, "I am speaking out against the death of a fellow man, a peaceful man who only wanted to live." (When Brenda received a letter from Peter telling her what he intended to do in memory of Dick, Brenda wrote him stating, "If only I had the courage to do things before, maybe this never would have happened . . . At any rate, I'll never be afraid to act on or stand by my convictions again.")

Editorials in support of Brenda appeared in newspapers from coast to coast. Father Kenney had been pressured from many in his parish and left St. Catherine's Church because of his support of Brenda. Tom Cavanaugh recalls, "When the Vietnam War came on and Brenda started to fight it, there was a big friction in the parish. The parishioners were split about fifty-fifty. The bishop called and told him he had to stop supporting Brenda and the others who were causing a stir about the war. Well, Father Kenney told the bishop he was not going to stop, because he was doing what he felt was right. So the bishop asked him what he should do and Father Kenney said he would give him his resignation.

"And he resigned. He moved from a beautiful home right outside the church in the most affluent neighborhood where he had not a worry, to a one-room apartment in the toughest, poorest part of town. He gave up everything for what he believed was right. It took an awful lot for him to stand up like that especially in this town."

The outpouring of attention Brenda received — positive and negative — propelled her to devote herself to do whatever she could to help end the war. In one of the many interviews she gave after Dick's death she said, "I am not a fanatic, nor a citizen who is disloyal to her country. But I do not believe in blind obedience to what is wrong and I think this war is wrong." She became very vocal in her support for the organization, Another Mother for Peace. She went to, and spoke at, peace marches and rallies in Washington, D.C., San Francisco, Chicago, and Manchester. Every where she went she wore a silver chain that had a small medal that read, "War is not healthy for children and other living things." She made herself and all aspects of her life open and available to the press.

Feature stories and interviews of her appeared in newspapers and on television shows across the country. In November of 1969, her story came to be known internationally when the BBC broadcast a one hour documentary in which she was the main focus. Robert MacNeil, the well-known and highly respected reporter, who interviewed Brenda for the program, remembers Brenda and her story in his book, *The Right Place at the Right Time,* like this: "In the end her story became the framework on which we hung all other people. Journalistically, it was a perfect story. It needed no hyping. Often a reporter is tempted to 'improve' the details of a story; to make quotes crisper, to bend the facts a little to make them 'better.' Brenda's story never lead us into that temptation because as it unfolded, it was a perfect and terrible parable for what the war was doing to the American people."

Robert MacNeil did all he could to make Brenda feel comfortable during the filming of the documentary. In fact Brenda has said, "Out of all the interviews I did and all the reporters I talked to, he (Robert MacNeil) was the only who did what he said he was going do. He was the only one who was totally honest with me. He was the only one who really cared about how I felt, the only who cared about how every time I talked about it, it was like reliving it, the only one who understood how truly hard it was for me to be twenty-one with a dead husband, an eighteen-month-old son and all this attention focused on me." However, not even Robert MacNeil could make Brenda feel comfortable with all the attention that was indiscriminately laced with either adoration and abomination.

Had Brenda done what she thought would bring her comfort, had she followed her instinct and feelings, she would have locked herself in her room, pulled the shades, crawled into bed pulled the covers over her head, squeezed her pillow, and screamed and cried until Dick came back to her. That was what she really wanted to do, but she knew that was not only impossible, but also selfish and senseless. Dick's death had been senseless and Brenda felt that many politicians as well as the government's chronic selfishness was keeping America in the war. She felt any sort of silence or complacency would only contribute to the continuation the war. She felt that if somehow, some way, by telling Dick's story she could save just one man, then maybe, just maybe, Dick would not have died for nothing.

Obviously, no matter what Brenda did there were many days she was left to wonder what purpose Dick's death could have possibly served. There was the day she walked into the living room at her parents house and there on the television were images of the 197th arriving home from Vietnam. She stood in front of the television paralyzed, unable to even blink, as the men were greeted by their wives and families. Her mind became numb as she watched everyone hugging, kissing, and crying tears of joy. She fell to her knees and touched the screen. She wondered if they had any idea how lucky they were. She cried to God, "Why?"

Jill remembers, "I remember seeing on the t.v. the plane landing. Then I remember seeing all those guys getting off the plane and hugging their families. And everyone there was showing their joy because they were so happy to see each other again. It was the hardest thing I ever watched in my life. It was so heart wrenching. How could it be so cruel?"

There was the day when an insurance agent Brenda had

never seen or spoken to came unannounced to her parents' house. He asked if he could speak to her privately. Brenda took him into the kitchen and cautiously sat down across the table from him. As he took his hat off she wondered what could he possibly want from her. Without making any eye contact he said, "Honey, I am sorry but you did not pay the premium on Richard's life insurance this past year so we can't pay you." Brenda's head felt like it was going to explode. What was he talking about? She had not called the insurance company or tried to make a claim. She stared at the nondescript man who had his eyes firmly focused on the table. "Who sent you here?" she demanded. "Who called you? Why are you telling me this? Do you think I want your money? I don't want your fucking money. I want my husband. Can you give me my husband back?" The man continued to stare at the table as he stood up. He had been prepared for her to be upset — but not like this. Brenda stood up, stepped toward him and looked intently at him with sheer anger and amazement. "Is this why you came here? To tell me I wasn't getting any money? GET OUT, GET OUT OF HERE RIGHT NOW. How dare you come here and tell me I am not getting any money. I DO NOT WANT MONEY! Money won't bring Dick back!" Brenda sobbed as Tom came into the kitchen and without a word escorted the man out. "I want my husband. The only thing I want is Dick."

There were days when Brenda would go to the mausoleum and just sit on the stone bench in front of the wall where Dick was entombed, waiting for a sign, waiting for something, anything that might indicate that Dick had kept the promise he made to come back to her if he was killed. Nancy Lou recalls how hard it was for her family to watch Brenda heading off for the cemetery with the hope in her heart only to return disappointed and confused. "It was just so sad. She just could not believe that Dick had not contacted her yet. I just think that Dick was just too good of a person to come back to her. I mean he knew if he came back to her in anyway she would never be able to move on with her life. If she thought in anyway he was there she would never, ever leave him."

And then there were the days when she would look at her son and all at once feel grateful, angry, happy, sad, hopeful, and discouraged. At any given moment she could look at Dickie and be filled with purpose and solace while in the same moment she could look at him and feel her heart shattering. The thought of Dickie never knowing his father was a glaring gash on her soul. At least she had known Dick. At least she had memories of him. At least she knew what an incredible father he would have been. At least, she KNEW how much Dick loved Dickie. Her soul ached for what her son had lost — for the love he would never know. She could not help but wonder why the innocents always had the most to lose in war.

Dickie was unquestionably, the single most important part of Brenda's life. She naturally felt bonded and dedicated to her son. However, she also felt an extraordinary connection to her child. Not only was he the only tangible piece of Dick that existed, but more importantly, he and Brenda had experienced and shared in so much in the eighteen months since he had entered the world: everything from his first breath, his first smile, his first words, his first steps, his first bath, his first swim, her first day as a widow, her first day as a single mother, and on and on. Not purposely, but undeniably, equally responsible for each other's life.

Brenda had given Dickie life and Dickie kept Brenda alive. Forever connected to one another by many things, but none stronger, than their undying love of a dead man.

28) Eternal Love

*"I truly believe that we made an error not of values
and intentions but of judgments and capabilities."*
Robert McNamara — 1995

*"His regret cannot be huge enough to balance the books for our
dead soldiers. The ghosts of those unlived lives circle close around
Mr. McNamara. Surely he must in every quiet and prosperous
moment hear the ceaseless whispers of those poor boys in the
infantry, dying in the tall grass, platoon by platoon, for no purpose. What he took from them cannot be repaid by prime-time
apology and stale tears three decades late."*
New York Times — editorial 1995

February 25, 1999 — 10:00 p.m.-4:00 a.m.

My Dearest Dick,
How I have missed you these past 30 years! I still cry so much when I think of you. I am sobbing as I write this. How can I still hurt so much from losing you so long ago . . . so many lifetimes ago?!

When Jami asked me to write this letter to you I could not answer her because I was trying to hold back years of tears. I was afraid if I told her yes that once I started to write to you I would start crying and never be able to stop.

I have been to a few therapists since you left me. They told me I needed to mourn to be able to get over you. They said I needed to cry. What they don't understand is that I could cry every moment of every day since you died and I still would not get over you. The pain in my heart will always be there as long as I am alive.

One of the most surprising things to me when you died was how my love for you only became stronger. I remember taking our marriage vows, "To love, honor and obey until death do you part," and I guess I always thought that when someone passed on, the love would also. But now I know that is NOT AT ALL the way that it is. It is very difficult to go through life when you are in love with a dead man. It makes it extremely difficult to have a loving relationship with some one else.

I live in paradise now, the island of St. Croix in the Virgin Islands. I have had a wonderful life. I think of you every day. Today as I was driving to town on the "highway" that hugs the Caribbean Sea, I just kept looking out at that beautiful turquoise water and all I could think of was how much you would have liked it here. I remember when we were dating and you told me about the trip you took to Jamaica with your family and how much you had loved it there. I remember that whenever you spoke of Jamaica I could feel the love you had for the culture in every word you spoke. I could feel the fondness and warmth you felt for the Jamaican people coming right from your heart. Things here are very similar to the way you described Jamaica to me: the people are warm and loving, the climate is perfect and the sun is always shining — which of course, makes me think of you because I always loved how you called me, "Sunshine." Oh how I wish you could spend just one day here with me.

I often think of the dichotomy of you having suffered the last year of your life on earth in hell and me now living out the rest of my life on this heavenly island. Through the years I have reread some of your letters from Vietnam. Dick, I cherished those letters when you were alive and there are not words to describe what they meant to me after you died. I kept them in their own chest, organized by the dates I received them and whenever I could find the strength (which was not very often) I would read some of them and EVERY TIME it just breaks my heart into little pieces — especially from the prospective of my life now.

I am now fifty years old. In addition to Dickie, I have two extremely precious sons: Sean and Chris. All three boys have been everything to me. They have made my world and life so precious. They are my whole life. I would do anything for them. But there is no way on this earth I would ever allow them to fight in a war. After carrying them in my body for nine months and feeding them from my breast, I feel that they are a part of me. I would do anything to keep them from harm.

I felt like I tried everything to keep you from harm, but nothing I did worked. I was young and inexperienced and no support, but I just can't help but constantly think there was something more I could have done to save you.

That year you were in Vietnam, I worried constantly. Every second, of every minute, of everyday and night, I worried about you being killed. And then, FINALLY at long last, you were on your way home and I was worry free. Right before I found out, I had picked up and packed some clothes for you so when I picked you up at the airport you could get out of your uniform and into your regular clothes — just like you said you wanted to. Charlotte and I had picked up Dickie from your parents house, and when we got to my parents, house I remember looking at your clothes as I got Dickie out of the car, and telling him that we had made it — that his daddy was going to be home in a few days. Charlotte and I were laughing about something as we walked into my parents house and the next thing I know my baby brother says, "Why are you laughing? Dick's dead." At first

I thought he was just being a brat and I lightheartedly said, "Jimmy, he's coming home in a couple days." I turned to walk away and then he started crying and said, "DICK'S DEAD!" I was holding our son and I felt like I was going to faint so I screamed for Charlotte to take Dickie. I grabbed Jimmy and started screaming at him to never say that, to never say anything like that. And then I just could not stand up. I had to sit down. I never in my life felt I was going to faint until that moment.

Even though it was just a few days, it seemed like an eternity from the time I found out, until they finally brought you and the four others home to us. They brought your body to the Manchester Airport. The same airport where I would pick you up when I was pregnant with Dickie when you would come home from Fort Bragg on weekends.

As I stood there holding Dickie I could not believe instead of running to greet you, instead of sprinting to hold you, I was waiting for them to bring you to me in a coffin. All five coffins were draped with the American flag. All sorts of politicians were present. All of them there for the free publicity, all of them feigning sympathy. They had NO IDEA of the tortuous pain we felt. After all the bull shit at the airport they brought your coffin to the funeral home.

Dick, they sent a military delegation to the funeral home to carry your coffin!!! So when I got to the funeral home I asked the five young boys if any of them knew you when you were alive. They all said no. It was Labor Day weekend — a time to enjoy life — not mourn it. I looked at those five young men and asked them where they would rather be: enjoying the holiday weekend with their family and friends or carrying an unknown person's coffin? They all looked down at the floor and then I told them to leave. Your friends and relatives carried you to your resting place.

Dick, when I went into the room where your coffin was I almost collapsed. If I had not been holding our son I'm sure I would have. Your coffin was closed and the flag was still on it. I just could not believe what I was seeing, so I had them take the flag off. Then I asked them to open the casket. When they did open it you were in the uniform you wanted to burn. Your hair was slicked back with grease and you were enclosed in glass!! I told them I wanted the glass taken off. They said that because of foreign Vietnamese diseases, it was impossible to take off. I told him he could take it off or I would. Somehow that glass came off. Then I had you dressed in your favorite suit and your hair fixed the right way. I put my favorite picture of you holding Dickie in with you. I also put in a sunflower as a symbol of our love of life, our love of nature and our love of each other. Today the fragrance that I wear is called "Sunflower."

Dick, we had so little time together on this earth. However our time together was so full of the entire universe. Oh how we climbed mountains and then rolled back down in the grass; how we would sit in mountain huts with a fire going and fantasize it was our home; how we would sit on the rocks at night on the coast of Maine and talk for hours as the surf crashed around us; how we walked miles through blizzards warmed solely by our love for each other; how we would eat steamed clams by the bushel on the dock in York Harbor; how we'd make love on the beach at night in a sleeping bag; how we played in the surf from Maine to Mexico to Hawaii; how we skied under bright blue skies and would lie in the snow and name the white puffy clouds floating by; how we'd party by your pool and throw our champagne glasses in the pool and be amazed the how the glasses stood upright in the bottom of the pool; how we loved the sun and the sea and the sky and the snow; how we loved just being alive and living life to the fullest; how we loved each other for each other and nothing more. The chemistry between us was so powerful.

I could not eat for months after you died. It was like I was in a daze for the first year after you died. I felt like I wasn't even part of my own body — like I was watching someone who looked like me going through the motions of each day. One month after your funeral I moved out of my parents house and into my own apartment. The nicest apartment I could afford was right next to the funeral home where we had your wake. The windows in the apartment overlooked the last place that I held you, touched you, kissed you and shed my tears on your stiff lifeless body. The only thing that kept me going was our beautiful, wonderful son. If it were not for him, I think I would have died also. Actually I know I would have died — he kept me alive when you died. I knew that no matter how terrible I felt, that I had to go on for him.

In the middle of writing this book I found the last five letters I wrote to you that came back to me unopened after you died. It was just too painful for me to open them, even thirty years later. I sent them to Jami and she used them in the book. I still have not been able to look at them. I can only read what is in the book. I just don't have the strength to read them in my own handwriting.

One thing that really shocked me when I did read them in the book is that I had blocked out the accident Dickie had the day you died. I was in the basement of my parents house washing the clothes I was going to bring when I picked you up and Dickie was playing by the shower that was down there and he tripped and fell on his face. He must have slipped and his smacked his mouth against the metal edge. Oh Dick, I was so terrified because his little mouth was full of blood and there was blood everywhere. I totally panicked because I was all alone and I could not stop the bleeding and poor Dickie was screaming bloody murder. I called my father, hysterical, and he rushed home to help me. As I read the last letter I wrote you describing what happened, I realized that he was hurt at the same time you were killed!!! How bizarre . . . your very last sign to me.

My days were filled with Dickie. He was fifteen months old

when you died. Nothing hurt me more than knowing what he lost by never getting to know you. Even though I knew in my heart that I would never be able to fill the hole that was left in his heart and soul by your death, I tried to fill every day of his life with as much joy and fun as possible. I had a seat put on the back of my bike and we did a lot of biking. In the winter we skied and went hiking and sledding. He was such an active child! He would just was go, go, go, nonstop. He had a little Tyke-Bike that he zoomed around EVERYWHERE on. He loved to play with matchbox cars. He would spend hours lining them up preciously.

It hurts so much that you never got to see him. You would be so proud. He has so many of your mannerisms — it's truly uncanny. I always had thought that mannerisms were learned, but now I know, they are inherited. He really is a reflection of the two of us. His eyes are yours except for the color — which is the same as mine. His smile is yours — charming, warm and inviting. His nose is a combination of us both. His body is yours — the same height AND weight. His soul is kind, fair, compassionate, and he has your charisma.

Unfortunately, I was never able to talk to him about you without crying. I just could not talk about you to him without my heart just shattering into little pieces. He knows so little about you because he never wanted to upset me or see me cry and I just could not find the strength to talk to him about what he lost when you died. I am not the only one though. NO ONE in my family or yours can talk about you without crying — even now — thirty years after you left us.

I feel so bad there is so much Dickie doesn't know because I couldn't talk about it. But since we started to write this book not only has Dickie learned things about you, but also most everyone has been able to talk about you. Yes, everyone still cries a lot but it is so good to talk at long last. Because I never could talk to Dickie about you, with this book he has begun to learn some things. For example, even though he grew up just a couple miles from Manchester, he never knew that the Amoskeag Bridge in Manchester was dedicated in your honor and the others who died. It wasn't until last year that Dickie knew that there was an amazing painting of a white cross with your, Roger, Giaetan, Richard, and Guy's full names on it. The cross is bathed in brilliant sunlight that has broken through dark clouds. At the foot of the cross are five flag-draped caskets. It's called "Light Shining Out of Darkness." A man from Manchester named Oscar Durand painted it in your honor just six weeks after you died. I even went to the first viewing of it in Manchester and I have thought about you and it every time I drove by the Manchester National Guard Armory. But, it was only recently, I was able to tell Dickie about it. Those examples are just the tip of the iceberg. Almost everyday Dickie is learning something about you. I mean, he had no idea, he was the same height and weight as you, until we were able to obtain your military records and he read them. He had always thought you were bigger than him.

Oh Dick, how I miss you as I sit here and cry as I write this. I have dreamed of you so many times and every time I do I don't want to wake up. There are two recurrent dreams I have had over the years. One is, you come home and you are living with your parents and you will not talk to me. I call and call but you will not take my calls. I tell your parents if I could just see you and talk to you everything would be okay but no matter what I do I can't get to you. I know you are there but I just can't get to you. The other dream is you ring the doorbell at the house I lived in for twenty years and when I answer the door you just stand there. You don't talk to me or anything, and then you just disappear.

I can hardly bear to think about the last time we were together. It took me two years to talk to Jami about it and even then it destroyed me for days. I am haunted by the fact that instead of enjoying each other and our time together, I should have bought you a wig and a dress and put you on a plane to Canada or somewhere where you would have been safe.

My charm bracelet that you gave me is one of my most treasured possessions, because it came from you. I put our wedding rings on it. But, Dick I am convinced, that the black coral pineapple that you gave me is a bad luck piece. I am convinced that taking black corral from an island is extremely bad luck. I felt this so strongly when you died. Later on, I was with various friends on trips or vacations and they would buy black corral and I would try so hard to talk them out of it. Well, every single one had something real bad happen to them within a year. Two had close relatives die, one went to prison and one was critically hurt. Oh how I wish you I had not taken that charm off the island.

Okay, I am going to tell you about my life since you left. At the end of October in 1969 I went on out to dinner with Jack Doherty. I had known him from my freshman year at U.N.H. We had a few friends in common and I had set him up with a girlfriend of mine back when I was at U.N.H. Anyway, we went to a quaint Italian restaurant in the north end of Boston where they served their own wine in old-fashioned bottles down in the basement. It was a lovely dinner. We headed back to Manchester after dinner and I cried the entire sixty miles from Boston to Manchester. I cried over losing you. I cried because I was not having dinner with you. I cried for Dickie. I just cried and cried. But what was amazing about Jack was that nothing seemed to bother him. He just let me cry and talk about you.

That winter he invited me to his ski house in Stowe, Vermont, for a weekend. I told him I would only go if I could bring my son. It was fine by him — he was the oldest of six children, so he was used to little ones. When he arrived to pick me up the entire living room of my apartment was filled with Dickie's paraphernalia — his full size playpen, his car seat, his stroller, a back pack, his Tyke Bike, all kinds of his toys, his suitcase. Again Jack did not blink an eye. He just started grabbing things and proceeded to load everything into the truck he had brought.

We had a great weekend. We skied from the top of Mount Mansfield, each of us taking turns with Dickie in his baby pack on our backs. We went cross-country skiing at the Trapp Family Lodge with Dickie on our backs. Everywhere we went and everything we did we had Dickie with us. Jack was really wonderful to both Dickie and me. We started to see each other after that trip on a regular basis. Jack would come by my apartment and take us out to lunch or he would come by and take Dickie out to breakfast in the mornings, so I could sleep in. You know how I liked to sleep in!

So, Dickie and I lived in the apartment next to the funeral home until the end of May 1970. The first of June I rented a house next to the beach in Ogunquit, Maine with three girlfriends. Oh what a ball we and that summer!! Dickie spent everyday on the beach and of course everybody loved him and was so protective of him. On his second birthday he and I woke up to "Today is Your Birthday," by the Beatles blasting out of the radio. There was a fire ablaze in the stone fireplace in our beautiful seaside cottage — what a day! What a summer!

Now, as the summer ended I had to think of what I was going to do with my life. I decided to go back to school at U.N.H. I rented an apartment in Dover that was about seven miles from school. In those days single motherhood and day care were rare. Dickie was two and I was worried about leaving him with anyone. I constantly worried about him. I did not realize until years later how much I obsessed and worried about him and Sean and Chris. You see Dick, the day you died was the first day in over a year that I did not worry myself sick about you. It was the first day I felt safe and look what happened!!

After that I was terrified to ever feel anything but worried about everything I loved because the minute I had stopped worrying about you — you died. It really sucks to go through life always thinking the worst is going to happen and that if you don't think that way, something really bad WILL happen. It was VERY hard for me to get over that. I have not completely, but I am getting better.

Anyway I found a wonderful woman my age, whose husband was a student, to take care of Dickie while I was in my classes. She even had a little girl Dickie's age. I took an extra course each semester and went to summer school so I could graduate a semester early.

When Dickie was three I had to find different day care for him. So I found a place that was about seven miles from U.N.H. in the other direction from our house. So, everyday I drove from Dover to Durham (7 miles) to Newmarket (7 miles) to Durham (7 miles) to Dover (7 miles). Being so busy kept my mind and body occupied, but at times it was so difficult to get Dickie ready, to do my homework, to give Dickie the love and attention he deserved, and had become used to, to remember all of Dickie's things as well as all my school things, and the all the driving really made me nervous.

There was this one time that Dickie got really sick and was in the hospital with pneumonia. It was finals week and in one of my classes my professor had said if anyone was late for, or missed the final, they would, no matter how well they had done previously, fail the course. I had spent most of the night before with Dickie at the hospital and went back first thing in the morning to see him again. Anyway, I was running late and a dog ran out in front of my car. I ran right over him in my little car and he got stuck underneath. I had to get out and pull the dog out. He ran away and seemed okay, but it shook me up even more than I already was.

Of course, now I was really late and I was speeding through town and I got pulled over. Well I was totally hysterical by the time the officer came up to the window. He looked at me and I started to cry even harder. He was not really fazed by it and rather facetiously he asked me what was wrong. I looked at him and yelled, "My husband was killed in Vietnam, my son is in the hospital with pneumonia, I just ran over some poor dog and if I am late for class I am going to fail my mid-term and now you are going to write me a ticket." I was really sobbing and he just looked at me funny, started to slowly back away from me like he was scared of me or something and said, "Uh just be careful." Then he just about ran back to his car.

Obviously, I did not get a ticket. I ended up getting to class on time. Dickie got much better and was able to come home not too long after that. Days like that were so hard without you but, the weird thing is, the hardest days of all, were the ones that were fun. Every thing I did that was fun or any time Dickie would laugh or anything like that, I would think of you and feel so sad that you were not there with us. Words could never express how much I miss you.

Okay back to my life. I graduated from U.N.H. in January of 1973. By that time Jack and I had been seeing each other three years. We decided to move to Manchester where he worked. That April we took a trip to St. John in the U.S. Virgin Islands. We stayed in a national park campground and I had never seen a more beautiful place on earth. Nothing — not Hawaii, not Mexico, not California, not Florida, nothing compared. The clear emerald water, the pure blue sky, the green lush jungle, the colorful fish, the wild donkeys, the aroma of the rain forest, everything about it was incredible. So rich, yet so simple, and pure. I did not want to leave. I wanted to stay there, settle there. I knew we would never get rich there, but we would always be happy. We did not stay. We went back to civilization as scheduled, but I knew I was going to go back there one day to live.

When we returned we decided to buy a house. Dickie was

going to be 5 that June and I wanted him to be able to be settled into one school system. Once he started school I did not want to move him. So, we looked and looked all around the suburbs of Manchester and nothing really got me excited. Finally I saw an ad for an antique farmhouse in the North End of Manchester. I called the realtor and went and looked at it. Again it just did not do it for me, but the realtor told me about an antique cape in Bedford. Well, I fell in love with it immediately. The moment we drove up to it I knew it was the one. It just caught my soul. It had been built in the 1780's and needed lots of T.L.C. but we purchased it immediately. After we purchased the house we found out that my great uncle, Paul Cavanaugh and his family, had lived there until he was killed in a car crash in 1922. It was kind of eerie and comforting at the same time.

The house was in the center of Bedford which was (and is) a quaint, pastoral suburb of Manchester. There were cows grazing across the street from us. There was a church on the hill across the street, whose bells peacefully chimed every hour. There was a general store just a short walk down the road. The post office and library were right across the field from the cows and the church. In short, it was the perfect, picturesque New England village.

Dickie started school that fall in Bedford and Jack and I literally tore the house apart and rebuilt it from the inside out. We planted a huge garden in the back and grew all our vegetables for the winter. We got a wonderful German Sheppard named Willie who was so kind to and protective of Dickie. (He used to walk Dickie to his bus stop and then always be there to meet Dickie and walk him home in the afternoon.) One thing I did not want, was for Dickie to be an only child, so I want off the birth control pill and conceived my second son, Sean, the spring of 1974.

I was very leery of marriage — after I lost you I thought I

never could or would marry again. But Jack made me realize that it would be the best thing for us and our children. On June 1, 1974, Jack and I were quietly married, accompanied by just my parents and Dickie, in the old church in York Village, Maine.

On December 17, 1974, Sean was born. He was a beautiful strawberry-blonde baby with my brown eyes. He was such a precious doll then and now. I am so proud of my sons. They are the most important and best thing in my life. When Sean started school I began teaching at the local school. It was the perfect job — just the mornings — so I could be home with my children in the afternoon.

In January of 1976 my mother called crying, from St. Croix. She said, "You won't believe what your father has done! He bought a condo for us! You have to come and see it right now!"

I said, "Mom, we can't. We have jobs, kids, pets and a house to take care of."

She said, "Brenda you MUST come down and be with us and see what your father has done for us!"

So, we went to St. Croix, and I, of course, fell in love with the Virgin Islands all over again. Consequently, every year we went to St. Croix for a few weeks each winter. Jack could not always take the time off from work, however, I felt I needed to go with my boys' no matter what. I felt we all needed (particularly me) and could use a break from those cold, gray New England winters and the warm weather and sunshine of St. Croix was the perfect solution.

I spent the summers with my boys, my parents, my siblings, my nieces and nephews at the beach house that you too loved so much. It was always so much fun being with my family. I know you understand because you loved it so much too. I remember how much fun we had at the beach — how you would play baseball with Jimmy or chase Nancy Lou and Mike around while I would lie on the sand, working on my tan and waiting for my turn to play with you. I always thought of you as I filled my days playing with Dickie and Sean on the beach.

At the end of 1977 Jack and I decided to have another child. I went off the pill again and Chris was conceived while we were vacationing in St. Croix. We named him Christian after the town of Christeansted — one of the two towns on the island. It was a difficult pregnancy. When I was five months pregnant I began to hemorrhage after a night of dancing. I awoke in the wee hours of the morning in a pool of blood. Jack rushed me to the hospital (60 miles away). I spent a few days in the hospital until the bleeding stopped. They said I could go home ONLY if I stayed OFF my feet the rest of the pregnancy! I felt fine, so the next four months of not being allowed to move around much was tortuous. I read a lot and spent a lot of time sitting and putting our vegetables up for the winter.

On November 4, 1978 Christian came into our lives. He took his time but again I was blessed with a precious and gorgeous baby boy. How incredibly fortunate I felt to have such wonderful, healthy and perfect sons.

With three sons, our little farmhouse seemed very small, so we bought five acres about a mile from our house. We built a post-and-beam brick Cape in an attempt to retain the feeling that our first house had. Our new home was a thousand square feet!(!!) with a huge brick fire place in the kitchen which was the heart of our home. Because the house was so big I was able to fill it with lots of Uncle Harrison's antiques. Over the years we added a screened porch and built-in swimming pool. We played lots of ball games in the pool and entertained a lot. Every one of the kids' friends always wanted to come to our house it seemed. The house was always filled with kids, dogs and cats. Our home had a lot of life.

We bought a condo in North Conway. The great thing about North Conway is it is a four-season resort and so we spent a lot of time there — playing golf, tennis, skiing, biking, hiking, canoeing, etc. During Christmas vacations Jill and her husband Dave would come up with their two sons (Davis who is the same age as Chris and Dana who is two years younger) during Christmas vacation and we would have MANY good times and laughs. I had so much fun doing things with my three boys. Jack had to work a lot, so on Friday afternoons I would pick up the boys from school and head straight to North Conway with them. Jack would come up whenever he could, but it seemed like me and the boys spent a lot of time just the four of us.

In 1989 we bought a condo close to my parents place in St. Croix and I was in love with the island. My boys were getting older (Dickie was finishing college, Sean was going in high school and Chris was really involved in school sports) and had tired of doing things with their "old" mother. Jack was still working very hard and I was at a point that I wanted him and I to spend more time together — our children were not so dependent on us anymore, we had achieved a financially comfortable life style and I really wanted him to relax and love the island like I did. I really felt like we were drifting apart and I wanted to connect with him. So I asked him to come and spend a week with me at our new condo for my 40th birthday. He was unable to come down and it just devastated me.

Really, I should not have let that hurt me so much. I mean when I first met Jack I asked him how much vacation time he had and he said the company he worked for (his father had owned it, and eventually Jack took it over and really made it grow and made very successful) did not have vacation time. So, it should not have been a surprise or hurtful to me that work was so important to him. It's just that after the relationship you and I had, Dick — spending every spare minute together — I was unable to accept anything else. I could not help but compare our love and life together with the one I was living. And even though I knew it was not fair to do so, I could not help but think of you and our love.

We tried to make our marriage work for another seven years. We went to counseling. In fact the last time we went to the therapist I left the office crying — I knew from that session that our marriage was over (although we stayed together another three years) and I cried all that night. The next morning of course I looked like hell and it was obvious I had been crying. Poor Dickie had just come home from college for the summer and he had brought a girl with him and she had spent the night. Well Dickie thought I had been crying because of him — because he had brought this girl home with him. Oh Dick, he is like you in so many ways; he is so sensitive and caring and fun-loving and EVERYONE who meets him can not help but like him. He just makes people feel at ease. He is athletic, independent and self-sufficient. But above all he has such a warm and caring way about him. He is just such a kind and gentle soul —just like you were. Dick, you would be so proud of him. I know that I am and I know Jack is too. Jack was an amazing and wonderful father to Dickie. He was so kind and loving to him and they still are very close. They both appreciate one another in way I'm sure few people could ever understand.

Unfortunately in 1996 I filed for divorce from Jack after I was diagnosed with melanoma. After I lost you, I realized how short life really is and I had tried to make the most of every minute. And then, suddenly, one morning I woke up and I was 46 years old, my boys were grown, my husband had no plans of slowing down from work or any intention of retiring anytime soon and a deadly disease had taken up residency within me. I decided it was time for both Jack and I to get on with our separate lives. It was the most difficult thing that I ever consciously chose to do. I had to own up to the fact that I had never given Jack the love he deserved. After you died I had nothing left to give anyone. Even as I write this I know that I loved him but I am just not capable of showing it. I wish I could be more warm and loving, but I am afraid that part of me died with you.

Amazingly Jack and I lived together through the whole divorce proceedings. We would go to court during the day and then come home and have dinner together. Dickie came out (he lives in California now) to help me get through it and it is really of no surprise that he was the one who was able to do what neither Jack or me or our attorneys could do — devise a settlement that both Jack and I could live with. In the mornings Dickie would ride to court with me and then in the afternoon he would ride back to the house with Jack. As I have said before he is just the most fair, honest, loving and likable person you could ever meet. Nancy Lou says she sees you whenever she sees Dickie.

So here I am in the tropics. My parents are close by in the condo they bought 25 years ago. My father dissolved the dealership in 1992. He and my mother spend the winter in St. Croix and the summer at the beach house you so loved. I can no longer tolerate sitting in the sun like I used to for hours because of the melanoma. Fortunately I had caught it early. It had not spread. My dermatologist removed the area skin around the original biopsy. I am free of it now but I am very careful around the sun. I play lots of tennis and golf and, of course, I still love to swim in the sea. I work part-time in a store in town. My parents are here and I do things with them every day. I have learned to sail and I have my captains license for up to a 50-ton vessel. I miss my boys terribly but they are all doing well.

My brother Tommy is battling cancer — non Hodgkin's lymphoma and is in the hospital as I write this. He is having massive doses of chemotherapy and is expected to be in the hospital for a month. Tommy has two truly terrific daughters, Brenna, 23 and Catelin, 21. They have been so wonderful to him throughout this illness.

As I said, Jill has two boys and has been happily married for 26 years. She lives in York Beach and sells cars in Portsmouth. She is a great golfer and skier.

Nancy Lou married her childhood sweetheart, Ric, and has two sweet girls — Erica, 7, and Cayleigh, 5.

Mike is living in York Beach and selling cars in Portsmouth as well.

Jimmy has stayed single all these years. I think your death had the most impact on him after me. He has been so supportive and helpful to Tommy throughout his illness too. We all have fabulous times together at the beach house. My parents, myself, my boys and their girlfriends, my brothers, my sisters, my nieces and nephews, we all just have such good times together. We celebrated the 100th anniversary of the beach house being in our family this summer. We are still a very close and supportive family.

Dickie graduated from college in 1991. He moved west to ski and he now is a realtor in Lake Tahoe, California. This past summer he bought his first house. He has been with his girlfriend four years and I just love her. She really adores him and loves him so much. I know I keep saying this but, you would be so proud of Dickie. He has your charisma — he just charms everyone he meets — men and women alike.

Sean is a brew master at a local pub on Lake Winapaeasake. His girlfriend, Steph is finishing her teaching degree. She is such a bright (4.0 average), beautiful and warm girl. I love and adore her.

Chris is a junior at Rollins College in Florida. He plays baseball and golf and is very talented at both. I tease and tell him if he is drafted for the major leagues he will have to take care of his poor old mother.

Your parents sold the house you grew up in and now live in a beautiful part of Florida — New Smyrna Beach. They have a magnificent condo right on the white sand beach. Your father sold the bakery 1977. I am sure it broke his heart not to be turning it over to you. When you died his hope for the future died.

Charlotte and Chick recently celebrated their thirtieth wedding anniversary. They live in Bedford and have two wonderful and loving children. Your nephew, that you never had a chance to meet, Brandon, is 28. He recently moved to California and is working for a yeast company your father owns. Tatum, your niece, you never had a chance to know, is 24. She lives in Arizona working as an early education teacher.

Well, that is how my last thirty years have been. I spend 7 or 8 months here in St. Croix overlooking the Caribbean sea, watching the goats grazing on the hills, the pelicans passing by. Every day I sit in awe of the rainbows, the birds, the blue sky and the sea. I have lots of friends to do things with and I love having my parents close by. I usually travel to New England in June and stay through the summer. I divide most of my time between North Conway and the beach house. Yes, I still eat steamed clams by the sea, but most of the time I am alone.

I am so thankful that I have such a loving, enjoyable family to share my life with. The most important thing I have learned in life is, that family is the most precious, most special and the greatest gift in life. It truly is the most fulfilling and rich part of life. Bearing and raising my children has been the most rewarding and enriching part of my life. NOTHING is more precious to me than my family. I recently came across a quote by Suzanne Somers, which really summarizes my feelings about life: "Life is a beautiful thing and nothing ever stays the same. If you can raise a child who can take part in your life, part of what you have taught him, and run like hell, there is nothing that should bring you more joy. NOTHING!"

I am so sad you are not here to share that joy. You would feel so proud and delighted and joyous about your son.

So Dick that is my life since you left me. My broken and tattered heart never did recover. You were my life, my joy and my whole being when you left me thirty years ago. There are no words to thank you for the gift of our son. He is so much like you and without him I could not have gone on to live this wonderful life I just told you about.

> UNTIL YOU AND I MEET AGAIN, KNOW THAT I HAVE LIVED MY WHOLE LIFE LOVING YOU . . . A DEAD YOUNG MAN . . . A SWEET LAMB WHO WAS LED TO SLAUGHTER . . . I ALWAYS HAVE AND ALWAYS WILL LOVE YOU MY DARLING. FOREVER YOURS
>
> LOVE, Brenda

29) The Bond of Father and Son

May 14, 2000/November 15, 2000

Dear Dad,

It seems odd that this is the first time I have ever written to you as I have spoken and prayed to you so many times throughout my life.

Although I never knew you, I believe that because we are connected as father and son, there is a unique chemistry (pardon the pun) between us.

As I know you are aware, I've had a good amount of close calls in my time. (Car and motorcycle wrecks, ski wrecks and several other ugly and dangerous situations . . . to name a few.) I truly believe the ONLY reason I've made it through these times is due to you saving me and thus as a direct result of your ultimate sacrifice. When I think about it, your death was so unfair. You were so young and had everything going for you. If I think about the politics of Vietnam, I just go out of my mind with anger at our country and the bull shit. I'll leave it at that, as I think you know my thoughts on the entire issue.

I don't know when it was or how old I was when I realized my father was not alive and had been killed in a war. I guess sometime before I was ten years old or so. It's hard to say because that subject is so difficult to understand at a young age.

As I grew older, not many around me spoke of you; as I came to learn later, it was because it pained them so much and maybe they thought it would be painful and hurtful to me to talk about you. But, I wish they had, so I could have had a better understanding of my father. Some of the only times I could get information from out of people was when they were drunk, and then it usually got really emotional.

Mem (as you know I call your mom and dad Mem and Pep), and Mom were the exception when it came to you. Mom was always open to any questions I had about you and she would always share her memories and feelings about you. That women loved you more than possible and the hurt she carries with her to this day is devastating. Just writing this brings tears to my eyes, probably because of the love the three of us have.

Mem and Pep also have lived their lives with a tremendous amount of inner sadness, you can almost see a piece of them missing. Growing up, Mem would bring me to the mausoleum and share your shortened life with me, your son. Unfortunately, you not being around created a void between Mem, Pep and me. I'm not sure why we haven't been able to overcome it.

As I write this, the sun has just come over the ridge and illuminated my desk at my home. This makes me think you are listening, as we only get about an hour of direct sun a day at the house and it is always very special. Due to you creating me, I am a very lucky person today; my life is fulfilling. I live in a great place and am able to ski to my hearts content. I've shacked up with a super chick. Because of Jami, I've gotten to know you better and learn more about you. Basically Jami is a godsend. I couldn't be a luckier guy. I must have received all of your good luck you left behind.

It is amazing how much you impacted people throughout your short-lived life. (And not just family.) Your battalions 20th reunion was probably the most emotional event I've ever attended. Strangers literally walked up to me for hours on end, embraced and cried. Their feelings entered me and made me cry. People you served with, just recognized me as being your son, and the love they transpired was unbelievable.

The only time I've gone to the Wall was amazing as well. (Many friends of mine had been to the Wall and brought me etchings of your name.) After looking for your name with my brother Sean, and not being able to spot it, I went to the thick directory book, randomly opened it up and exactly where my thumb was, was your name. Thanks for saving me time.

Obviously I've missed you a great deal over the years. I was extremely fortunate Mom found such an incredible, strong man with great values in Jack. Of course we had our difficulties, but I believe because of him — and the traits I inherited from you — I've been able to succeed in life. Jack and Mom created a wealthy youth for me and I would be less than honest if I did not say that sometimes, growing up, I wondered if I was better off growing up in the family I was in rather than with you and Mom. I know — what horrible thoughts — but I couldn't help it.

Over the years I realized what an unbelievable life I would have had if you were my dad. Not only would I have been able to call you Dad, but, many life situations would have been encompassing you.

It is unfair that I have been blessed by you because you were killed. It blows me away the tears that I cry when I never even knew you — that says something — but I'm not sure what. Whether it is the void by not being here, sadness for your death, or what — but I miss you and always will and hope that you will always be there and continue to keep tabs on me.

I Love You Dad,

Your son,
Dick

Epilogue

My Darling Dick,

    I used to love writing to you, sharing the happenings of my life when we were apart. I now find it so painful and difficult since you left me. However, I need to update you on my life since my last letter in February of 1999. It has been three years already.

    As I sit here in paradise, I am looking out at the turquoise sea with two, bright white sailboats floating by Buck Island that is just so green and lush right now. Palm trees are swaying in the soft trade winds and they are framed by bright red flowers. Yet, I sit here with tears streaming down my face, thinking of you, and wishing you were here.

    My family, as you know, continues to be my greatest joy in life. My parents are here in St. Croix for the winter. We played golf yesterday morning. It's such a privilege to still have them and enjoy life with them!

    During the summer we still gather at the beach house in Maine that you so loved. We sit on the veranda in old rocking chairs that so many generations have sat in and swap stories of past and present. It is difficult to believe that I am now the elderly generation; part of the generation you and I thought was so old when we would sit and chat before you left for Vietnam. Everyone still loves to spend as much time as possible there. (Just like you always did.) There is just something magical about it. Now the sixth generation is about to embark in this wonderful old house by the sea.

Wondrously, we now have the most beautiful granddaughter, Calli James Genest. She was born October 20, 2001. What an absolute treasure and the GREATEST gift that Dickie and Jami could ever give us. Calli is so beautiful with her gorgeous red hair and sparkling violet eyes. She has your contagious smile . . . you would burst with joy at the sight of her.

Jami gave me the honor of being present at Calli's birth. Calli presented herself "bottoms up" . . . she was breech. Jami was so strong and stoic . . . she had no medication and delivered Calli totally naturally.

I was so proud of Dickie at the birth because when Jami thought she could no longer persevere in the delivery, Dickie grabbed her hand, convinced her that she could do it and gave her the strength and fortitude to PUSH on. I was extremely proud of both of them. Being there was so thrilling . . . to watch Calli emerge into this world at midnight brightened my world profusely; yet it was a bittersweet joy because the hole in my heart aches that you are not here to share in her life and beauty.

Calli is so lucky because she has two parents who absolutely adore her and will always be there for her. Dickie really tickled me a few days after she was born. He was holding Calli and he looked down at her and said, "I going golfing now, I wish I could take you with me today, but you are too little, but next year at this time you won't be too little and you'll get to go with your dad."

Calli looks so much like you and Dickie did as babies. It is just amazing to me the resemblance through two generations. My only regret is that we do not live close by one another. Calli is so precious, I just want to hold and cuddle and kiss her all day. Dickie, Jami and Calli are coming here for a month this winter. My parents can hardly wait to see their first great-grandchild and I can't wait to get my hands on her again. They also plan on coming to Maine this summer and we are just thrilled that we will be able to see Calli grow. I am going to get a little seat put on the back of my bike so I can take her for morning rides to the Nubble Lighthouse like I used to do with Dickie when he was a baby. I can hardly wait to play with her on the beach and just watch her grow!!

This Christmas was one of great happiness for me. I learned my second son, Sean, and his wife, Stephanie, are expecting. Their little treasure is due around June 11th. They live in York, close to the beach house, so these little cousins will be romping on the porch together this summer. Sean and Steph had the most spectacular wedding overlooking the Atlantic at sunset in September 2000. It was picture perfect with the Nubble in the distant background. I am so anxious to hold their little boy who will be Finnigan Gabriel Doherty.

My youngest son, Chris, and his fiancée, Gwen, built a gorgeous house in Florida. Chris injured his ankle playing college baseball and after three surgeries to correct it, he is no longer able to play baseball. So, his lifelong dream and hard work were destroyed. I was so proud of him because instead of bemoaning the loss of his dreams and becoming depressed — he moved on and decided to become a golf teaching pro. His great news to me at Christmas was that he and Gwen became engaged. Chris could not have found a more perfect life partner. It is so thrilling to see my three boys have grown into such wonderful, caring, confident, responsible, young men. It is so hard to fathom that my "babies" are now older than you when you died!!

In my last letter to you I told you that my brother Tommy was diagnosed with non-Hodgkin's lymphoma. After a long battle and a bone marrow transplant, he is now in remission and has never looked better in his life. He is going to be a grandfather . . . and is so thrilled. His daughter Brenna and her husband-to-be Chip are expecting a baby in July. It is going to be so fantastic to have three babies at the beach house this summer for all the family to dote over. Tommy's other daughter, Caitlin, graduated with honors from UNH and lives in Nashua with her wonderful boyfriend Todd.

My sister, Jill, and her husband, David, still live close to the beach house and are doing well and looking great. Their sons, Davis and Dana are now grown men .. they are both over 6 feet 2 inches tall, sandy blonde, funny and handsome. Davis is living and surfing in Hawaii and Dana is going to school in Florida.

My brother, Mike is still selling cars and living with his significant other, Robin who is a flight attendant with American Airlines.

How the world has changed in the past thirty years. On September 11, a most horrific event took place. Terrorists took over American Airlines and United Airlines planes and purposely crashed two of the planes into the World Trade Center towers in New York City and one plane into the Pentagon. The fourth plane was kept from harming anyone on the ground by heroic passengers. Thousands of people were killed. So many lives ruined. Watching the events on TV that morning brought the horror of your death back again. I cried most of that day . . . for those lost and those who survived them. The pain for so many people . . . unimaginable!!! That day has changed the world forever. Now we are at war in Afghanistan. When I watch the news it brings it ALL back to me. Showing troops having Christmas dinner and thinking of your last Christmas. It makes me sad all over again.

I digress, anyway, my sister Nancy Lou and her husband Ric's little girls, Erica and Cayleigh, are quickly growing into wonderful young ladies. I have so much fun with them and get so much joy doing things with them. I had them with me for a week in North Conway this summer. We went horseback riding, kayaking, swung from ropes along the river, went on water slides, rode alpine slides down mountains and went to the top of Mt. Washington. Of course when we were on top of Mt. Washington I thought of you and the time we climbed it. Anyway, Ric was diagnosed with non-Hodgkin's lymphoma this past spring. He is currently in treatment and seems to be doing well. They will be here the same time as Dickie and Jami and will get to see Calli for the first time. The girls are so excited to see the baby.

Your sister Charlotte and her husband Chick have moved to Florida to be near your parents. I think it is of great comfort to your parents to have them so near and to be able to do so many things with them. Your father gave everyone quite a scare in September. Right before the attacks of September 11th he was in Las Vegas with your mother, Charlotte and Chick and he collapsed at a party. Luckily a friend of his, who is a doctor, was at the party and was able to resuscitate him. Because of the attacks on 9/11 they were not able to fly back to Florida and he ended up having to have quintuplet by-pass surgery in Las Vegas. It must have been so hard on your mother. What a blessing that Charlotte and Chick were there to help. Your father is doing much better now, back home and playing golf regularly. Everyone is amazed and relieved by his recovery. I know your parents are thrilled about Calli and are very anxious to see and hold her.

Charlotte and Chick's children — your nephew Brandon and niece Tatum — are doing very well. Brandon married a beautiful blonde California girl, Lisa, in June of 2000. They now live about an hour from Dickie and Brandon is still working for the yeast company. Tatum is back in New Hampshire and married her beau Chris in September. Again, I just can't believe all these "babies" have grown up.

Last but not least, my brother Jimmy — he continues to sell cars and build houses. Last summer instead of Jimmy, I went with Tommy to deliver a car. We were on old route 101 (it was the main road to the beach when you were here) by Epping, New Hampshire when Tommy pointed out an old general store where Jimmy makes Tommy stop whenever they travel that route. He makes Tommy stop there so he can buy a candy bar and a soda pop . . . because whenever you would bring Jimmy up to the beach you would stop there and buy him a candy bar and pop. I just learned this 35 years later and it brought tears to my eyes. What an impact you had on so many people's lives with your small acts of kindness. Jimmy is going to be 40 years old soon and yet that act so many years ago still means so much to him.

I also just learned what killed you this past year. After years and years of trying, I was finally able to get a copy of your individual Deceased Personnel File — a detailed report of the accident and your death. I had to hire an attorney and use the Freedom of Information Act. It has been so hard not knowing what happened to you for all of these years. And even though I knew it would be painful to find out, I just had to know. Well of course once I read it I cried for days and days. I guess the force of the explosion caused a massive head injury that killed you.

Dick, it was so shocking and heartbreaking to see a diagram of your injuries. What was absolutely uncanny was, you had a deep cut on your chin in the same spot that Dickie did when he fell at my parents house the day you died. The report said you died about 2:30 in the afternoon — I'm pretty sure that is when Dickie fell because I know we got home from shopping about 1:30 and by the time I got Dickie some lunch and went down to do laundry it had to be around 2:30. What I think is even more remarkable, is that because of the international date line, you were already dead when Dickie fell, but he fell at 2:30 p.m., August 26 and you had died at 2:30 p.m., August 26. It is just so unbelievable to me that Dickie fell and cut himself in the same place on the same day at the same time that you died. As I said in my last letter, it must have been your last message to me.

Okay, back to my life — I am still a charter yacht captain. Jim, the wonderful man I have been dating these past several years, and I have a business called "Shabeen Charters." We do day sails on his beautiful 42' Hunter sailboat. I still play a lot of golf and tennis but try and stay out of the mid-day sun. Since I had melanoma, I am careful with the sun. I was lucky to catch it early and do not want a reoccurrence.

I still miss you dreadfully. Since 9/11/01 there is so much talk of closure for families. When will people learn that there is no closure for such devastating losses?! The pain of a wounded heart is forever.

All my love always,

Brenda